EMPOWERING YOU, TRANSFORMING LIVES!

REBECCA HALL GRUYTER, Compiler
#1 International Best Selling Author

Copyright © 2018 by Rebecca Hall Gruyter
All rights reserved. No part of this publication may be reproduced, distributed or transmitted in any form or by any means, including photocopying, recording or other electronic or mechanical methods, without the prior written permission of the publisher, except in the case of brief quotations embodied in reviews and certain other non-commercial uses permitted by copyright law. For permission requests please contact RHG Media Productions
Published 2018
Printed in the United States of America

Print ISBN: 978-1-7328885-1-7
Publisher Information:
RHG Media Productions
25495 Southwick Drive #103
Hayward, CA 94544

www.YourPurposeDrivenPractice.com

CONTENTS

Foreword 5

January 9

February 43

March 73

April 107

May 139

June 173

July 205

August 239

September 273

October 305

November 339

December 371

A Note from Rebecca 405

By Subject 407

Learn More About our Authors 411

Closing Thoughts 451

FOREWORD
"EMPOWERING YOU, TRANSFORMING LIVES!"

BY: REBECCA HALL GRUYTER, BOOK COMPILER

Thank you for leaning into Empowering YOU, Transforming Lives! I'm honored and excited to bring this powerful book to you, featuring over 40 experts that are committed to helping you **SHINE** powerfully in your life! Our vision is that this amazing collection of 365 inspirations will walk beside you and support you each and every day of the year, year after year. Many of us have been powerfully served by daily inspiration books and now we are honored to have the opportunity to walk beside you and support you on a daily basis.

As a women's empowerment leader, I know a lot about being disempowered and how to overcome that in order to step into your passion, power, and gifts so that you **SHINE**! I celebrate you saying 'yes' to this book and to yourself! It is a courageous act to say 'yes' to you and to be willing to let others walk beside you to support and cheer you on in life.

I discovered life is not a solo journey and the more we can walk beside each other and cheer each other on the rich and more powerful our journey is. I believe transformation and living a life on purpose takes place in the mindful choices we make on a day to day basis. As those choices add up to our week, our month, and our life. This daily inspiration book is designed to support you in stopping, pausing, and reflecting each day. Pouring into you encouragement, truth, motivation, and support into you on a day to day basis. As Zig Ziglar says *"People often say that motivation doesn't last. Well, neither does bathing. That's why we recommend it daily."* ☺

In sharing their inspirations, our authors will equip and empower you to discover your value, align to your purpose, step forward, and choose to **SHINE**! I believe this book is a living and interactive book that will speak wisdom, encouragement, and power into your life. Your heart will be touched and you will be motivated and to take action to step forward powerfully in your life. I want to invite you to pause, take a deep breath, and be ready to receive these powerful messages so they can ignite a fire in you, inspire courage in you, and focus your purpose in your life to encourage you to take action now and **SHINE**!

I'm passionate about women stepping forward and sharing their wisdom, heart, lives, and stories because I know firsthand what it like to come from a much disempowered place. I experienced all types of abuse during my most formative years – the tender ages of five to thirteen. I actually continued to visit that abusive environment until the age of eighteen. This environment of abuse made me believe false messages like: "I am not okay," "there is something wrong with me," that it must be "my fault," and that it is "NOT safe to be seen or heard." As a result, I became an expert in hiding. When I was finally rescued by my birth father and placed in his home with my stepmother (who became the mother of my heart), I was able start my healing journey. On this journey, I discovered that these previous beliefs I had embraced in that unsafe environment were actually lies. I discovered that I am beautifully and wonderfully made (just like you), on purpose and for a purpose; that I matter and am needed just as I am; that it wasn't my fault; and ultimately that it is safe to be seen, heard, and **SHINE**!

So my mission - the calling of my heart - is to help others understand same truths: **We are all beautifully and wonderfully made and needed just as we are.** When we step forward and share the gift of us, it makes a difference in our lives and in the lives of those around us. This means we have to be willing to be seen on the same level that we are wanting to serve and make a difference in the world. **The more you SHINE, the more you are paving the way for others while sharing the amazing gift of you with the world.**

We each need others to encourage us, to speak wisdom and truth into us, to love us and cheer us on, and to help us stand up again when we fall. This book will walk beside you to help you run and not grow weary, to complete all that you are called to complete, and to live on purpose and with great purpose.

In creating this book, I asked each heart-centered and powerful co-author to share a daily inspiration to support you, one day and one choice at a time. As they share from their respective journeys with you, they share what they have learned. They share their wisdom and what they wish someone had encouraged them with or whispered in their ear - especially in those dark and challenging times. They are committed to pouring into you, to equip and empower you in your life. Throughout the inspirations you will feel a consistent and transparent heartbeat to support you in very real ways as the authors often share what they wish they would have known. We want to make your path and journey easier for you step forward and **SHINE**! As the book compiler, I'm so proud of what each co-author has shared in their chapters, and am honored to have each of them leaning in to support you. I am equally honored that you have said "yes" to our book and are entrusting us to support you on your journey.

Now it's your turn. Are you going to lean in and learn from the wisdom within this book? Will you let us walk beside you on your journey of life? We want to lift you up, support you, encourage, and empower you. It is your choice. We want to be equip and empower you to take action, move forward and share your gifts with the world. You can choose to open the pages and let them pour into you, or you can put this book on a shelf. My heart and prayer is that you will say "yes" to you and lean into the powerful messages of hope that are waiting to pour into you, your heart, and your life.

You have unique gifts, talents, abilities, stories, journeys, and perspectives that you alone can bring forward. Those in your life need you, your message, your wisdom, your perspective, gifts, talents, and heart. When we shrink back or hide, the world becomes less vibrant and we all miss out. Be willing to share the gift of you with those around you and with the world! Be willing to be seen on the same level you are willing/wanting to serve.

Here is how to get the most out of this powerful book. It is divided it three sections, each one designed to meet you exactly where you are at and to support you each and every day of the year. **The first section** you will find the daily inspiration in order of the calendar year, each month and day of the year. **The second section** you will find all a subject section that you can look up a particular are or subject that you are wanting support in and it will list the inspirations that can support you in that particular area. **The third section** you will find all our beautiful authors pictures, biographies, and their contact information. I know that they would love to hear from you and have you follow and connect with them. I encourage you to "friend" and follow those authors with whom you feel a powerful resonance and connection so that they can continue to pour into and support you on your journey in life.

Now the next step is yours. Drink-in the stories and messages that are within these pages to serve, support, and inspire you. Take the time to pause, read, and reflect. Listen to the powerful messages of hope that are waiting for you within the pages of this book. It's not an accident that you purchased this book and are opening it to read right now, today. I invite you to lean in and truly receive the messages and wisdom that will speak to your heart and soul that you will find in these transformational and dynamic pages. Enjoy this rich collection of wisdom, love, and encouragement.

-----Rebecca Hall Gruyter, Book Compiler

Founder/Owner of Your Purpose Driven Practice and CEO of RHG Media Productions

Rebecca Hall Gruyter is an Influencer and Empowerment Leader committed to bringing Experts and Influencers forward so that together we can lean in and make the world a better place one heart and life at a time. She is the owner of *Your Purpose Driven Practice*, creator of the *Women's Empowerment Series* events/TV show, the *Speaker Talent Search*™, and *Your Success Formula*™. Rebecca is an in-demand speaker, an expert money coach, and a frequent guest expert on success panels, tele-summits, TV, and radio shows.

As the CEO of *RHG Media Productions*™, Rebecca launched the international TV Network (www.RHGTVNetwork.com) to bring even more positive and transformational programming to the world. In July 2017 she launched the Global RHG Magazine & TV Guide bringing inspirational influences to the world and their messages! In January 2018, she expanded RHG Publishing to now help individual authors bring their books forward as best sellers so they can be positioned as they bring their powerful book forward.

Rebecca is a popular and syndicated radio talk show host, #1 bestselling author (multiple times), and publisher who wants to help YOU impact the world powerfully!

(925) 787-1572
Rebecca@YourPurposeDrivenPractice.com
www.facebook.com/rhallgruyter **(Facebook)**
www.YourPurposeDrivenPractice.com **(Main Website)**
www.RHGTVNetwork.com **(TV Network)**
www.SpeakerTalentSearch.com
www.EmpoweringWomenTransformingLives.com
(Weekly Radio Show)
www.MeetWithRebecca.com
(Calendar link to schedule a time to talk with Rebecca)

January

1.

Living On Purpose and With Purpose

Welcome to a new year of your purpose-driven life! What does this actually mean?

Your time, energy, gifts, talents, and resources are precious. Choose how you are going to spend - and share - these precious gifts that make YOU who you are and how you're gifted to show up in this world. Yes, "choose!" You get to choose how to spend them on purpose and with great purpose, each and every day. And when you do, you expand them and bring even more meaning to your life and to the world!

How do you do that? Here is a key practice:

- **Stop, pause, and evaluate the day** before you. Look at where you are and where you want to be. Then you can make a plan to get there - for your day, your week, or your month.
- **Stay intentional and mindful** as you do this, knowing you have choice. Go through your day with this in mind - "I am making choices all day, every day, with mindfulness and purpose."
- **Choose to move forward** those things that matter most to you.

This simple practice will create a life of more ease, more productivity, more action, more wonderful things coming back to you. When you are living a purpose-driven life, you are doing this not just for yourself, but also for those you are serving and interacting with - your employees, children, family, clients, pets, community.

Can you picture how much more strongly and easily you could show up in those places, lovingly and powerfully?

~Daily Inspiration by Rebecca Hall Gruyter, Influencer & Empowerment Leader

2.

Being You Authentically

"Be yourself; everyone else is already taken."
– OSCAR WILDE

Who are you? What mask are you wearing?

As you begin this new year, you have a choice to toss aside the mask of how other people see you, rid yourself of the conditioning behaviors passed down through the generations, and become uniquely you. The choice to shine, to sparkle, to be more than you were, to be more authentically you! I want you to be able to show the world exactly who you are without the fear of being shamed or judged. To have the freedom of being vulnerable without the thoughts of getting hurt. To tell your truth and not be criticized for this truth. Today, choose to allow your authentic self to come out and play. Find the courage to look deep inside and express your desires and dreams. Remove the mask of being someone everybody else thinks you should be. As you make this choice to be you without the fear, you begin to come alive and live from this authentic world that you have created tossing away the mask of conditioning and smallness. You have this within you to express yourself, to be bold and daring, to celebrate who you are! Choose you!

One step...

Write out all your desires and dreams without any critiquing. Allow your heart to soar with ideas. Then choose what is one step you can take toward the dream/desire that you feel most connected with and do that. It is with baby steps that you create your authentic self!

~Daily Inspiration by Denise Hansard, Empowerment Expert

3.

Desires Align with Your Highest Purpose

Each January, we are encouraged to make New Year's Resolutions. We make a list of all the things we think we should start or stop doing. We may even feel guilt or shame for past failures. Nevertheless, we tell ourselves that this year will be different.

In reality, we create and recreate our lives every moment through our thoughts and feelings. Rather than making a list, I invite you to take some quiet time and ask yourself "Who am I?" "Who do I want to become?" "What gifts do I have to share?" What does my soul yearn to express?"

Now imagine that you are stepping into this greatness expression of yourself and you are wildly successful. Hold this vision for a few moments. What do you see? Where are you? What are you doing? Who have you become?

As you answer these questions, notice your feelings. Do you feel joy? Happiness? Relief? Use these feelings to anchor yourself in this high vibration. **Know that as you vibrate with your highest expression, the Universe will automatically refine your desires to align with your highest purpose every day of the year.**

~Daily Inspiration by Olivia Parr-Rud, Corporate Love Ambassador

4.

Thought for the Day

"Every great dream begins with a dreamer. Always remember, you have within you the strength, the patience, and the passion to reach for the stars to change the world."
– HARRIET TUBMAN

5.

Be Brave

Being technologically challenged, I am often at the mercy of others when it comes to anything more complicated than email and basic word processing. White-knuckled, I created a video audition for a coveted spot in a focus group. My technical advisor, my 13-year-old, helped me with the editing. Unbeknownst to me, she took advantage of my ignorance and snuck in an extra slide at the end of the video. Bright neon blue letters on a black background read: *"This is Ruth's daughter. Pick my mom:) She is super nice and has the courage to do things that I could never do. She didn't tell me to say this. SHHHHHH!"*

As I was reviewing my video application, I saw the message that my daughter snuck in. I laughed and chose to leave it in my video. I thought it would say a great deal about my character in ways that I never would.

My daughter's words got me thinking. She saw me take risks while creating a new business and putting myself out into the world. Sometimes it took gut-wrenching courage on my part; apparently, she had seen that. Later that week, I was considering becoming a radio host for a network offering shows about spirituality. I was unsure if I had what it took. I remembered my daughter's words. If I was as brave as she thought I was, would I do that weekly podcast? Yes, I would! **Just knowing that she thought I was brave gave me a stronger backbone. I can be as courageous as my daughter believes me to be.**

Is there something you wish you were bold enough to try? I believe that you can be that brave!

"You will not always be strong, but you can always be brave."
- BEAU TAPLIN

~Daily Inspiration by Dr. Ruth Anderson, Spiritual Counselor

6.

Thought for the Day

"The best way to predict the future is to create it."
- ABRAHAM LINCOLN

7.

Be an extremist today!

Merriam-Webster defines extremity as "an intense degree; a drastic or desperate act or measure". This definition conjures up scary images of eminent danger, pain, or overwhelming sorrow.

But maybe it shouldn't. Martin Luther King Jr. wrote "Letter from Birmingham Jail" in response to being called an extremist. He was initially disappointed in that label, but the more he thought about it he began to realize it was a compliment. In the letter he refers to the extreme position of Martin Luther, John Bunyan, Abraham Lincoln and Thomas Jefferson. These men, as well as others he mentioned took extreme positions in their stand for equality and righteousness. He then says "Perhaps the South, the nation and the world are in dire need of creative extremists".

We need to be extreme in our pursuit of justice, our demonstrations of love, and our development of character. We should practice creative extremity with acts of kindness, loving gentleness, and acceptance. **Extremity shouldn't, as another definition says, be a "limb of the body," but should embody our way of living.**

Being an extremist does not necessarily mean doing big things. In the book *Give a Little* by Wendy Smith she quotes Pattrick M. Rooney of the Center on Philanthropy as saying *"of the approximately 62 billion dollars raised after the catastrophic tsunami in 2004, more of the monies came from individuals that donated $50 or less than any corporation or government."* Little things can have a great impact.

How can you begin living extremely today? Be willing to fully smile, really smile (commit to it extremely), at everyone you meet today and watch their responses. You will be amused and encouraged by what you see. Some will look at you in puzzlement. Do I know you? Some will genuinely smile and others will do that polite smile and quickly look away. There might even be some who won't smile at you.

Maybe you can be extreme in your kindness by holding a door for someone, helping grab an item from the top shelf, or paying for the coffee of the person behind you. The more you do these small acts, the more extreme you will find to do!

Live extremely thankful and giving lives today. It will change you and our world.

~Daily Inspiration by Elda Robinson, Teacher

8.

The Power of VISION

If you are going to succeed at anything in life you MUST know your outcome. You absolutely must get laser focused on your goal. Determine with complete clarity where you want to be. **Having vision is getting clear on your mission and the steps it takes to get there.**

What is your business? Your mission? What are the pain points that you have a solution for? Who do you serve? What is your zone of genius, that thing you do better than anyone else?

Where are you at with your vision? On a scale of zero to 10 with zero being you have no clue what your purpose or your vision is and 10 being absolutely clarity of what you want. Spend time today getting clear on your mission and the next step you can take to get one step closer.

~Daily Inspiration by Mary Shores, Author and Speaker

9.

The Art of Being Scrappy

No one talks about it, serves it up as something to be proud of or truly lets the world know that many of life's accomplishments are grounded in the seldom owned word; scrappy. **It's not glamorous or elite, and certainly doesn't sound noble. However, when we reflect on some of the greatest achievements in the world, I believe a dose of scrappiness played a part in the success.**

Think about Oprah Winfrey, Thomas Edison and J.K. Rowling. Have you heard the phrase, "knowledge is power"? **In reality, it's applied knowledge that makes things happen.** It's a common belief that success factors stem from intelligence or talent; those with the most degrees, highest I.Q. or gifted are most likely to succeed. I'm not knocking the super intelligent or highly educated; however, I will say that **some of the most successful and joyous people I know are those who put their knowledge into action, they stick with it when it's dark and challenging and when the obstacles are coming at them**. At first, we may miss the value of being scrappy.

A clear example of this came to mind when I was speaking with my mentor, Kimberly Zink, CEO of Klemmer Leadership Seminars and advised her that I'd been offered the role of hosting a radio show on behalf of Klemmer entitled "The Compassionate Samurai Business Hour" on Voice America Talk Radio. I mentioned there were others in the company who are more gifted, and she reminded me I was the one who got out of my chair, took action and made it happen. That's being scrappy! **I look at being scrappy now as that secret sauce, that element of surprise and that little something extra inside of me that says, "you've got this".** As you reflect today, where do you let your scrappiness shine?

~Daily Inspiration by Kathy Fairbanks, Radio Show Host

10.

New Year, New Day, New Start

"Sometimes to change a situation you are in requires you to take a giant leap. But, you won't be able to fly unless you are willing to transform."
– SUZY KASSEM, Rise Up and Salute the
Sun: The Writings of Suzy Kassem

The New Year is an opportunity to re-start; it offers the chance for a do-over, a reboot and a clean slate. The process in which one year ends and another begins is really nothing more than one day ending and another day beginning.

We love to celebrate a new year coming in with toasts, resolutions, and kisses at midnight, but do we also celebrate ourselves for the past year's accomplishments and successes?

As humans, we are changing every day and researchers believe we renew ourselves approximately every seven years though cellular rejuvenation. Many of these changes go unnoticed, like our hair falling out at 100 strands per day to make room for new growth and our skin regenerating itself every 27 days. Still, there is one part of us that does not renew as automatically as we would like - and that is our thoughts. This includes how we think about ourselves, our lives and our accomplishments, as well as, our beliefs. Therefore, it's important to acknowledge at least three successes you had last year and feel gratitude for those successes. Recall the feelings you had when you accomplished your goals. **Today, and for the rest of this year, trust that while the rest of our bodies are in a constant state of transformation, we must be conscious and open to letting our thoughts transform as we leap into the new year as well.**

~Daily Inspiration by Bonnie Bonadeo, The Connection Coach

11.

Send Out Ripples of Light and SHINE!

"Step out of hiding onto the Center Stage of your life."
- REBECCA HALL GRUYTER

The calling of my heart is to help others know how valuable, gifted and wonderfully made they are - and that means you! This is because I know, deeply, that you are a light that can shine so brightly that it can be seen even in the darkness. You can be the light of hope and encouragement for another! Whether it's in your business, volunteer work, relationships or strangers, you can send out rippling rays of light wherever you are.

~Daily Inspiration by Rebecca Hall Gruyter, Influencer & Empowerment Leader

12.

Live Your Dream - Your Way!

"Live the Life of Your Dreams: Be brave enough to live the life of your dreams according to your vision and purpose instead of the expectations and opinions of others."
– ROY T. BENNETT, *The Light in the Heart*

One question I love to ask my clients is: "What is your *why*?" I get all kinds of answers, everywhere between those with an amount of money involved to those with nothing short of changing the world. What I mean by this question is in Roy Bennett's quote – What do you dream? What is your vision for the future? What is the purpose of your life?

We often take our dreams, stash them in a pretty box, tie it with a fabulous bow ... and put it in the closet behind the ski equipment we haven't used in forever. We may look up at that box from time to time while we're busy with so many other things. Or forget about it entirely, until one day we ask, "Is this all there is?"

Let's take that dream out of the closet now, and really begin to live it!

Living your dream takes vision, not resolutions, not goals, but true vision. What will your future be like with your vision realized? Use all of your senses – sight, smell, hearing, taste, and feeling – to describe it. Put your thoughts in a letter to your future self. Read it out loud, often, and with feeling and commitment.

Begin to live your life on your purpose and with your own vision – not what others say, think or feel about what you should be doing. Be courageous and live that dream!

~*Daily Inspiration by Linda Patten, Leadership Expert*

13.

Source is Always Divine Order

Since Order is the first Law of the Universe, you know there could not be a Universe unless its various parts were kept in perfect order. Divine Order reflects the underlying harmony, order and balance from the vast cosmos to the mundane of your life. It operates consistently to bring all the parts of your life into its Highest Light. The moment you have Faith and cooperate with this Truth, insight is revealed to you and whatever is in your Divine Plan begins to manifest effortlessly.

There are no accidents — all things within your life are sent to you in perfect order and for a Divine Purpose, either to enrich your Soul with Spiritual Substance or to bring a deeper and truer quality of conscious awareness through Soul lessons learned. When you have Absolute Faith in Divine Order and a Plan, even though it is unseen, you will realize it is always working in your favor moving you towards your Greatest Good.

Today embrace Divine Order in all aspects of your life.

~Daily Inspiration by Kathleen E. Sims, D.D., C.H.T.

14.

Thought for the Day

*"Nothing is impossible,
the word itself says 'I'm possible'!"*
- AUDREY HEPBURN

15.

Stop Being the Best Kept Secret

This is your year - You are a beautiful, generous, gifted person ... who might be someone *that not many people know about* (meaning, a best kept secret).

Are you top of mind for those people who need your positive impact? Can they easily find you, see you, and hear you?

These are important questions to answer, because I've discovered that if they cannot see you and hear you, then you cannot help them. This is why I believe **visibility is so very important**, so that it's easy for people to find you.

This is also true: **There is no one out there who is magically going to put you on a stage and then all your dreams are going to come true.** If you want to make a difference, you have to lead your own effort. If your visibility is low, then it's up to you to raise it - not anyone else but you.

The people who need your positive impact are waiting for you because YOU ARE NEEDED! Believe me, people need you! People are hurting. People are discouraged. People are losing hope. People are praying and dreaming for somebody just like you, to share with them your love, insight, wisdom, and powerful gifts.

Can you make a commitment today to make yourself visible? To shine brightly enough so that your people can see your loving hand outstretched to help them?

Yes! No more hiding!

~Daily Inspiration by Rebecca Hall Gruyter, Influencer & Empowerment Leader

16.

Tranquility

Tranquility is where everyone is free to find solace in their own way. The tranquility that is found by the avid scuba diver in Hawaii may be different then the climber who scales Mount Everest. Yet, both experiences can be viewed as heightened and energized, what can be categorized as a spiritual phenomenon. The simple act of walking on grass through a park can be relaxing and therapeutic for some individuals. By allowing the blades of grass to mesh between their toes and feel the earth beneath them, they would feel connected with nature.

You have witnessed tranquility on the faces of your children while they're sound asleep, dreaming ever so peacefully. However, you find tranquility whether it's with oils, by spiritual means, your religious beliefs, extreme sports, simple walks in the park or gazing up at the stars at night the world is a better place because of peaceful, happy, content people like you.

Remember to carve out time each day for some tranquility, and carry it with you throughout the day.

~Daily Inspiration by Cassandra Garabedian, Stylist

17.

Thought for the Day

"Seventy percent of success in life is showing up."
– WOODY ALLEN

18.

Step Into Your True Potential

It is important to know that your goals impact your definition of success. Whatever level of success you want to reach pertains to your goals.

Make sure your goals are up to par with your potential and how you truly define success. Look forward, not back. Do not judge your past decisions with the knowledge you hold now, rather think of the future decisions you will be capable of handling with better discernment.

Look at your situation from a different angle and find what has led you there. Your past will only be relevant if it affects your future goals. As Rudy Ruettiger said, "Reality…is the enemy of fantasies but not of dreams." We all have tremendous potential! What can you do today to set a goal to help you step further into your potential?

~Daily Inspiration by Pastor Nicolas Pacheco

19.

Change Your Life...Just Ask.

Your life can change today, by simply asking for what you want. You see, people can't read your mind; we just don't have that kind of power. **But the power is simple and it`s in you. You need to remember and be willing ask.**

If you are looking for that new client today, pick up the phone and call them, or text them, and tell them how great they are and how honored you would be to earn their business.

People every day are looking for something great to do, or to buy, to enhance their lives or the lives of others. So just ask, because if you don't ask the answer always will be "NO," or someone else will ask. Ask for what you want, make those calls, and get started today!

~Daily Inspiration by Inguss

20.

Let Support In

*"If you want to go fast, go alone.
If you want to go far, go together."*
- AFRICAN PROVERB

As a strong, sometimes stubborn, independent woman, I was never comfortable reaching out for help. It always seemed easier to grind my way through challenges. I didn't realize that this mindset actually made life much harder, not easier at all.

Starting my own business, required me to shift into a new mindset that was unfamiliar, but golden for success, which is this: **It's not only okay to reach out for support, it's *essential* for the big dreams, the big results, the big love you wish to pour into the world** whether you own a business, or not.

Plus, it's way more fun! And fun is allowed ;) As with any fear, the key to stepping beyond our comfort zone is, tiny, baby steps. (And we're all in "baby phase" anytime we begin something new).

In addition to empowering my daughter, my dream is to help women share their love, gifts and talents in the world now, more than ever, in their own unique way. The world needs the financial dream in your heart, to come true.

So... next time, fear holds you back from doing something your heart is calling you to do, I invite you to try these four tips instead:

1. **Trust your heart.**
2. **Tend to your emotions**
3. **Take tiny, baby steps**
4. **Trust in the support of a person or group for accountability, positivity and valuable input for growth and success.**

To your beautiful dreams and financial happy-ever-after!

~Daily Inspiration by Marlene Elizabeth, Author of **MONEYWINGS™**

21.

Worth the Wait

There are two types of people in life: those who live life aggressively and those who wait patiently. Both of them have the opportunity to live wonderful lives.

For those who are willing to wait things out, there are many opportunities given to those who wait patiently.

For example, coal mines, over time sometimes reveal diamonds. Oysters offer pearls after a certain period of time given the right circumstances. Some things are worth the wait.

I encourage you to be patient, have a longer-term view, be open to gems that will serve you. Remember true jewels can take a bit more time but are worth it in the long run…..because you are worth it.

~Daily Inspiration by Kri' Shawn Terrell, Motivational Speaker

22.

Resurface from the Clutter

At the age of 60 I recognize the need to release my past. Emotionally there are some tougher issues, but for the releasing it is a feeling of success. As a border line hoarder I know it's hard to let go. It took many confrontations and thinking my husband would divorce me because our house is one big mess. My "Stuff" was actually adding to my depression and causing overwhelm. I never knew where to begin, but once I began it was freeing.

"Things" are not easy to let go but as you are willing to release you will feel great relief and accomplishment.

*You will feel freer and the air will feel lighter.
*You will find your home again.
*Your embarrassment is lifted
(*I recommend hiring a professional organizer because they keep you focused and guide you to sort your "stuff" systematically.*)
Things to let go of:
*Photos from your child's first years and he is now 35. Take a picture and recycle the original.
*Emotions and thoughts that no longer serve.
*Toys in good condition from their younger years. Give them away or sell them.
* Ancient Divorce papers. Shred them to release the past.
*Boxes of outdated papers or recipes you never used.
*VHS Videos are outdated. Donate them.
*The clothing you hoped to eventually fit into is just taking up space. Buy new ones when you reach your desired weight. (*When the clutter and your "stuff" is gone you will find your weight whittle away much faster.*)

Trust in the process and know you will feel better once you accomplished this. What are you willing to let go of? Once you complete your clearing consider rewarding yourself.

~Daily Inspiration by Catherine M Laub, Advocate for Mental Health

23.

Our Own Point of View

*"If you change the way you look at things,
the things you look at do change."*
-WAYNE DYER

Or, in other words, it is not what you see, but how you see it.

Many of us have a tendency to immediately look for what is wrong, all the time, everywhere.

Our question for you is this: What would your life be like if you were to choose to look for what is right, as well--in any situation or with any person, particularly in your family? Asking the question "What is right?" often gives us a bigger view of any given situation or person.

Our tip:

1. Start with people or situations that are easy.
2. What can you do to remind yourself to also look for what is right?

You will find that looking for what is right is a gift you give yourself and everybody around you.
Have fun!

(The question "Am I looking for what is right or what is wrong?" is from Debbie Ford's book *The Right Questions*.)

~Daily Inspiration by Mooniek Seebregts and Martina Caviezel, The Parent Empowerment Coaches

24.

Thought for the Day

"If you're offered a seat on a rocket ship, don't ask what seat! Just get on."
- SHERYL SANDBERG

25.

You are the author of your life!

January brings to mind new beginnings and offers us an opportunity to rewrite our story. I was not encouraged to be a writer because it wasn't practical. However, I never let go of my dream. I rewrote my story and while I was a thirty-year-old college freshman, I achieved my goal of achieving a degree in journalism.

Spend fifteen minutes reflecting on **how you are making choices to create who you are right now.** Record in your journal where you are now and give voice to the person you want to be. Your words have the power to bring you from where you are to where you want to be.

~Daily Inspiration by Mary E. Knippel, Your Writing Mentor

26.

Thought for the Day

"Two roads diverged in a wood, and I—I took the one less traveled by, And that has made all the different."
– ROBERT FROST

27.

Radiance is a Choice

If you want a different future, you must evolve beyond the state of being that created your past.

Whether it is a new year or a new day, every new beginning starts with a choice. You can choose to begin the day thinking of all the things you want, everything you need to do, and all that you want to change in your life. But this mindset of lack will leave you believing that joy and fulfillment isn't something you have, but something you need to find. This perspective will fill your day with anxiety, stress and disappointment.

Luckily, there is another choice. You can choose to begin the day quieting your mind, surrendering to the stillness of the moment, and sinking in to the deepest parts of your being. When you sink deep within yourself, beyond the challenges and the circumstances of your life, you uncover the most radiant part of you. This radiance holds the source of your joy, your love, and your true power. When you connect to this place, you know who you truly are from the depths of your being. You know your purpose. You know your gifts. You know your truth. You will feel that everything and everyone in your life is a gift. You too, are a gift.

When you begin the day from this place of Radiance, you come from a state of wholeness and strength. You see beyond the superficial distractions in your life and are inspired by your deeper purpose. You feel inspired to share your most powerful gifts, and uplift the people in your life with your inner light. Abundance, love and joy become your life, and you are free.

~Daily Inspiration by Ron Coquia, Radiance Coach

28.

Gratitude is a Choice

Gratitude helps us see what is there instead of what isn't. Being grateful will heal your Mind, *Body, and Spirit*. **Once practiced, gratitude will help you to attract more to be grateful for.**

Start simple by saying as you breathe in:
I am grateful for my breath and then build on it ...
Questions you can journal to help find gratitude:
Who was kind to you today?
What did you enjoy doing today?
What made you smile today?

~Daily Inspiration by Carmell Pelly, Empowerment Leader

29.

Thought for the Day

"You must be the change you wish to see in the world."
- GANDHI

30.

Set and Achieve Goals!

January, for most of us, is about what we want to achieve with our goals. Some of us have continued to write the same goals year after year, right? People have asked me many times how is it that I have achieved so much? They are referring to the nearly forty goals I have achieved over the past three years. Some of those goals are: writing three books, publishing three workbooks, writing three co-authored books, launching and syndicating a podcast, and many more.

One of those nine publications is called Goal For It – 30 Paths to Imagine More Success, which shares all of my secrets of goal achievement. There actually is a formula I wrote out that it makes it very simple to understand the components to finishing very complex goals such as writing a book that can be published!

Focus and determination are two coveted factors for a high level of goal achievement. After achieving all those goals over a three year period, my already high levels of self-esteem and confidence skyrocketed. It also helped when the co-owner of a multi-million dollar international corporation told me that my work was brilliant and impressive! I was able to do this because I leaned into the formula to complete my goals.

I realized that when you achieve a goal that rewards you with fabulous accolades, your self-esteem and confidence levels can catapult you to higher levels in both areas. With that mindset shift, your business can skyrocket and remove all self-imposed limits!

Here are my top three tips to help you set goals and truly achieve them:

- Know your value
- Allow mindset shift when accolades are given
- Analyze how you can increase your new mind-set into up-leveled progression

Now "Goal For It!" It's up to you.

~Daily Inspiration by Syndee Hendricks, Certified Business Consultant and Intuitive Coach

31.

Come Out of Hiding and SHINE!

This means that **we can't hide behind the roles that we play, our credentials, or our limiting beliefs.** These things (which we believe are protecting us) actually block people from truly hearing and experiencing us - the very people who need us are separated from us.

The only way to be found is for you to **be willing to take off all that stuff that is blocking the connection**. The only way to truly make a positive difference in the world is to **be willing to be seen, authentically and transparently.**

I invite you today to look at ways in which you might be hiding a little bit. Please do this without self-judgment or criticism, and always with self-love.

And then ask: In what ways could I step out of hiding onto the Center Stage of my life, just a little bit more?

A great first step is to decide on an action you could take - today - to lean into making a difference for another, to shine your light for them.

~Daily Inspiration by Rebecca Hall Gruyter, Influencer & Empowerment Leader

February

1.

Be Willing to Say YES

*"Be willing to say yes to those things that matter
most and commit to bringing them forward."*
- REBECCA HALL GRUYTER

Have you ever bumped against this -You committed to doing something that later turns out not to serve you? It demanded too much time, fell out of alignment with your comfort or purpose, and became someone else's priority or vision instead of your own?

I understand! In those times we are not taking a leadership position in our own lives! **How can we commit to bringing forward those things that matter most if we don't have clear boundaries?**

Here are some practices to consider: **Choose when and where you can say 'yes' powerfully** by first checking if it's truly supporting your goal(s).

Pause and check in with your opportunities. Ask yourself: Why am I attending this event? Why am I producing this thing? Why am I working on this person's project? Make sure that the 'why' is actually supportive of and in alignment with you, not just because someone else wants you to or asked you to (which can be great, but is it helping you move forward to that which you're being called to bring forth?).

If you find that you are doing that thing for someone else and it's not creating room for the things you're wanting to bring forward, then (gently and lovingly) do not accept. And create space and room to say yes to those things that truly matter to you.

~Daily Inspiration by Rebecca Hall Gruyter, Influencer & Empowerment Leader

2.

Unconditional Love

The power of love
mysterious and wondrous
like double rainbow

February is often thought of as the month of Love. In the U.S. we have Valentine's Day in the middle of the month. For some of us we have a partner and look forward to celebrating with our special someone. Maybe we don't currently have a romantic partner. Whichever is true for you, it makes a big difference when we empower ourselves and focus on **self-love**. When we **love ourselves unconditionally** we feel more empowered and have better experiences in life. One of my favorite authors, Marci Shimoff, suggests that we become **love philanthropists** rather than **love beggars**. We can start by filling up our own cup of love and then let it spill over onto everyone else.

What can you do today to demonstrate **unconditional self-love**? Do you love yourself regardless of how you feel, or what actions you take? Can you look in the mirror and say to yourself "[your name] I love you just the way you are"?

~Daily Inspiration by Bonnie May Best, Wellness Consultant

3.

Connection Matters

When is the last time you talked to a stranger? **Connection doesn't just happen it must be deliberate.** We are all different. So we probably think it might be difficult to start a conversation with a stranger who doesn't look like you. It is not! We must not ignore the differences but acknowledge them. It can be discouraging if you are not making the connections you desire. The good news is you can change that by being willing to initiate connection.

I met someone I wanted to make a connection with but she was closed off. But I really wanted to connect with her. I decided to approach her when the time was right and simply ask her non-threatening questions. For example, "How long have you worked here?" or "Do you drink tea also?" She opened right up and we became friends. **We never know who we are passing by when we don't reach out and connect. I know fear is the main reason people don't speak to strangers, we fear we may say the wrong thing. Fear is a liar. Open up, connect to the universe and make a new connection.**

~Daily Inspiration by Tresté Loving, Racial Equity Expert

4.

Chocolatey

As a school teacher I get many mugs, but one of my favorite coffee mugs is one I found at a thrift store. It says I have **O**bsessive **C**hocolate **D**isorder! I freely admit to being a chocoholic.

First, there is the rich, intense dark chocolate. The hint of bitterness enhances the deep flavor that evokes memories of dark forests and hidden ponds. This chocolate is made to be savored. Second is the smooth, softer essence that milk chocolate gives. It melts in your mouth and reminds one of Mom's Christmas fudge. There is no bitterness in this type of chocolate.

Many chocolate purists insist that white chocolate isn't really chocolate. It doesn't have the full bodied flavor of dark chocolate or the sweet, gentle taste of milk chocolate. It has a unique, unexpected flavor all its own. Forest Gump said "Life is like a box of chocolates. You never know what you are going to get". Sometimes life is like dark chocolate. It is intense, and often accompanied with bitterness. Take time to savor these experiences. Use them to learn more about yourself. Evaluate your direction and see if you need to make changes. Realize you are strong enough to deal with whatever you are currently going through.

Sometimes life is like the sweetness of milk chocolate. Things are going well and there are no issues. Don't rush through these times. Enjoy them to the fullest, and remember them when life gets more complicated. White chocolate reminds us of the total unexpected things in life. These moments that take our breath away, leave us in awe, and make us laugh or even cry. These moments are treasures to hold in remembrance; gems to be enjoyed anytime.

There is one very important thing to remember about chocolate. To be its best it needs to be tempered. Tempering involves being heated and cooled until the correct consistency and look is achieved. If chocolate is not tempered it will be dull, crumbly, streaky, and have no snap! In our lives we are often heated, cooled and stirred up. And, hopefully, through this process, we become snappy and shine! **Embrace each rich, chocolatey moment.**

Enough talk about chocolate, go find some and treat yourself. No guilt involved.

~Daily Inspiration by Elda Robinson, Teacher

5.

Thought for the Day

"Fearlessness is like a muscle. I know from my own life that the more I exercise it the more natural it becomes to not let my fears run me."
- ARIANNA HUFFINGTON

6.

You are Grounded, Loved, and are Enough

Train your mind in these truths by writing affirmations and posting them everywhere so that you can easily see them. On your mirror, your fridge, in your car and in your wallet. **Be mindful about what you are choosing to believe.**
Example:

- I am a beautiful and strong person. I can tackle anything that comes my way today.
- I am a confident person. I am going to rock it today.
- I am going to be my best self-today. I will stay positive and kind.

Keep a journal of your affirmations and write in it daily. When we learn to love ourselves in all situations, we learn to be the best version of ourselves. We become more compassionate towards ourselves, and we stop judging ourselves based on our past decisions or actions. We learn from our mistakes and move on to the next moment. It becomes easier to adapt to changes and we begin to bounce back from hardships faster.

~Daily Inspiration by Carmell Pelly, Empowerment Leader

7.

Living at a Higher Vibrational Frequency

Everything is made of molecules and those molecules are made of positive and negative charges that hold them together or pull them apart by Source energy. It stands to reason that our vibrational energy will ebb and flow, increase and decrease as well, depending on the energy sources around us and within us. **What you think and more importantly, what you feel at any moment in time determines at what vibrational frequency you are vibrating at.** We pull energy towards us and push it away depending on the vibrational energy frequency we are vibrating at any moment in time.

Consciously keeping your energy vibration at higher frequencies will attract more of what you want to you and will affect the people around you as well. Have you ever noticed that when you are feeling great, that things just seem to go your way? Like you get "Rock Star" parking, even when you're in a hurry and might be running late for that appointment—but because you are feeling awesome—there's a parking spot right in front waiting for you.

The opposite can happen too. Doesn't it seem that you hit every red light on those days you're already in a bad mood?! It might sound crazy but try it next time—shift your focus and your vibrational energy to one of gratitude, love, joy (all higher vibrational energy levels)—this might take a bit of concentrated focus on day that is not going your way—and see if you start attracting something better.

Surrounding yourself with higher vibrational energy people will increase your vibration. When we are surrounded with people who are sending out amazing energy—we naturally gravitate towards them and consequently our vibration is increased just by being in their proximal space. There is power in proximity.

~Daily Inspiration by Carmen Bryant, Entrepreneur & Success Coach

8.

LOVE. Make It Your Business.

Large corporations are among the most powerful entities on the planet. Imagine if we could infuse them with love!

Good news! Research strongly suggests that companies who encourage loving behavior actually make higher profits. Yes, companies whose leaders model and encourage compassion, connection, and caring, are actually more successful in the long run. It turns out that our high-tech, fast-paced, global economy requires more agility and resilience to thrive. This agility and resilience emerges from employees who feel seen, valued, and connected, i.e. "loved."

If you work in the corporate world, I invite you to open your heart and connect deeply with your coworkers and your customers. Not only will you feel more joy and creativity. You will help infuse the planet with more love while helping your company achieve even greater success!

~Daily Inspiration by Olivia Parr-Rud, Corporate Love Ambassador

9.

Fall in Love and Like with Yourself

"One morning, in February 1986, out of nowhere, I experienced a realization. In an instant, I discovered that when I believed my stressful thoughts, I suffered, but when I questioned them, I didn't suffer"
– BRYON KATIE

Our thoughts and words hold so much power and energy that we may think we are on track to accomplish something and then suddenly, our actions seem to betray us. Words hold energy – for example, "like" holds more power than "love", "don't" holds more power than "do" and "stop" holds more power than "start." It's important to use those words that have a higher vibration to help us manifest our dreams and desires. Did you know that we have an estimated 12,000-60,000 thoughts per day and 98% are pretty much the same thoughts we had yesterday?

Let's take love as an example, there have been many articles and books written on why it is so important to love yourself, but do you actually *like* yourself? Would you be friends with yourself? Self-Love and self like would be defined as knowing you're not perfect, have flaws, bad days and appreciate yourself for who you are anyway. If you answered yes, I do love myself, then why in just the last week did you beat yourself up for doing or not doing something? Maybe you said something in your head or even out loud, like, "that was stupid of me, why do I keep doing this to myself?" Could it be possible that you don't like yourself? In order to dig deeper, ask yourself these questions today: What do I like about me? What don't I like about me? Are the things I dislike about myself preventing me from having the love I desire for myself and others? **Today, make one new choice to stop an action that you don't like vs. starting a new one, or don't do something vs. doing something and see if you can shift the power in your commitment to be madly in love and like with yourself!**

~Daily Inspiration by Bonnie Bonadeo, The Connection Coach

10.

Your True Self Is Love & Joy

Within you the love that is your birthright is discovered, affirming the Truth that you are Love, and Joy is your Natural state. When you tap into the unconditional love within you it awakens your Natural Joy. The heart-felt inspiration of your deepest Spiritualized feelings is what gives your life meaning and the experience for which you have long searched.

You can now realize the Truth that all meaning and its Real experience resides within you. It is Eternally available if you are willing to walk on the Path of healing all obstacles that appear before you eclipsing this Truth. You thus quietly, gently, and powerfully, through thought, word and deed, express God to all through you, and claim your birthright of Joy. As a result, you express your Authentic Self and others have an experience of Who you really are: A radiating center of Light, Love and Joy.

Today live from the knowledge that you are the Gift of Love and Joy waiting to be given.

~Daily Inspiration by Kathleen E. Sims, D.D., C.H.T.

11.

Show up for Yourself

I believe when you show up for yourself and make yourself a priority, you position yourself in the world as someone of tremendous value.

It took being diagnosed with breast cancer twice before I woke up to the fact that I am the only one who can make myself a priority and love me for who I am. **You are the only one who can decide that you are a priority in your life.** Spend fifteen minutes reflecting on how you prioritize people, tasks, and commitments (both personal and professional). Pay particular attention to where you are on that list. Record in your journal where you are now and give voice to the person you want to be. Your words have the power to bring you from where you are to where you want to be.

~Daily Inspiration by Mary E. Knippel, Your Writing Mentor

12.

You Are Sooo Beautiful!

In this "month of love," I want to share a little gift with you, something special that we do at the Women's Empowerment events I host. I believe in life is about connection, not perfection. I celebrate those differences, quirks, and "imperfections" we all have that make us who we are. But we don't always celebrate our own moments of "imperfection," do we? In face I believe we are each beautifully, wonderfully and uniquely made....and it's those "differences" that enrich our life and the lives of those around us.

Frequently, when we make a "misstep", say the wrong word, show up in an "imperfect" way we get embarrassed, start to focus on what we view as imperfect....breaking the human connection we just made with another. In those moments we start up that conversation in our heads: I can't believe I said that! They'll never listen to me again! Oh my goodness, I tripped in front of all these people! What was I thinking? And on and on...

In those moments, I invite you to **switch from self-critical chatter to saying: "You are sooo beautiful!!"** It instantly brightens everything, brings us back into connection, and can make us smile. Not only embracing and loving all of who you are, but also making it okay to be authentic and "imperfect" for all of those around you. Reminding them and yourself that you are beautiful and wonderful...especially in those moments where you take the guard down and let people truly see you and celebrate you when you shine and when you stumble. All serves, is beautiful, builds connections, and allows us to truly and deeply connect.

I have all my guests in the whole room practice saying this together: "You are sooooo beautiful!" to each other, wholeheartedly and making eye contact. You can imagine the wonderful energy and love that's created in the room! When someone shares this gift with you because they see something wonderful in you...remember to take it in. **Receive that gift and that truth they see in you.**

Remember in those "imperfect" moments that YOU ARE SOOOOO BEAUTIFUL! Remembering how beautiful and wonderful and lovable we are.

~Daily Inspiration by Rebecca Hall Gruyter, Influencer & Empowerment Leader

13.

Thought for the Day

"The only place success comes before work is in the dictionary."
– VINCE LOMBARDI

14.

Love What You See in the Mirror

February is my favorite month for many reasons:

- It's a short month
- Spring is just ahead
- Valentine's Day and LOVE!

Some of us are fortunate enough to find romantic love early in our transition to adulthood, but many are not so fortunate. Though in that process we are given lessons to learn, the lessons about love begin much sooner than when we discover that first romantic love. One of the things I learned as a child from my faith and from my parents was how important integrity is in life. Simply put, it is about doing the right thing when no one is looking. The big payoff is that when you look in the mirror you not only like what you see, but also you have your own personal respect and admiration – both of which are priceless. That's right! You can't buy either one.

In my book Insights from an Intuitive, I share that integrity is your code of ethics, and true character means walking the talk of that code. We can all think we live our lives with a higher mind in daily life but, the truth is, that it is not an easy task. It's really about balance — walking the tightrope of knowing your standards of integrity, and the delivery of those standards through your actions is what becomes your character—good, bad, or indifferent.

For everyday life, knowing and living your code of ethics or mission statement serves well to keep yourself in alignment. Through a higher understanding of your integrity and character, you become very empowered and liberated. And, of course, you will love what you see in the mirror every day...free of charge.

I want you to discover how to love yourself and what you see in the mirror every day...by walking in alignment with who you truly are.

~Daily Inspiration by Syndee Hendricks, Certified Business Consultant and Intuitive Coach

15.

The Power of FOCUS

Always focus on what you WANT instead of what you DON'T want. Your focus is like your flashlight. *What you focus on grows.*

When you know your outcome, you are developing the muscle of end-result thinking. This is a mind-set that encourages you to always keep your end-result goals in mind while you're moving throughout life. Strengthening this muscle will, over time, make it easier to identify the *yes* and *no* answers when you're faced with choices, because you'll see what takes you either closer to or farther from your desired end result. Pause today and say yes to those things that will get you closer to the result you desire.

~ Daily Inspiration by Mary Shores, Author and Speaker

16.

Keep Going, You Are Almost There

Your best success is that which is up ahead of you. Become determined to master your life and direct your thoughts to only those things, situations and associations that serve your Highest Good. **Infuse Value into your Experience and show promise for Progressively Positive Outcomes.**

Manifesting Progressively Positive Outcomes starts with making better choices in regards to our associations and endeavors. Seek out, search for and serve only Your Highest Good. Start Living and BEING the Cause that you know you truly are and allow your Soul Full Cosmic Expression by giving it Full Operational Control of your daily life, **for Optimal Living. Start Happening to Life instead of Life Happening to You.** Step out of your comfort zone and believe your best is still worth striving for and within your realistic reach. Make the necessary adjustments to align yourself with that which will progress you forward and closer to your Highest Good Goal Realization. Trust Yourself.

Affirmation:
I AM Manifesting Progressively Positive Outcomes, in all my endeavors, associations and situations. I AM seeking out opportunities that perfectly align with my Highest Good Goals and Desires. I AM allowing my Soul Full Operational Control of My Daily Life.

~Daily Inspiration by Mark Edward Pyle, Manifestation Expert

17.

The Power is Within You!

Do you know the power that is within you? The strength and resilience which is inside of you? The amazing fortitude you have deep down inside. I promise you it is there. You just need to reach down and tap into it. You must take time to know you. To tap into your inner strength and power. Each of us has the power of change inside of us. We just have to be willing to go deep down inside and find your power. Today, stop, pause and connect to your strength and power. Then go forth and SHINE!

~Daily Inspiration by Teresa Hawley Howard, Empowerment Leader

18.

Relationships

Imagine wanting to know how a tree behaves in a storm, so climbing up one and clinging to it for dear life as a storm rages! Or decide to perch precariously on a rock while Yosemite Falls rushes by. John Muir's appetite for learning about nature was almost insatiable. His books are insightful and inspiring. As interesting as it would be to talk to him, I'd rather talk to his wife, Louie Stentzel Muir.

Louie, an accomplished musician and excellent student, lived with her parents after her school years. During that time she learned a great deal about growing fruits and flowers from her horticultural father. When John Muir went on his explorations, she very capably managed their ranch and finances. She chose to do these things rather than travel with her husband. We get a glimpse into the kind of relationship they had in a letter she wrote in 1888. "Dear John, A ranch that needs and takes the sacrifice of a noble life or work, ought to be flung away beyond all reach... The Alaska book and the Yosemite book, dear John, must be written and you need to be your own self, well and strong to make them worthy of you." She began downsizing their ranch to help him better focus on his passion for discovery.

Their life together demonstrates what the old-fashioned word helpmate is, partners in the true sense. Louie lived life exercising her strengths which enabled John to live and use his. Their kind of relationship could be applied in all areas of life. **Imagine what changes could be accomplished in our world if we lived our lives doing what we do best, encouraging and supporting others to do their best.** It wouldn't matter who got the credit or who was in the spotlight. If your teammate or partner was the one flying, then you would be the one creating the enabling wind. Who can you make their best by being at your best?

~Daily Inspiration by Elda Robinson, Teacher

19.

We Are the Change

*"When we are no longer able to change a situation,
we are challenged to change ourselves."*
-VIKTOR FRANKL

In today's world, adopting a personal practice that actualizes Viktor Frankl's wise words could be misconstrued as apathy. It is not. If, after working toward changing a situation (personal or otherwise), we are unsuccessful, it is always a good idea to take a step back and look to ourselves for answers and/or solutions.

Asking ourselves, **"What is it that worries, angers, offends, or saddens me?" is only the beginning of the process. We must also ask ourselves: "If I cannot change what it is that I have identified, can I change how I act or react to it?"** And, the answers we get to this second question are where we usually find ourselves challenged.

Why? **Because, it is not easy to see or understand that what we do on a personal or micro level—like drops of water falling into an empty bucket—has as the potential to add up over time.** The result? We find ourselves with the equivalent of a bucket filled with life saving water—the ability to change things on a large scale or macro level. And, our next step is to take the time to honestly look inward and ask ourselves whether we need to change our intentions, the way we think (our perspective), our actions, or all of the above? It is then that we are ready to actualize change in ourselves and in our world. **We are the change...with each thought, word, and deed...we are the change we want to see in our world.**

~Daily Inspiration by Dr. Nancy Tarr Hart

20.

What's Your Recovery Quotient?

Living in a world of modern medicine, high-tech and global access seems to provide a number or measurement for everything. **So, when it comes to relationships, what's your recovery quotient?** A recovery quotient is the amount of time and resources it takes to get back to baseline after an unpleasant event has occurred. If we think of this in terms of algebra the formula would look something like this:

Recovery Quotient = <u>**Event or Circumstance**</u>
Time Required to Get Back to Baseline

One of the key takeaways I've discovered, after attending and now working with the team at Klemmer Leadership Seminars, is the importance in becoming a detective around my relationships. One common denominator to the equation is "me" and only I can control the way I respond to people, places or circumstances. In the Klemmer seminars, one of the dynamic modules delivered is entitled the 3Rs, which represent resentment, resistance and revenge. Although discovery of the 3Rs has been life-changing, the true beauty in the training comes from the tools of exiting out of the 3Rs. The quicker and healthier way this is accomplished, the more productive I become. Nelson Mandela said, "resentment is like drinking poison and then hoping it will kill your enemies."

An effective tool I began using this year is something called, "the junk journal" where I jot down each time I have a negative thought of myself or others into the "junk journal". (This includes anything I'm resistant to or resentful of). The journal has two columns; one for the person involved and the 2nd column for the topic. After a short time, I typically notice a trend around a certain person or thing that's taking up valuable brain and heart space. It then becomes crystal clear what action needs to be taken to address this trend. **Remember to be compassionate as you research your recovery quotient.**

~Daily Inspiration by Kathy Fairbanks, Radio Show Host

21.

How Did I Get Here?

Ever look back and say, "WOW, how'd I get here?"

I recently found myself having business meetings via phone conference while sitting on a beautiful beach in Florida. I'm from rainy, cold, Washington State. Not to mention I grew up "less fortunate," pretty much labeled "white trash" and lucky if didn't end up homeless or strung out on drugs. The fact was, according to what had been handed to me in life… this is not where I was "supposed to be."

Now there have been plenty of times when I have thought, "How did I get here?" To be honest, most of those times were not because I was on some tropical beach. Most of the times have been when I was in a state of darkness, and when I found myself asking that question.

Have you ever asked this question "How did I get here?" And listened to the answer? **I discovered when I started asking the question, and truly listening to the answer, it made a profound difference in my life.** Discovering the answer of "how" I had gotten there… sometimes it was just circumstances of life, sometimes it was at the hand of another, and sometimes it was just because I had allowed myself to choose that path. Regardless of the method used, the one thing I discovered is that I ALWAYS have a choice of what to do with what I've been given. I held strong to that truth, reminded myself of it often, and then determined to set my sights on the light of where I wanted to be.

It's not always easy. As a matter of fact, it is so hard sometimes it seems like you break. You are more powerful than the "breaks," and you have the choice to choose better.

Every day you make choices on who you'll be and how you'll live this life. Decide now, purposely seek after, and point yourself in the direction that will lead you to where, and who you want to be. Give yourself credit for how far you've already come, remember you're on a journey. Before you know it, you'll be "having meetings on a beach."

~*Daily Inspiration by Julz DeFant, RDH*

22.

Move Forward Powerfully with Clarity and Purpose.

We can move forward powerfully each day if we have clarity and purpose. In Buddhist circles, there is a well-known saying likening the mind to water. The saying is *'the mind is like water. When it is turbulent, it's difficult to see. When it's calm, everything becomes clear'*. If you discover you continually dwell on negative thoughts, quickly shift out of that destructive mindset and refocus on positive thoughts. By removing the thoughts that cause your mind turbulence and anxiety, you can clearly focus on more important matters, and pursuing them with purpose.

Just imagine a marathon runner in mid-race deciding to focus on negative events that happened a week ago, or worse, years ago rather than focusing on winning the race or crossing the finish line. If the runner loses focus on the race, the runner will slow down, and possibly become disheartened, ultimately dropping out of the race. The runner lost clarity and purpose and could no longer move powerfully in their pursuit of winning the race. It is the same with us. Every day we are presented with choices that can help or hinder us in moving powerfully with clarity with purpose.

You are powerful and you have purpose! Do not let life's distractions, negative thoughts, or your internal dialogue stop you from living your life to its full potential. Move forward with clarity and purpose!

~Daily Inspiration by Adrian Jefferson Chofor

23.

Thought for the Day

"Patience, persistence and perspiration make an unbeatable combination for success."
– NAPOLEON HILL

24.

Are You Giving Love or Needing Love?

Ah, relationships! Those beautiful, life-affirming, fun, annoying, hurtful, pesky relationships. Can't live with them, can't live without them ...

What do we do when relationships challenge us, hurt us, call into question our beliefs, throw us off our path to our purpose and joy? We can't change the people (as much as we'd like to!), but we *can* reframe our response to them, which will bring us back into alignment with our values, purpose and path.

At a time in my life when I felt desperately confused and saddened by the way I was being treated, a spiritual mentor told me: **"In any given moment, a person is in one of two states – either giving love or in need of love."** It sounded crazy at the time (you may have to sit with it for a while as I did...) but has since become a guiding principle in my life. The person showing "bad" behavior is simply needing love in that moment because they are acting from their own demons. Our tendency is to respond to the person in kind, which only sucks us into their fear and escalates the situation, sometimes to dangerous levels.

What if we recognized in that moment that this person isn't out to hurt us? Rather, they're simply acting out of fear (the opposite of love) expressing as anger, lack, not being enough, greed, selfishness, judgment and the like. What is true in this moment is, as challenging as it can be to see, that they are feeling unloved.

What breaks the chain? Switching to giving love. In fact, at the deepest level love and fear can't exist at the same time. Like sneezing with your eyes open - can't do it! By the way, ALL of us experience both states, several times a day, whether or not we are aware of it. After all, we're only human. **But isn't it great to know that these are our choices?**

Here's to loving relationships - always!

~Daily Inspiration by Bettyanne Green, Content Marketing Strategist

25.

Stress Prevention

Now that the holidays are over it is time to plan for a stress free year. If you experienced stress during the holidays take a step back and focus on the things that went well. Once you have those positive thoughts, apply them to the coming year.

Extend any traditions throughout the year. If you baked cookies think about doing it every few months, and the more the merrier to help bake. If you made decorations find a way to create new ones for each season. If it is entertainment you enjoyed, find local college events to support the children as they grow into their roles as actors.

Remember to play uplifting music when you feel stressed because it builds your pleasure endorphins. There is subliminal music you can play at any time. Play in the background while going about your day. There are various uplifting categories to choose for support. Keep a journal of only happy moments and things you are grateful for. Make a vision board to create your dreams and display it where you will see it often.

Practice Feng Shui and set up your home for positive energy.

Use meditation daily to build your spiritual skeleton.

Use the color turquoise to recharge your spirits during times of mental stress and tiredness. It controls and heals the emotions creating emotional balance and stability.

Write positive affirmations on turquoise color paper and post them through the house or place of employment. It can be as simple as "I AM HAPPY" or "I AM CALM"

Plan on what works for you to relieve stress before it creeps up on you. When you plan ahead it makes any stressful situation go more smoothly and helps to keep you calm.

~Daily Inspiration by Catherine M Laub, Advocate for Mental Health

26.

Laying on the Road Won't Help

Reflecting on moving homes, when asked how the move went, my reply was "I could have laid on the road."

Obviously I'm speaking figuratively and obviously I wouldn't do that.

But sometimes things do get the better of us and we feel like we have absolutely no control over the outcomes and consequences.

So I thought I'd share a few strategies that might help in those rare situations when you may feel like laying on the road:

1. Find something you can be grateful for; anything that will bring a smile to your face and a happy feeling to raise your vibration.
2. Acknowledge the success you have enjoyed so far. It could be with a particular project or anything from your past, where you have overcome challenges or simply achieved goals. This will give you confidence that you can overcome these challenges as well.
3. Find something you can control or take action on and implement that. This will help you make progress as well as keep your mind off what's not working.
4. Accept how you are feeling at the moment and know that "this too will pass".
5. Make a note of your challenges so that when the time comes to share these stories to inspire others, you'll have all the nitty gritty details that you might otherwise forget, which are critical for others to imagine and relate to.

I know for myself, I'm looking at our current challenges and saying to myself, "Well, this is all part of the journey and will make a great story when we share how we went from here to here and how you can too".

Take heart, if you're experiencing challenges, it's not forever and remember, and laying on the road won't help.

~Daily Inspiration by Shirley Dalton, Business Expert

27.

Enjoy This Not-So-Sweet Indulgence

It's February, this month is all about matters of the heart--from National Love Your Pet Day to Valentine's Day.

And that brings us to the topic of chocolate--one of our favorite guilty pleasures! In fact, we spend nearly $20 million on this food during Valentine's week. And why not, it's the ultimate feel-good indulgence!

But science is now telling us this food--especially the dark version--could be good for our health. Dark chocolate contains a class of nutrients called flavonoids. These naturally-occurring chemicals have both antioxidant and anti-inflammatory properties. Dark chocolate's consumption has been linked to lowering blood pressure, supporting heart and brain health, and possibly lowering the risk of diabetes.

But like all desserts, it is possible to get too much of a good thing.

So here's the skinny on dark chocolate consumption: Purchase a product that has 70% cocoa (with a lower percentage, you won't get the health benefits; a higher percentage delivers a more bitter taste) and limit portion size. Break off one small square (about 1.5" by 1.5", only 62 calories and 3 grams of sugar), then re-wrap the package and put it back on the shelf. Now you're ready to sit down and thoroughly savor this rich, decadent reward! So send yourself some love wrapped in a chocolate hug; it's the perfect way to celebrate the end of a special day!

~Daily Inspiration by Lisa Harris, MS, RD, Fitness Pro

28.

What the World Needs...Is More of You

I believe every single person has been given unique talents, abilities, gifts, and dreams. My vision is for everyone to have the chance to show up in just the way they are gifted to serve.

The world needs YOU, in all your unique and wonderful ways!

I envision a big, beautiful gift box that I am handing to you right now. It is filled with reminders of who you are, how wonderful you are, and the many ways that the world needs YOU. Take a moment to think about what it is inside the box - all the things that you love about yourself and others love about you, all the things that you were brought here to give to the world!

Take another moment to think about the joy and fun you have had – with your friends, with loved ones, or all by yourself (which is a precious gift itself!). Laughter and joy are present-moment experiences that bring our world together. The world can never have enough of our joy and laughter. The world can never have enough of YOU! **Remember to share the gift of YOU!**

~Daily Inspiration by Rebecca Hall Gruyter, Influencer & Empowerment Leader

March

1.

What are You Preparing to Grow in This Year?

Remember back in January when you had lots of energy about your projects, looked forward to making them happen, got some movement going? March is now the time to think about that soil in which your seeds of ideas, projects, creations are being planted.

"April showers that bring May flowers" start with the plans, seeds, soil, and space in order to grow into a rose! Are you preparing now for the coming time of growth that happens in April and May?

Pay attention to what you are preparing for growth.
- What are you spending time and energy on?
- Are there other people planting seeds that may not be part of your vision and plan for your garden?
- Are you pausing, breathing, and clearing out space that will allow your seedlings to send down roots?

Pay attention to what you are planting. What are you building into your life?
- This is the season to plan your garden on purpose, so that as you go forward in your life, you are focusing on the things that matter to you.
- Tap into the energy of preparing and planting that will grow into what you want to bring forward in this year.
- Protect your time and protect your space, so that your seeds will have room and roots to grow and flourish come harvest time!

~Daily Inspiration by Rebecca Hall Gruyter, Influencer & Empowerment Leader

2.

Let's Get Persnickety

When I visualize this word I see a person, wrapped in self-righteousness, with haughty, condemning eyes and a small, puckered -up mouth, looking down on others. I am sure you have at least one in your life. The first definition of persnickety is fussy, someone who majors on the minors. But, persnickety also means "requiring great precision". This is the persnickety I want to encourage us to embrace.

A 125 million-dollar Mars space probe missed the mark because someone didn't check the work. Propulsion engineers typically express force in pounds, but usually convert to newtons for space missions. Engineers at NASA assumed the conversion had been made, and didn't check.

A chef needs to be precise. There is a poem by an unknown author that gives us the hilarious results. After all the substitutions, the poem ends with "My friend gave me the recipe -she said you couldn't beat it. There must be something wrong with her, I couldn't even eat it."

Take a few minutes today and think about the precision that is needed to do many of the jobs we have. Then **deliberately choose to live today precisely and purposefully.** Examine yourself and see where darkness is lurking that needs to be banished. Expect experiences that will stretch you, frustrate you, or maybe even leave you awestruck. Meet them head on, intentionally, and draw every ounce of energy from them to make your light stronger. Expand your horizons and look for someone who could use some light, the wisdom and knowledge you have. By doing that you will create a light wave, like a ripple, that will result in a better world. Let's all live with a bit more precision and embrace your inner persnickety.

~Daily Inspiration by Elda Robinson, Teacher

3.

You are the Master of Your Universe

You are both the Cause and the Effect of everything in your life. As Cause, you are responsible for forming all your experiences according to the levels of your thoughts. All your thoughts, when fueled by your feelings, move energy into motion, subsequently causing you to behave as you do. The effect of this is reflected in what you attract.

Your mind is an impartial machine, automatically receiving both positive and negative input as a neutral force, manufacturing all the raw material of your mind — thoughts + feelings = energy of "like-kind". You now know that there are no accidents in the Universe. You always receive that which you ask for and people respond exactly as you see them, because they are mirrors of your

Today choose your thoughts with great discernment and Purpose.

~Daily Inspiration by Kathleen E. Sims, D.D., C.H.T.

4.

Leadership Lessons

Here are some lessons I learned in leadership. As a pastor, I have discovered these powerful truths about leadership that I hope will serve you too:

1. **It's Okay to Fail.** It is important to learn from your failures and to grow as a person. Many fail twice, the first time from a lack of knowledge and the second from lack of growth. Embrace your failures as an opportunity to learn and grow. What is something have learned from a failure/mistake that can now help you and others?

2. **Invest in your growth.** It is indispensable in the process of becoming a better person. Commit your time and money into your future; that includes fully committing yourself to a specific calendar and investing in things that will help you grow, rather than keep you from reaching your full potential. How are you investing in your growth?

3. **Be willing to follow**. I believe great leaders also know how to be great followers. If you want to succeed you must be able and willing to follow others who are more experienced than you are and know the way. This will help you costly mistakes you would not have made if you had followed the example of others who have gone before you. Who are you following and learning from today?

~Daily Inspiration by Pastor Nicolas C Pacheco

5.

Sometimes "No" Really Means "Not Yet"

I remember the time that I got to ride with my grandfather his tractor as it lurched over the rough terrain on his farm. Now my grandfather was a man that I wanted to emulate, and at the age of 10, I asked if I could drive the tractor. I had been studying his every move, noticing how he put in the clutch when he needed to shift gears, and giving it gas at just the right time…I *knew* I could do it!

I will never forget when he looked down at me, put his hand on my head, and said *"you can't drive the tractor, you are too little"*. I was crushed! What I **really heard**, was that there was something **wrong** with me…that no matter how hard I prepared myself, I would **never** be able to do certain "grown-up" things because I was <u>**alway**</u>s going to be "too little"!

As I grew in strength and height there did come a time that my grandfather asked me to drive the tractor! With my grandfather's strong hand on mine, he guided me through the intricate dance of the clutch and gas.

I finally understood that my grandfather never meant that being "too little" was to be a lesson of lifelong inferiority. He meant that **for now**, I was "too little". If he had let me drive at the age of 10, I surely would have been a miserable failure (imagine *that* life lesson!). He knew when it would be my time…not because of a <u>**fault within**</u> me, but because of a <u>**strength within**</u> me.

How many times have our childhood brains done the best they could to interpret what a respected parent figure said and gotten in all wrong? Yet with our childhood interpretation, we move forward in life believing that negative interpretation to be an infallible truth!

So remember: When life starts throwing a lot of "no's" at us (didn't get that promotion or that new position) it doesn't mean that something is wrong with us, it just means that "**I'm not ready**…. **yet**!"

~Daily Inspiration by John F. Hall, MBA, Author, Business Owner

6.

Thought for the Day

"Life is 10% what happens to me and 90% of how I react to it."
– CHARLES SWINDOLL

7.

Trust in Love

My daughter was two weeks shy of turning one when we adopted her. She was found at a bus station in a bustling city in China when she was 3 1/2 months old. After that, she was in an orphanage for eight long months sharing caregivers with many other babies. When she finally landed in our family, she had the option of holding her heart closed for fear of being hurt again. Or she had the option of opening her heart to us, allowing us to reach her and allowing her to love us in turn. Luckily she showed great levels of resilience and chose to let us in.

If you have been hurt by the loss of love, please find your inner resilience and allow yourself to open your heart so that others might love you.

As Maya Angelou wrote, "Have enough courage to trust love one more time, and always one more time."

~Daily Inspiration by Dr. Ruth Anderson, Spiritual Counselor

8.

The Power of STORY

The story you tell yourself about yourself becomes your identity! Tell the story that connects you to the magic of life. You must stop telling the harmful stories from your past. Those stories don't serve you and keep you swirling in a fog of despair and overwhelm.

Instead, **harness the power of your story to tell your success stories.** Each time you relive a success story that actually does serve you, you'll receive a jolt of happiness hormones. You create your own story, so only tell stories that serve and empower you. You'll be able to create magic. So choose your story of powerful success.

~Daily Inspiration by Mary Shores, Author and Speaker

9.

Spring Forward

"Courage, dear heart"
- C.S. LEWIS

Spring is a great time of renewal and rebirth, new beginnings. I often think of it as the beginning of a new year. This is a powerful time to reinvent yourself (to shed the old, allow all you have invested in yourself to blossom and sprout). Have courage to step forward into the year powerfully. Be willing to feel the fear, transform it into excitement and anticipation and step forward anyway. I've learned it's necessary to stretch outside your comfort zone. Recently, I read a poem that stated that courage is a muscle, which makes perfect sense to me. We need to continue to work at building it up and use it to push through to greater heights.

Say hello to a stranger, ask for the raise, submit your resume. Just go for it!

How are you building your courage muscle today? What fears can you change into excitement?

~Daily Inspiration by Jaimie Harnagel, Certified Reiki Master and Shamanic Practitioner

10.

Abundance is a Natural State

The truth is that *Abundance* is a natural state. Nature has no limits. There is enough for everyone. Realizing this for the world begins with *You*. When I started out, I didn't have much, but I believed in possibility. I was broke, uneducated, and unskilled. I cringe to think about the life I'd be living if I had allowed a lack mentality create my reality.

Somehow, I believed that while the odds seemed to be against me, they were irrelevant. I knew intuitively that life confirms beliefs–whatever they are. I believed that ultimately I would have personal and professional success. When you cultivate an abundance mindset, take action to bring it into manifestation, and allow this mindset to reach a place of life-wide well-being Emotionally, Physically, Spiritually, and Financially. You will become a powerful force, able to bring abundance into the lives of others.

This is the motivation behind my work. I know that the collective *"we"* can do more good in the world than I ever could.

So take a few minutes and imagine how that would feel. Imagine and what it would look like, then write it down. This is your destination.

~*Daily Inspiration by Carmell Pelly, Empowerment Leader*

11.

Let go my EGO

Ego … that part of you, your mind, that controls the conversations going on in your head all the time … the conversation between your conscious and subconscious thoughts. Or a person's sense of self-esteem or self-importance.

When I was growing up, I used humor to deflect attention away from me as I never wanted anyone to see how unworthy I felt. My sister saw this humor as a means for me to become the center of attention. She would tell me, "it is not always about you."

What she saw as my "ego" was my means of protecting myself from hurt or pain. Neither of us were wrong. The ego's sole purpose is to protect you, to keep you safe. It doesn't always do this in an empowering way.

The ego is neither good nor bad. It just is. It is how it shows up in thoughts and behaviors that put definition to it. The ego's main job is to make you feel safe. Ego is a place of constriction and is opposed to change or growth.

When ego drives your actions, you are not in a place of feeling complete as love is not a part of the ego. Ego is the reason you can't move forward. If ego is trying to stop you, how do you rid the needs of the ego and not be afraid. This is counter-intuitive as the ego wants you to say "no" first and then think about it later – this is the safe way. Take a leap of faith, say "yes" without the "how" stopping you. Identify when the ego is doing the talking. **Decide to intentionally come from your heart.** Take that step into the unknown outside of your comfort zone where beautiful things happen.

~Daily Inspiration by Denise Hansard, Empowerment Expert

12.

Thought for the Day

"You miss 100% of the shots you don't take."
– WAYNE GRETZKY

13.

Gratitude Starts It All

Endeavor and believe that you are worthy and deserved. Elevate and establish your self worth with Positive Affirmations that encourage your ascension. Trust your intuition as your guide and believe that you are deserving of Progressively Positive Outcomes in all your associations, situations and endeavors. **Start each day with the affirmation** "I AM Grateful for…" and begin to appreciate the simple things that really matter to you.

Pick something new each day to BE Grateful for and seek out endeavors that feed your gratitude, in positive and balanced ways. **STAY GRATEFUL and Empower yourself with Purpose Reminders that feed your Soul.** *Release* yourself from negative thought patterns and behaviors and allow yourself to replace them with positive and progressive thought patterns and behaviors. **CHANGE YOUR THOUGHTS AND YOU CHANGE YOUR REALITY.**

Affirmation:
I AM Grateful I AM Who I Desire to Be. I AM Worthy and Deserved of all Recognition that I AM Receiving. I AM Empowering MySoulSelf with Purpose Reminders. I AM Positive and Progressive, in My Thought and Behavior Patterns.

~Daily Inspiration by Mark Edward Pyle, Manifestation Expert

14.

Seeding and Nurturing Your Vision

March is a glorious time of rebirth and renewal! It presents the perfect opportunity to reimagine and reseed your highest vision of yourself. But as you know, you can't just throw seeds onto the ground and expect healthy growth. **You must also provide healthy soil and nurture your vision.**

I invite you to visualize your life as you step into your soul purpose. Where are you living? What are your surroundings? Are you alone? Are you living with others? Are you near water? Surrounded by trees?

Now consider where you are currently living. Does it match the ideal surroundings that you visualized? If you discover that your current situation is not ideal for the expression of your soul purpose, relax. Just getting clarity around your ideal surroundings is a powerful first step.

I invite you to spend a few minutes each morning visualizing your ideal surroundings and feeling the joy that your soul purpose brings you. Then pay attention to what shows up in your life. As you focus on your ideal living situation and feel the joy of expressing your soul purpose, the Universe conspires to support you in magical ways.

~Daily Inspiration by Olivia Parr-Rud, Corporate Love Ambassador

15.

Spring Forward and SHINE!

"You can have roots and wings."
- JAKE, IN SWEET HOME ALABAMA

There's something about a seed knowing what it is, knowing what it's going to become. It starts digging its roots in deep so that it can grow and shine as it's made to do. That describes us as well! We can lean into who we truly are, what we truly need, and who we are truly made to be. Sometimes it's hidden deep down under old stories and messages we've received, but we are gifted to serve with all our unique talents, abilities, and dreams - just like the rose has been gifted with color, scent, delicate petals, and strong stems.

I believe "you can have roots and wings" like Jake says in the movie *Sweet Home Alabama*. In fact, we NEED both to SHINE. We have roots that we send down deep into the earth, a foundation for the actions that will support us in bringing forward what we are called to do and be. Our roots are our plans, our talents, our resources, and the loving people who support us. Our deep roots help us weather the storms of life as we grow and blossom.

We also have wings - dreams, goals, callings that pull us to fly! Our wings take us to new opportunities to SHINE and to light the path for others. We're able to spring forward to SHINE because we have our roots to support us.

Today, let's celebrate our roots and our wings, and all the gifts we've been given to share! **Let your roots go deep and your wings give flight to your dreams, passion and purpose.**

~Daily Inspiration by Rebecca Hall Gruyter, Influencer & Empowerment Leader

16.

Personal Power

*"You would worry a lot less about what people think
of you, if you realized how seldom they do."*
-ELEANOR ROOSEVELT

This is one of my favorite reminders to stop looking outside myself for validation. Today, I invite you to take a deep breath, quiet your mind, look inward, and think about what you want your day to be about. Ask yourself: What do I want to accomplish today, who do I want to connect with today, or even, how do I want to FEEL today?

It's up to you. The less you worry about what others think, the more personal power you can keep to determine the quality of your own life.

~Daily Inspiration by Dr. Liz Lyster

17.

Thought for the Day

"When everything seems to be going against you, remember that the airplane takes off against the wind, not with it."
- HENRY FORD

18.

Fix Your Focus

Focus is defined as "The center of interest or activity." (Dictionary.com: focus) Sometimes in your life, you'll find that your focus can be centered on various distractions, i.e. setback, finances, divorce, health concerns and more.

It is very common to fix all of your thoughts on what is disturbing your peace. However, this can lead to feeling exhausted, anxious, depressed, angry and even suicidal. In order to take advantage of the day, you must learn to re-channel your focus on the positive.

Here are some tips to help you **FOCUS:**

F: Forward thinking! - There is nothing you can change about what happened. What you can do is release yourself and your future by letting go of the past and plan to move forward.

O: Optimism is KEY! - Choose to be optimistic in EVERY situation! If you are dealing with a diagnosis, be thankful you know what you're dealing with and focus on healing. . If you finances are shaky, be grateful for what you have a look at how you can bring in more. If your family is struggling, be grateful they are still with you. If you are dealing with grief, cherish the memories you had with the people who have left your life. Optimism is KEY for your focus to be where it needs to be for your success!

C: Control Your Thoughts! - In order to remain focus, choose to focus on thoughts that will feed you and guide you into your success in every area of your life.

U: Understand the Big Picture of Life! - Life will get better. Opportunities will come. Life comes in seasons, so embrace your season while focusing on the next opportunity!

S: Success is YOURS! – As you fix your focus, your life will align again with purpose!

~Daily Inspiration by India White, Author and Inspirational Speaker

19.

Move On Down the Road

I look at where I have been and where I am going during this time of year. The road I am on seems to get longer with wild turns that catch me off guard. But I enjoy the curves. The curves keep my mind sharp and ensure I don't get complacent in my professional life and with my husband. I also strengthen my resolve to be a better rendition of myself as I journey down my road.

It is my road and no matter how much I might like to travel someone else's road I cannot. No one can travel my road either. We each get to travel our own road. Make sure you are moving in the right direction, evolving as you go, and at a pace that will get you to your destination. **We must remember that we all have our role in this world and unlike a Broadway play, no one can play your role. Enjoy your travel as you move on down your road.**

~Daily Inspiration by Tresté Loving, Racial Equity Expert

20.

Questions – Empowering or Disempowering?

My favorite quote is **"Yesterday is history, tomorrow is a mystery, today is a gift, that's why we call it the present."** (This has been quoted by many people. It is considered Widely Misattributed. It seems that no one knows who first said it.)

Perhaps you're thinking "Wow, two months of the year are gone!" You may be asking yourself: "Why is it so difficult to follow through on my plans to make this year better?" "Why haven't I done what I said I would do?"

In my life journey I've learned that there are questions which empower and questions that disempower. The two questions above focus on what is wrong, what is not going well. The questions and answers make us feel bad ourselves. I've learned to rephrase my questions so that I feel empowered. For example, I would prefer to ask "How can I get back on track, so that I can make this a wonderful year?" Consider that an airplane is usually off course most of the time as it flies toward its destination. There are many course corrections in order to ensure that the plane gets to the right destination. Another empowering question might be "What is the best next step right now to get back on track and move forward?"

How can you use **empowering questions** instead of those that disempower you?

~Daily Inspiration by Bonnie May Best, Wellness Consultant

21.

Thought for the Day

*"Mediocrity will never do.
You are capable of something better."*
- GORDON B. HINCKLEY

22.

What You Do Today Is Important

What you do today is important because you are exchanging a day of your life for it. When tomorrow comes, this day will be gone forever; in its place is something that you have left behind... let it be something good."
- MAC ANDERSON

Be BRAVE. Self-limiting beliefs are like sticky goblins --they become so much a part of you, you don't even realize they're there. When you're stuck in frustration, unable to move past your fears and tempted to settle - don't. Instead, ask yourself, "what if..." One of the bravest questions I asked is "what if I can be spiritual *and* wealthy?" The truth set me free. "A comfort zone is a beautiful thing, but nothing ever grows there". Friend courage.

The HEART of financial success lies in relationships.
I cannot emphasize this enough: know your value and self-worth. Honor your feminine leader qualities to create, nurture and transform! Women are especially gifted in building relationships. You are empowered to generate amazing income and impact in the world. Know that you already have *everything* to begin and you'll experience financial freedom quicker than you can imagine.

You AND I cannot accomplish great things alone. We need others to achieve the greatness we were born to share. Brain science reveals the valuable ways we need a support team to shine in our full potential as individuals and as a society. The beauty of "left brain", "right brain", male and female teams working together is essential for creating unlimited possibilities to thrive.

Honor your BLAZING zone of genius (and the strengths of those around you). Everybody has a gift - trust yours. I've always seen the world through eyes of faith and innovation, but greatly undervalued these strengths based on the opinions of others. As a result, my world became very small and financially unstable. When I learned to be vulnerable in safe places to connect with others, opportunities "magically" appeared. **Live in your unique design and you'll soon ignite a flourishing, joyful life.**

~Daily Inspiration by Marlene Elizabeth, Author of MONEYWINGS™

23.

You are the Hero(ine)

You are the hero(ine) of your story and all of your experiences are a part of your legacy.

During this Women's History Month, take a look at the legacy you are creating with your commitment as a caring human being modeling compassion and generosity in your daily life. A legacy often means a financial inheritance, but in this instance, legacy refers to a heritage of values, traditions and cherished memories. My grandmother loved to bake and she passed that knack to tweak a recipe to make it her own with a sprinkle of cinnamon, or a handful of walnuts, on to my mother who passed it on to me.

Who taught you to bake, sew, perhaps your legacy involved learning to play an instrument or a sport? **What part of their legacy will you pass on with your unique twist to the story?** Spend fifteen minutes reflecting on where you are in your life right now. Record in your journal where you are now and give voice to the person you want to be. **Your words have the power to bring you from where you are to where you want to be.**

~Daily Inspiration by Mary E. Knippel, Your Writing Mentor

24.

Thought for the Day

"I'm convinced that about half of what separates the successful entrepreneurs from the non-successful ones is pure perseverance."
- STEVE JOBS

25.

From Out of The Moss, We Renew

Burn-out is a very real challenge that we face. With our daily in-and-out of responsibilities, repeatedly doing the same things over and over again, some level of burn-out is inevitable. It has the potential to bring about a blanket depression, negative attitudes, loss of production, and can destroy your relationships, self-esteem, and ability to thrive. Like a slow-growing moss, it spreads and spreads until it's so thick that you are left struggling just-to-get-through-each-day... just like Tom's roof.

Tom, our elderly next-door neighbor, had a roof that was in need of some serious attention. Being right next door, we had a prime view of his moss-covered roof. Just about any time guests came over, they would comment on the severity of it. We worried about it caving in on him and how the eyesore would impact the sale of our own home.

Over the years, the moss had just slowly grown. Each year it spread little by little until eventually it had covered and weighed down every inch. Just like moss, there are things in our lives that, inch by inch, start to cover who we truly are and weigh us down. How do we get back to that shiny new surface that enables us to live our days feeling secure, confident, and strong? Through Renewal.

When you work on renewing yourself, you begin to take who you have become, and weed through the "moss" of life in order to get back to who you truly are.

Equip yourself with strategies that allow yourself to SHINE, be grateful for the blessings in your life, take time to breathe... seek after renewal and let the moss be gone. **By enabling yourself to be renewed, you will be allowing yourself the strength to reach your full potential and make a positive difference in the lives around you.**

~Daily Inspiration by Julz DeFant, RDH

26.

Thought for the Day

"Most people fail in life not because they aim too high and miss, but because they aim too low and hit."
- LES BROWN

27.

Commitment vs. Compliance

It sounds straightforward, right? Compliance comes from a mindset of "have to" and Commitment comes from a mindset of "totally surrendered to a choice you have made". However, when this plays out in life, it's not always easy to see which side of the fence one is playing from. It simply seems that any time in my life when I've said "yes" when I really felt like "no" was the best answer for me, it comes back to bite me.

One of the greatest gifts of my life has been attending and now working with the team at Klemmer Leadership Seminars. **One way to discover which side of the commitment/compliance fence you're playing on is to run through the following test:**

- Is this my goal or someone else's?
- Am I committed to the goal or moving forward out of compliance alone?
- If committed to the goal, what's my "why behind the why?" (This could be several layers deep.)
- What are the anticipated obstacles to overcome?
- What are the upsides and downsides of achieving this goal?
- Where will I tap into the best research for tools, support and general leverage to lighten my load?
- If I'm responding out of compliance, what would it take to shift to a committed mindset.
- Have I discovered the WIIFM? "What's in It for Me".
- These same questions may be utilized for others when enrolling a team into action for **their** reasons.

Remember that leaders generate true commitment in those around them, instead of compliance.

~Daily Inspiration by Kathy Fairbanks, Radio Show Host

28.

Nature's Inspiration

The things that inspire us are the things that bring us joy. That is because in that moment we are accessing our soul's desire.

For me, nature is a big inspiration. The sun on my face is rejuvenating; it gives me warm energy. Watching the leaves change colors also fills me with a joy like no other. The colors bring in inspiration and creativity, which lead me to a place where I create beautiful color combinations in beadwork. When I feel that joy shoot up into my stomach, I completely light up.

Allow nature to be *your* inspiration. Make time to notice the changes Mother Nature brings about. Make an effort to be outside today, no matter the weather; take 10 minutes to feel - whether it's the sun on your face, rain, snow or the breeze against your skin. Breathe in the sweetness. Hear the sounds of nature and know you are part of it all. You are not alone. Just these few precious moments will ground you. Be open and allow these moments to give you clarity and inspiration.

Take a few moments today to reflect on what brings you inspiration. And how can you encourage and inspire others?

~Daily Inspiration by Jaimie Harnagel, Certified Reiki Master and Shamanic Practitioner

29.

My Father Told Me He Loves Me

At age Eighty-three Daddy left us suddenly. His birthday was March 25th. He had health issues due to a heart condition for many years. The last time I saw him was in May.

December 5, 2012, I had a dream from Daddy. He told me "Please just let me die". A few days later he was hospitalized with pneumonia. Tony (my husband) and I were attending a party but had to visit Daddy first. I knew I may not get to see him again.

We kissed Daddy goodbye and said we love him. Daddy responded back he loves us too. **He never told me that until this moment.** My dream was confirmed and I knew his time was near.

The next day I was busy and didn't get to visit him. Tuesday I was called to assist my mother, who had the flu. While there the doctor called. Daddy had an incident and was revived, but in a coma.

I spent the next four days around the clock in the hospital lobby because I knew what was coming. Saturday, December 15, 2012, twenty-three of us gathered around Daddy as the nurse unplugged his life support. However, he didn't seem to be gone. The monitor still showed a heart rate because of his defribulator. Daddy comes to me often in dreams so his heart is still beating for me. **My inspiration is: Even when the life support instruments showed his body was gone, he has remained with me in sprit.**

When someone you love has an illness make sure you spend time with them. When they are gone pay attention to your dreams because they visit us often.

~Daily Inspiration by Catherine M Laub, Advocate for Mental Health

30.

Thought for the Day

"You become what you believe."
– OPRAH WINFREY

31.

When Things Get Stormy

"March...in like a lion and out like a lamb."
- 19TH-CENTURY PROVERB

For many parts of the world, the weather in March is very unpredictable. The same can be true in our businesses and lives - at any time of the year! Something unexpected, an unhappy surprise or twist, hits us and throws us off-course, just like those sudden storms in March. Are there storms brewing in your life or business? What is your plan to weather these storms when they do arise, so that you stay on the path to bring forth that which you are called to do?

Growing up, my family always had an "emergency toolkit" handy in case the power went out or one of us got hurt. I found we can have our own **emergency toolkit to help us through stressful and stormy situations.** For example, I keep essential oils in it that I can use wherever I am to bring me calm and steadiness. I have practices (prayer, breathing, journaling, taking a break) that help me stop, pause, center, focus so that I can move forward on purpose even in unexpected situations.

I also have my **"emergency helpline" - friends I know I can call to help me center myself** by talking me down or reminding me of my truth. I also bring in support when I need it, the people on whom I can rely to stand beside me, practically and profoundly. I encourage you to build your list too. ☺

Remember **life is not a solo journey**, none of us were meant to do it all on own, so be willing to reach out and walk beside another...and let them walk beside you too.

~Daily Inspiration by Rebecca Hall Gruyter, Influencer & Empowerment Leader

April

1.

How do You Set Yourself Up for Success?

Your time and energy are so very precious. It can be easy to make a commitment and just go full speed ahead on a business activity, like a networking event, without really thinking about it. At these moments, do you ask yourself: Why am I going? What do I want to get out of this? What kind of follow-up am I prepared to do? You want to think about your objective and goals before jumping into something, to make sure that you're not creating more work for yourself rather than bringing true value.

Take some time to visualize the activity or project first: Picture yourself there, see what you are doing and what you expect the results to be. Give yourself permission to evaluate whether or not it's a good use of your time, to make sure that you are doing things on purpose and with purpose. If you do decide to make the commitment, do another visualization so you can plan to get the most out of the experience. **Your time and energy are precious. Use them and spend them on purpose and with purpose.**

~Daily Inspiration by Rebecca Hall Gruyter, Influencer & Empowerment Leader

2.

Three Success Tips to Grow MONEYWINGS™

Unfold your financial potential, one brave feather at a time.

One of the most successful women I heard speak gave a lesson full of key points. At the end of her talk, each point led to her core message: "If you believe, you will succeed." She led a billion-dollar company. (Rarely did I blink as she spoke.) Janice Bryant Howroyd is the 1st African American to lead a billion-dollar business. Her presentation inspired me to share two more success tips with my clients that I've learned over the years as a mama-preneur:

#1 90% of success is in how you show up. Be ever-mindful of your thoughts, words, actions and habits for they lead to your character and destiny. Create an environment around you that supports your success including your physical space, mindset, routines, and the people you allow (and don't allow) into your space. **Surround yourself with those who believe in you and energize you to blossom. Sit in the driver's seat - take full responsibility for your life and well-being.**

#2 Live in your full potential to shine. Avoid "comparison-its". The illusion I followed trying to be like everyone else only lead me in circles! Move forward instead, pouring your energy and focus into being someone you love. Know your purpose, your clear desired outcome and daily inspired actions to achieve it. Be the honest channel you can only be, and then allow the Universe to take care of the rest. (You'll be astounded at the miracles you'll experience!)

~Daily Inspiration by Marlene Elizabeth, Author of MONEYWINGS™

3.

Thought for the Day

"Remember no one can make you feel inferior without your consent."
– ELEANOR ROOSEVELT

4.

Make Fear Your Friend

What are you afraid of? How does it make you feel? Instead of letting your fear get the best of you, find out how to fully experience it, name it, get to know it and take it by the hand so it can become your friend and ally.

Everyone knows fear. It can come in an instant and throw you into chaos, yet it can also save your life. Fear is a natural response to physical danger, but it can also be self-created, such as the fear of:

- *failure*
- *being out of control*
- *being different*
- *being lonely*
- *You may fear love because you fear being rejected*

This self-generated fear is found in its acronym: F.E.A.R. or False Evidence Appearing Real. It appears real, even though it is a fear of the future and is not happening now. As long as you push away, deny or ignore fear, it will hold you captive and keep you emotionally frozen, unable to move forward. Sooo, What can we do?

Allow fear in and make friends with it. Fear is a powerful emotion that demands understanding and patience. But trying to block it will simply create further anxiety.

The next time fear arises try this simple breathing exercise
Fear comes—you breathe and let go.
Fear comes—you see how the mind needs reassurance and tenderness.
Fear comes—replace it with love.

When you do this, you are inviting the fearful and anxious parts of yourself to get to know each other; to sit down for a cup of tea together, to release the fear and feel the love and acceptance takes its place.

~*Daily Inspiration by Carmell Pelly, Empowerment Leader*

5.

Overcoming the Darkness

Since my dark night of the soul in 2014, I experienced many positive changes and much growth. We all face the darkness at some point but it doesn't affect everyone the same way. For me it was drastic and during a crisis moment.

This was a crucial turning point and the only way to go was up. There are so many ways to overcome the symptoms and move forward and shine. For me this time of darkness was the beginning of a new and better life. I share this message not for sympathy, but for inspiration to guide you to the best you can be. I realized the moment I was taken to the hospital things would get better. Three days earlier I prayed to God and my Angels to help me feel better and get off some of my twenty-two medications. This was the answer.

God wanted me to experience the full extent of the darkness so I could relate to others when I speak with them. For me it was both mental and physical symptoms that fed off each other. Each person is different. I am grateful for my life and the opportunity to reach out and lift others up. Here is what I've discovered:

You are absolutely wanted, needed and make a difference by being you. Commit today to sharing your gifts and talents in a positive way. Be willing to be the light for another.

~Daily Inspiration by Catherine M Laub, Advocate for Mental Health

6.

Success is YOURS!

Success is defined as, "the favorable or prosperous termination of attempts or endeavors; the accomplishment of one's goals." (Dictionary.com- http://www.dictionary.com/browse/success)

When we think of success, we tend to think of someone winning a gold medal, an orchestra finishing its performance, a college graduate or etc. The main experience that each of these events mentioned previously have in common is that a goal was made and the goal was met with a successful outcome. In order to have success, you must be determined to see success in whatever you are pursuing. YOU must be persuaded that no matter what they are facing as an obstacle towards their success that success will be YOUR!

So, let me encourage you today that success is YOURS!

Here are some helpful tips for you to embrace YOUR Success:

1. **Remember that the Best is Yet to Come!** – Sometimes you have to continue to look up and remain positive and remember that your best days are still ahead of you!
2. **Fight the Urge to be Average!** – It can be tempting to settle for less than you've desired. Be encouraged and overcome that temptation and come out on the other side as VICTORIOUS!
3. **Plan and Receive!** – Your efforts are not in vain! Continue to invest in your dreams until you are able to receive complete success in every area!
4. **Celebrate the Small Victories!** – As you begin to receive success in various areas, take time to celebrate the small victories! You deserve this!
5. **Refuse to Quit**- Never give up! That is not an option. You only have one option: SUCCEED!!

No matter where you are on your journey, it's never too late to start. Choose to make steps towards your success and make it happen!

~Daily Inspiration by India White, Author and Inspirational Speaker

7.

Living in Expectation

We are more than we realize. We are fertile. What you invest in yourself you will in time reap. Whether it be money, kind words, seed offering, it will grow. It's all on how you look at it. I want to invite you to live in expectation...expect and believe in growth.

Invest in yourself and others. Expect and welcome growth...in both yourself and others. How are you investing in yourself and others today? Are you living in expectation? Today, find a way to invest more in yourself and others while leaning in with great excitement and expectation of growth in your life.

~Daily Inspiration by Kri' Shawn Terrell, Motivational Speaker

8.

Thought for the Day

*"When I stand before God at the end of my life,
I would hope that I would not have a single bit of talent
left and could say, I used everything you gave me."*
– ERMA BOMBECK

9.

Collaborate, Lead and Grow!

*"I can promise you that women working together
– linked, informed and educated – can bring peace
and prosperity to this forsaken planet."*
– ISABEL ALLENDE

After the quiet winter, spring is the season of prosperity and the start of new things. It is also the time for connection to others, thus this quote. As we watch the early spring flowers break through frozen ground and begin to bud, we recognize how much hope there is in that ability to break through.

While it looks like a solitary effort, there is much going on below the surface. There is connection – seed, soil, sand, water, ice, bugs and worms, together conspiring for this tiny seedling to pop through and reach up to the sun. *We know the value of collaboration and working together to create unbelievable wonders. We create movements that change the world.* The more visible we are in our desire to change, the more we come together in community.

Whether the thing you want to change is bringing a neighborhood watch to your community or campaigning for more women in elected government positions or working to end abuse of any type, you need to draw your allies to you to help, support, bring visibility and more, to the work you do. That is when true prosperity begins to grow like those brave spring flowers.

What movement will you start or put your effort and energy into? Dare to Lead!

~Daily Inspiration by Linda Patten, Leadership Expert

10.

Loving & Leveraging Life

One of the most productive tools anyone can adopt in business is mastering the art of leveraging. I'm always saddened when I work with a client who continues to show up as if it's their first day on the job and that they must start from scratch each day. There's never been a better time in history to leverage the use of templates. If I complete a task, spreadsheet, or project more than once, I create a system in order not to start from scratch each time I'm casting a vision for the project.

Once there's clarity around the project I'll set up a goal achievement template, which will most likely come from a previously used template. Then I track my results from start to finish, both from a "staying on course" perspective and from a "course-correction" perspective. Templates are one thing; leveraging people is a different. When it comes to leverage and people, it's essential that there's a balanced exchange; not necessarily an equal exchange. Maya Angelou shares when comes to people and leverage **"I've learned that people will forget what you said, people will forget what you did, but people will never forget how you made them feel."**

Maintenance is a subset of leverage. I recently received a call from a sales manager I worked with fourteen years ago requesting a work reference. Providing a reference was easy, as Michael was a dream employee. Later I realized one of the reasons it was so easy was because Michael stayed in touch every six months. I know that if fourteen years had transpired without communication, my reference would have been positive, but may have lacked enthusiasm or relevance. Leverage is simply an advanced form of human connection.

Here's to your success…keep knocking 'em alive!

~Daily Inspiration by Kathy Fairbanks, Radio Show Host

11.

Thought for the Day

*"When life gets you down
do you wanna know what you've gotta do?
Just keep swimming!"*
– DORY, FINDING NEMO

12.

Be Mindful of the Seeds that You Are Planting

"Bloom where you are planted and SHINE!"
- REBECCA HALL GRUYTER

What seeds are you planting for your life and business this spring? Are you allowing great things to grow? Or, do you have things so packed on your schedule that you can't see through the weeds or have the space to grow? This can create what my dad would call "root-bound" plants, when there's no room for the roots to stretch out and expand and grow like they are meant to do.

I invite you to be very mindful of the seeds that you're planting now, and to give them the intention, space, and love that will allow them to grow. Here are some practices to help you:

Be unattached to the "how." This allows the "how" to show up in unexpected (and wonderful) ways, especially if you're going where you haven't gone before! Be open to letting things unfold and trust that your needs will be made and "how" will show up. Be willing to receive the "how" even if it shows up in an unexpected way.

Slow down and look around. Especially when you are creating something new, it's so important to take time to slow down so that you can keep SHINING, stepping forward, and making sure you see the next step on your path. Remember to notice the growth and check to make sure your feet are on your path and moving in the right direction for you and your goals.

Stay mindful of who you are, and what you are bringing forth every day. Never lose your values or your power. Keep your eye - and your heart - on your purpose. Why? Because you are creating something beautiful, and the world needs what you have to offer!

~Daily Inspiration by Rebecca Hall Gruyter, Influencer & Empowerment Leader

13.

Transformation

"Change is inevitable, but transformation is by conscious choice."
– HEATHER ASH AMARA

They say the transformed people can help transform others, but does the caterpillar get coached by the butterfly on his journey? As humans evolve we continue to gain more knowledge and fill our brains with more data. The more we analyze and attempt to make logical choices, the less we use our natural instincts to grow and prosper. Human beings are classified as animals and we have an instinct to survive, procreate and evolve, but would we know how to do this today without Google?

I recently moved from the desert of Arizona to the hospitable south of Georgia. This is my first time being able to witness the entire process of seasons changing. I've watched the trees go dormant and lose their leaves, and for months could not imagine that they could come back to life with such energy, strength and power. It's amazing watching plants bloom so beautifully and within days become green, luscious leaves that will thrive for the next few seasons. I curiously wondered how the animals, insects and trees know to evolve, and yet, we as individuals struggle with simple, often trivial changes. We rely on logic to make the best choices or go outside of ourselves and look to others to guide us in our decisions. However, we must realize that like the plants that surround us, we also have the very power, strength and know-how within ourselves to grow, evolve and flourish.

Today, I encourage you to reflect on your life and see the evidence of your past transformations. If you are currently struggling with a challenge, allow your inner caterpillar to guide you. Go within and trust your instincts to help you make decisions and realize that your next transformation is less than a season away.

~Daily Inspiration by Bonnie Bonadeo, The Connection Coach

14.

Flow through Fear

As we take steps to explore new possibilities in the season of Spring, we can encounter one of the biggest obstacles to making positive changes in our lives – fear. Although fear is what stops most of us from taking the actions to live the life we desire, fear is not the enemy.

Fear is simply what you feel when you try to cross the boundaries of your beliefs. Many of us know the three instinctive responses to fear – fight, flight, and freeze, but many of us don't realize that there is a fourth way to respond to fear that can transform your life - **FLOW. When you FLOW through your fears, you experience the power of your Radiance.**

F – Feel the fear as sensations in your body. The more you ignore your fear, the stronger it gets, but when you acknowledge and honor your emotions, you come into alignment with your true power. By focusing on the sensations in your body, you receive the message your fear is telling you without getting trapped by your stories and thoughts. When you follow the movement of these sensations in your body, the feeling of fear will subside.

L – Let go of your desires that are triggering this fear just for a moment. Many times, fear comes from the heaviness of a desire trying to push though the parts of you that resist change. When you let go of desire, the pressure lifts, your awareness widens, and you open yourself up to greater possibilities you may not have been aware of.

O – Open to love. The most powerful response to fear is love. Love allows you to approach life's challenges from the perspective of joy and compassion, and connects you to your true inner power.

W – Witness and trust the Wisdom that emerges. From this place of love and clarity, powerful wisdom emerges that will guide you forward on a path that resonates with your greater truth and passion.

When you learn to **FLOW**, fear no longer is something you avoid. Fear becomes an invitation for growth, transformation, and living a Radiant life!

~Daily Inspiration by Ron Coquia, Radiance Coach

15.

Promote Your Purpose, Positively

Surround yourself with Progressively Positive People and Endeavors. Gravitate towards those people and endeavors that truly resonate with your Soul and align with your Highest Good Goals and Desires. Make continuing connections with the progressive people that promote Positivity, with the positive places that encourage progressive growth and with the progressive endeavors that positively promote your Purpose.

Become impassioned and driven to make the important connections count, and count for something tremendously prosperous. Examine all your associations and invest in those that pull you towards your own goals. Embrace your greatness and begin the steady march towards goal manifestation with confidence and clarity. Find the winners in your field and begin to follow them closely and incorporate the practices and techniques that advance you and your endeavors progressively forward.

Affirmation:
I AM surrounding myself with Progressively Positive People and Endeavors. I AM making continuing connections with People that Promote Positivity. I AM Embracing My Greatness. I AM Incorporating Winner Techniques and Practices that Advance Me and My Endeavors Progressively Forward.

~Daily Inspiration by Mark Edward Pyle, Manifestation Expert

16.

Thought for the Day

"The person who says it cannot be done should not interrupt the person who is doing it."
– CHINESE PROVERB

17.

A Friend Indeed

How many people go through life without experiencing the deep bond of a close friendship? Friends opening their hearts and minds, trusting one another that they're safe and can be vulnerable as they walk together along life's journey. **Take a moment to reflect on your friendships, what kind of friendships have you forged?**

Friendship has nothing to do with time and distance. The question I would like for you to examine is why do we have this chemistry with a select few people? How is it that our group of friends have now turned exclusive, only a few people we know and not scores of others?

We know common interests, history, common values, and equality are what draw people together as friends. **What do you think makes a "friend" worthy of the name, "friend?" What has been your experience with friendships?**

Relationships can be complex without boundaries. What is it that makes someone call another their true friend? Is it their commitment to their happiness? Always willing to put that friend's happiness before the relationship? Yes, but a true friend is much more.

A true friend would correct you and let you know when you're wrong. A true friend would not ask you to place the friendship before your principles nor compromise your principles for them or anything else. **A true friend is a good influencer who inspires you to live up to your highest potential.**

~Daily Inspiration by Cassandra Garabedian, Stylist

18.

Overcoming Challenges

*Climb above troubles
to view landscape with new eyes
a new perspective*

I have overcome many challenges in my life journey. **I've learned that it is helpful to find a way to rise above the challenge and view what is happening from a new perspective. There is always a silver lining.**

Many years ago, my car was stolen. I was with friends and they were surprised by my attitude. I realized that I'd been wanting a new car. The old car was beginning to need repairs. What I really wanted was a gold Mercedes instead of an old white Toyota. A few days after my car was taken I contacted my friend who was out of town –I was taking care of her home and dog – to let her know my car was gone. She offered to let me drive her gold Mercedes, since it was her second car and she didn't drive it much. I laughed and thanked God for giving me the answer to my prayers!

I believe that everything happens for a reason. I stop and ask "What is the lesson here?" "What is the blessing in this experience?"

Are you able to stop and ask questions that give you the opportunity to learn and grow through any challenges you face?

~Daily Inspiration by Bonnie May Best, Wellness Consultant

19.

Asking Better Questions

The questions we ask, of ourselves and others, determines the direction and outcome of our lives.

Better questions lead to better solutions and outcomes.

If you are having a less than desirable day, try asking yourself: "What can I do to make this day more enjoyable?"

When something you consider "bad" or "negative" happens, rather than asking, "*Why* did that happen?" try asking, "*How* can I respond to this?" or "*What* can I do now?" or "*What* do I need right now?" These questions help you to generate more constructive options.

For example, when you have work or a project you must accomplish, and are less than thrilled about, try asking yourself: "*How* can I make this fun/enjoyable/easy?"

Some other useful questions to ask yourself:

- How do I want to show up today?
- What am I excited about today?
- Who can I encourage or serve?
- What am I grateful for?

Some Essential Oils to help you in asking better questions:

Clary Sage - *The Oil of Clarity & Vision*
Encourages you to remain open to new ideas and perspectives.
Spearmint - *The Oil of Confident Speech*
Inspires clarity of thought and confident verbal expression.

~Daily Inspiration by Tish Reese, Health + Wellness Mentor

20.

Perfection

"If the minimum wasn't (sic) good enough, it wouldn't be called the minimum"
-ROD KACKLEY

Have you ever been frozen in doing a task because of a desire for perfection? Worse yet, even given up the task entirely because it didn't seem to be "good enough" or wasn't "perfect" enough to submit? Have you worked many extra hours on a project, tweaking and adjusting, to get that last 5 % completed to your acceptable level of perfection... feeling that to do less just wasn't high quality?

We need to consider what is truly the minimum quality **acceptable**. Now don't get me wrong, I am not suggesting mediocrity in our work (quite the opposite!). I am suggesting that there comes a time that we set the minimum quality "Good Enough" bar **high** enough to be EXACTLY that...**Good** Enough!

If the "minimum" is not adequate for providing a quality 90-95 percent of the needed information to the audience, then we would simply raise the "minimum bar"! **Being able to get the message out with 90-95 percent effectiveness sooner can be more powerful than taking the effort to put forth the "perfect" project later.**

Perfection often requires one to spend countless hours of re-wording, tweaking, and energy just for that last few (perhaps pretty, but unnecessary) percent. Would that extra effort needed to increase 5% to make it "perfect" have truly made a hugely profound difference to the recipients? After all, **for whom** are we creating the project? Is it for **ourselves** so we feel good about "perfection", or for the **recipients** who will use the information?

General George Patton is credited with saying **"A good plan, executed vigorously today, is better that a great plan next week."** He would much rather have a satisfactory, operational plan *now* than wait for a "perfectly honed" plan *later*.

The combination of early action and a 90% "Good" plan is better than late action on a "Perfected" plan.

So if we raise our minimum standard "bar" to a high enough level that is truly acceptable, and then work to that standard, we can free ourselves from the frozen inefficient trap of chasing often unattainable Perfection! It provides for a much better life!

~Daily Inspiration by John F. Hall, MBA, Author, Business Owner

21.

Thought for the Day

"I've learned that people will forget what you said, people will forget what you did, but people will never forget how you made them fee."
– MAYA ANGELOU

22.

Your Setback is Only One Scene in Your Story

On April 11, 2012 I sat in my car attempting, unsuccessfully, to calm my nerves as I waited for 'the call'. When the phone rang I quickly answered unaware the words to follow would change my life. "We received your test results and I'm sorry to tell you, **you have invasive ductile** carcinoma," the nurse on the other end explained. The words hung in the air and it wasn't until I said them out loud to my husband minutes later that it hit me, **I have breast cancer.**

Your setback is only one scene in your story, just like breast cancer is only one in mine. If you think about your life in terms of a movie, it is comprised of multiple scenes, both positive and negative. While you cannot predict the ending of your movie, you can have hope knowing that even the most negative situations are isolated to one part of your story. Remember the words of Jesus in John 16:33, "I have told you these things, so that you may have peace. In this world you will have trouble. But take heart, I have overcome the world!" Next time you find yourself living an unwanted scene, remember Jesus provided you with His peace and your setback is only one scene in your story.

~Daily Inspiration by Sunday Burquest, Women's Empowerment Speaker & Author

23.

Thought for the Day

"A friend is one that knows you as you are, understands where you have been, accepts what you have become, and still, gently, allows you to grow."
– WILLIAM SHAKESPEARE

24.

Spring Forward in Your Relationship with Money

Sometimes we have this "thing" about money. Many people know we have to deal with it, but we'd really rather not have to talk about it; we just hope that everything falls into place.

So we get disconnected from money. We leave money out of the conversation about our intentions, our goals, and our wants. Which makes it hard for money to support our intentions, goals and purpose.

I want to encourage you to instead purposely build a relationship, an ongoing conversation, with money. Let money in on what you want from it! Open your ears - listen to what's being offered to you. You can see what serves you and what does not: What do you really need? What are you wanting to build and create? What matters to you? Let money be part of what you are looking to build and create...a valued and trusted partner.

Discover how to connect with money, communicate with money, and build what matters most to you with money coming along side to support you. Remember, money doesn't get to direct the relationship - you get to choose. Choose to build a positive relationship with money.

~Daily Inspiration by Rebecca Hall Gruyter, Influencer & Empowerment Leader

25.

Seeking Validation

Maybe it's just me. Maybe you don't seek validation the way that I do. I am a writer, and I want people to acknowledge my writing. Good reviews always spur me on to write more. Sadly, I am aware that sometimes I need this form of validation for me to move forward in this work that I believe is my life calling. If this is my work, why do I need validation from others?

I know that people get criticized for following their calling all the time. Look at J.K. Rowling. The now famous author of the Harry Potter series was turned down by 12 different publishers before receiving validation by Bloomsbury Publishing.

The reality is that many others have lived their lives doing their life's work and it has never been acknowledged. But that doesn't mean it was not valuable, and it does not mean that the world didn't need that work to be done. Please do not wait for someone else to see the value in your work for you to step forward into your brilliance. **The world needs you to step up and be heard. Your validation may well need to come from within you. Be your own cheerleader!**

"When nobody else celebrates you, learn to celebrate yourself. When nobody else compliments you, then compliment yourself. It's not up to other people to keep you encouraged. It's up to you. Encouragement should come from the inside."
-JOEL OSTEEN

~Daily Inspiration by Dr. Ruth Anderson, Spiritual Counselor

26.

Thought for the Day

"I'm a success today because I had a friend who believed in me and I didn't have the heart to let him down."
– ABRAHAM LINCOLN

27.

When You Share YOU, the World is a Better Place

We sometimes get stuck in playing a supportive role lifting others up... while forgetting to bring our own gifts and talents forward, to stand up and shine our own light. It is a lovely thing to serve others, yet the world does not mean for us to shrink back from what we were made to do and be!

We make a difference by sharing all of who we are - our gifts, talents, core values, abilities - with others. When we share and SHINE, we make the world a better place, one heart and life at a time.

Doesn't that feel empowering? To stand up and stand out and bring **ALL** of who you are forward?

Take this powerful message and feeling with you throughout this beautiful spring day, opening yourself up to whatever may come your way, KNOWING you are making the world a better place...today!

~Daily Inspiration by Rebecca Hall Gruyter, Influencer & Empowerment Leader

28.

Your True Self Perceives Truth

When you realize that everything that happens to you can teach you something valuable, you become willing to look beyond appearances to the Divine Gift present in all things. You can now benefit from the lessons of the past to make a meaningful contribution to the present, and expand your Soul's learning on your journey of Evolution through all time.

To focus on the Light in another or any situation, is to focus on the Solution, which adds Substance to it, thus dissolving any problem you had perceived. When you see beyond negative appearances in this way, you can understand the Divine Purpose of an event and the Soul Lesson for which it was intended for your greater Good, therefore, accelerating your Path of growth and bringing forth More Light. When you see life from this perspective, you can accept the perfection in all people and circumstances, no matter the "seeming" appearances. Through this Perception Lens of Truth, you can now see the Light in yourself and others, thus bringing It forth into the world. Now your past experiences become sources of priceless gifts, which help you conduct your life from a new foundation of Self-love and appreciation.

Today practice seeing the world through the 'Eyes of God'.

~Daily Inspiration by Kathleen E. Sims, D.D., C.H.T.

29.

The Power of AUTHENTICITY

Tapping into the truest part of yourself is like putting your inner SUPERHERO in charge. Authenticity is the practice of choosing moment-to-moment how you portray yourself as you truly are in the world. We are all told that we need to live our life a certain way—*believe this, believe that, get a job, buy a house, be a success*, and so on, forever.

But that way of life may be in conflict with who you really are. **Regardless of what the rest of the world tells you, the only way to be completely fulfilled on a daily basis is to allow the real you to live in this world.** *Welcome* the real you; get to know yourself and your desires. When I learned to bring my personal beliefs and values to the core of my business everything changed rapidly. Share the gift of the authentic you with the world.

~Daily Inspiration by Mary Shores, Author and Speaker

30.

Thought for the Day

*"People often say that motivation doesn't last.
Well, neither does bathing.
That's why we recommend it daily."*
– ZIG ZIGLAR

May

1.

Nourish Your Own Mind-Body-Spirit Garden

I shared with a health professional recently how I can get into this place of going, going, going, and I forget to eat or take a break until I'm almost forced to stop and take care of myself.

She responded: "When you think of the massive quantities of things you are creating, that you are birthing, that you're producing... remember that you can't possibly do it on an empty tank. You have to be mindful of nourishing yourself to bring forth what you're meant to bring forth."

It really struck me! And I wonder if this applies to you too as well, with all you might be creating and growing in your life and business?

I am being mindful about nourishing myself, feeding my mind-body-soul-spirit (it's all connected!). I know I have to take the time periodically to look at what I'm doing in my business, and keep it in balance with my personal life and wellbeing - just like a well-tended garden - so it can flourish.

I invite you to look at this, too... **What are ways that you can build self-nourishment into your daily life?**

~Daily Inspiration by Rebecca Hall Gruyter, Influencer & Empowerment Leader

2.

Celebrate You!

Celebrate you by nurturing yourself.

Spend fifteen minutes observing how you can nurture yourself in such simple ways with a scented hand lotion, perhaps a massage, or a weekend getaway. I love having my feet rubbed and having pretty toenails. Once a month I put a little spring in my step with a pedicure. **What nurtures you? What makes you feel pampered, cherished, spoiled, and indulged?** Record in your journal where you are now and give voice to the person you want to be. Your words have the power to bring you from where you are to where you want to be.

~Daily Inspiration by Mary E. Knippel, Your Writing Mentor

3.

Thought for the Day

"A bird doesn't sing because it has an answer, it sings because it has a song."
– MAYA ANGELOU

4.

Be YOU!

There is only one of you. Know there may be people who look and act like you, but **the truth is that there is only one YOU. Be you with everything you do today, tomorrow, and every day.** Be an example to all in what you say, in the way you live, in your love, your faith, and your purity. **Your true actions will lift everyone around you.**

So many times we want to be someone else, have some superpowers, and more. But at those times when you want and wish to be one of them, you forget how powerful you actually are by truly being you. **Be you because you are outstanding, and you're absolutely needed just as you are!**

~Daily Inspiration by Inguss

5.

Go For Great!

"Don't tolerate – go for great!"
-DR. LIZ LYSTER

When doctors tell patients that they are "just" getting older, or that they "just" have to live with aches or pains or fatigue, it makes me cringe! **You do not have to tolerate not feeling your best. Don't settle for being told there's nothing that can be done. You can always take your health to the next level.**

Have you been tolerating any discomforts in your body? Whether it's nutrition, exercise, supplements or meditation, seek out steps you can take to make small improvements that add up to feeling your best. Today, it is your choice to claim your best life and health!

~Daily Inspiration by Dr. Liz Lyster

6.

Let It Be

"When people say 'Let it go' what they mean is 'Get over it,' and that's not a helpful thing to say. . . . We should probably say, 'Let it be.'"
– JON KABAT-ZINN

'Let it be'—probably a good first step; a reminder to stop the continually looping replays of "it" in our minds. Yet, it may be a better choice for us to try to understand "letting go" or "letting 'it' be" as "moving past it" until we are able to reach a point of an acceptance of sorts.

The acceptance may be miniscule, it could be complete, or it could fall somewhere on the spectrum between the two...and it is rarely an acceptance of the "it" itself. The acceptance is, more importantly, of the fact that "it" occurred and we are helpless to change that fact. **When this has been acknowledged and accepted, we are usually amazed to find that we have arrived at the point where we can truly move past "it" to allow for strength and healing to enter into our hearts and minds. We also are gifted with a window into our soul and the guidance it provides us—we can access our soul's wisdom.**

With the knowledge that we are continually participating in our soul's growth, we can choose to flourish or to languish, and there is no right or wrong. The choice is ours to make—always—and no matter which we choose, we are still participating in our soul's journey.

~Daily Inspiration by Dr. Nancy Tarr Hart

7.

Be Your Best

Joy comes from within
bubbling up like fresh water
well overflowing

My birthday is in May, which is why my middle name is May. I love both the spring and summer seasons. New life, new growth, an opportunity to explore new adventures, all of these remind me of those two seasons.

Many years ago I realized I struggled with my last name Best. How could I possibly live up to that name? I decided to change my attitude. I started playing with my name. Others around me started playing with it as well. **I now use the tag line in my business 'Be Your Best'.**

I discovered it is important to fill our own well fully so that we have enough to give others. This helps us be our best. Find a way today to fill 'you' up so that you can **"Be Your Best"**.

~Daily Inspiration by Bonnie May Best, Wellness Consultant

8.

You Are Ready

"Promise me, you will always remember: you're braver than you believe, and stronger than you seem, and smarter than you think"
– CHRISTOPHER ROBIN TO WINNIE THE
POOH, AS WRITTEN BY A.A. MILNE

Ah...what if these words are actually true? Imagine a world where we are **truly better t**han we *think* we are! Do we ever hold back from doing something because we don't think we can do it, or simply because we have never done it before?

Just because we <u>think</u> we can't do something, or have never done it before, does **NOT** mean that we **CAN'T** do it!! We are <u>much</u> <u>more</u> capable than we may think.

Have you ever *known* that someone could do something, but *they* couldn't see it? I remember when my daughter was learning to ride a bike. After a regimen of gradually raising the training wheels, there came a time that I **KNEW** beyond a doubt that she was ready to ride on her own. SHE didn't believe it! I ran alongside her while she was on the bike as she shouted "don't let go, don't let go!" The thing is, I had **already** let go and she was riding on her own!! She was in actuality *much more capable* than she believed!!

Perhaps we need to let ourselves believe that, no matter how good or bad we think we may be at something, we are **ACTUALLY better!!** What a nice thought!!

~Daily Inspiration by John F. Hall, MBA, Author, Business Owner

9.

Don't Judge A Book by Its Cover

The person you are meeting today started their journey long before your encounter with them.

A book cover is very important because it has to stand out among other publications, this is why so much money and time is spent on getting a book cover just right. It has to be visually captivating to the reader with a compelling title to grab the reader's interest. The more captivated the reader is by the cover, the more likely the reader will purchase the book and begin reading the contents. The reader will begin reading the story starting with the first page. If a reader decided to skip half of the book and start from the middle, they would miss out on key information about the characters and the plot. We know the beginning of the story lays the foundation of a plot and the development of the main characters. The main characters will be in the same place at the middle or end of the book as to where they started at the beginning, but learning key points or experiences of someone's life in the past can help us understand the how and why they ended up where there are in the present.

We are not defined by our past, and we should be careful not to judge people based on who they are today. The homeless person that we see daily could have at one time been considered a successful, wealthy person, but a life-changing experience altered their life's path. The successful, wealthy person that you admire today could have once been a homeless person that was once overlooked by many in society. **We all have a story. We all have a past. As we strive to build a brighter future, just remember the saying, 'don't judge a book by its cover'. Take the time to build sustainable relationships and get to know people on a deeper level.**

~Daily Inspiration by Adrian Jefferson Chofor, Global Personal Transformation Strategist

10.

Thought for the Day

"Our greatest weakness lies in giving up. The most certain way to succeed is always to try just one more time."
– THOMAS A. EDISON

11.

You Are Whole and Complete as You Are

When you uncover the false negative beliefs your ego has made up about your worth and identity, you can recognize your sabotaging patterns. You then begin to unravel and heal your compensating personality traits that cause you to feel like something is missing, and think you're not good enough. Realize that this part of yourself has been eclipsing the Essence of your Authentic Self, by 'seemingly' convincing you hiding will keep you safe in the world. When you acknowledge this, the Truth of your Real Self - which *Is Whole and Complete* - can now be easily revealed and accessed.

All you need to do is acknowledge the perfection of your Being. When you know for yourself the Truth of your Identity, you can recognize and appreciate the greatness of your intellect, and know it is a tool in service to your Higher Self and your Essence. You were created with everything inside that is required to have a life that works perfectly. You can see in the Light of this Truth that **you** have actually been seeking

'The One You Truly Are'.

Today affirm the search is over and you are whole and complete. Then courageously express your full potential in the world from your Heart and Soul.

~*Daily Inspiration by Kathleen E. Sims, D.D., C.H.T.*

12.

Messages from Three Moms

It was so very fortunate that I was on my own at 16! My mother announced that she was moving cross- country from Illinois to Idaho for a new job. It was her time as my father passed away two years earlier, and she had not found her single footing. Since I had a thirty-hour-per-week job through a school work program, college plans, and a boyfriend I planned to marry, I would be staying. Since I was a very determined young woman, she allowed me to stay at my Grandmother's home. Gram became my second mom. My boyfriend's mother, Mrs. Singer, became my third mom.

I considered myself very fortunate to have those three women in my life as mothers! On Mother's Day this month, I honor each of them for the gifts they bestowed upon me. As a young woman, I studied others to determine what qualities I admired about them so that I could mold my life in such a way so as to be proud of who I was, as well as who I was becoming.

First, my mother, Eldora, was a beautiful soul who I learned many things from: fairness, equality, generosity, philanthropy, and work ethic. Second is Gram. Gram was 76 years young when I moved into her spare room at age 16. During the week, I rarely saw her as I was nearly as busy as she was. The first lesson I learned from her was to live in integrity, and the second lesson I learned from Gram was how to persevere when tired or worn down. Third is Mrs. Singer. She was a beautiful woman with a flair of sophistication about her. Even at her home, she dressed appropriately, did her hair, and applied makeup before she started her day! Great lesson to present your best self every day.

Gratitude fills my heart this Mother's Day month as I think about each of these amazing women. They have all given me such important lessons, and have helped me live my life in such a way that I can truly be proud of the woman I have become! Happy Mother's Day!

~Daily Inspiration by Syndee Hendricks, Certified Business Consultant and Intuitive Coach

13.

Thought for the Day

"Everyone has inside them a piece of good news. The good news is you don't know how great you can be! How much you can love! What you can accomplish! And what your potential is."
– ANNE FRANK

14.

Listen to Yourself

When I was setting up my office I replaced the carpet. I had gone to considerable trouble to employ a Feng Shui specialist and a color specialist to ensure the office was just right.

I was waiting for the carpet layer to come and lay the carpet. It had been dispatched a week prior and was waiting at the warehouse.

My intuition kept saying, "Go and check it". Of course, I ignored it. "It'll be right", I told myself.

The day finally arrived. The carpet layer was here and so was the carpet. I opened the office and let him in. I was in the car, driving out the driveway when my intuition screamed at me, "CHECK IT".

"Oh, ok!" I parked the car, got out, walked over to the van, lifted the cover and nearly fainted.

You guessed it. It was the wrong color.

Panic stricken I raced back up the stairs. "Stop, stop! It's the wrong one." And down to the warehouse I flew (well, drove very quickly). Catastrophe averted for the time being, I had to wait another week and a half and then it was touch and go if the carpet layer could fit me in. It was very close to Christmas.

Finally the carpet was laid. Boy was I grateful to the carpet layer. He also seemed to appreciate the Christmas ham.

Moral of the story – LISTEN TO YOURSELF!
How often in business do we think others have the answers?
How often do we question ourselves, or procrastinate over taking action?
Not listening to myself cost me a couple of weeks in lost productivity as well as the pain of knowing that this could have been avoided.

Check in with yourself and listen to yourself. You'll probably find you're right!

~Daily Inspiration by Shirley Dalton, Business Expert

15.

Bee Kind

Bees touch down on a flower and then go buzzing around performing their random acts of "kindness" by pollinating our fruits and vegetables.

"As they go from flower to flower, that progression enriches the world."
-BERNADETTE KING

Perhaps we can take notes from observing bees. If they don't pollinate, then we don't receive the fruits of their labor. Instead of kindness, discouragement and despair can set in.

One day, while waiting in a line at the grocery store, I observed the lady checking out ahead of me. She was stressed, frantically searching the bottom of her bag for a dime, which she knew she had, but couldn't find in that moment. I pulled out a dime and gave it to her and her face lit up like I had given her ten dollars instead of ten cents!

She walked out of that store a little lighter and to be honest, so did I. Best ten cents I ever spent.

Kindness doesn't have to cost anything. Smiling at a stranger takes only a second and is free. Today, I challenge you, Dear Reader, to BEE Kind. Smile at every person you come across and watch as their faces light up in response. Open the door for someone or allow them to open the door for you. No politics, just feel the gratitude for this simple gesture. Perhaps, pay a toll for the next person or weed an elderly neighbor's yard. You get the idea.

Then sit and bask in the warm glow that comes from brightening someone's day.

~Daily Inspiration by Jaimie Harnagel, Certified Reiki Master and Shamanic Practitioner

16.

Choose What Matters Most

Do you let yourself be poured into by the things that help, nourish, and support you to **SHINE**?

Or, are you letting other things, perhaps other people's priorities, become your priority? It's so easy to get "too busy," become overwhelmed, and not be able to complete in a given day the priorities we set for that day. Does this sound familiar to you?

Part of the challenge is that we are so good at continuing to add things to our plate! We're talented, we want to give and to serve, we want to say "yes" to so many things and people...

This is a good time to stop and check in.

1. **Take just 30 seconds.** Write down what you currently have on your plate. Make a list of: what you have now, what's coming up, what needs to be finished, and what needs to be started.
2. **Now look at your list and notice**: What feels heavy? What feels pressured? What doesn't? It's good to know where you are feeling pulled or depleted, instead of feeling poured into.
3. **Reset your "shoulds."** It is very disempowering to say, "I have to, I should, I need to…" If you find yourself thinking those words, shift it to "I choose."
4. **Now choose what matters most to help you move forward.** We can get caught up in doing lots of things and forget to choose to do the most important ones to help us move forward on our goals.

Because, in reality, you are choosing - all the time. **You are empowered with choice to do the things that serve you and let you shine ever brighter. Choose to SHINE and fully share the gift of you!**

~Daily Inspiration by Rebecca Hall Gruyter, Influencer & Empowerment Leader

17.

Concentrate on the Feeling!

In the U.S., the weather is getting warmer, days are growing longer, and you're starting to think about outdoor activities--from working in the garden to planning a summer vacation.

Or...maybe you're just feeling guilty because you're still inside staring at your computer or cell phone.

But before you shame yourself into lacing up your running shoes, here's some advice my fitness clients, and research, have taught me: **Guilt and fear are not good reasons to exercise**. Don't force yourself to run or go to the gym because you need to drop 20 lb. or because you're following doctor's orders. While those motivations might get you started, your efforts **will not be sustainable** over the long haul.

Instead, find an activity you enjoy and concentrate on the fabulous feeling you get while doing it. Maybe you love a good yoga stretch, or the wind on your face when you're out on your bike. Perhaps you enjoy the feeling of success or even the muscle "pain" after completing a new workout (that discomfort will go away, I promise!).

Just concentrate on the here and now. Enjoy the activity and the ecstasy it creates for you. *That* feeling will help you continue moving, even when your TV wants you to sit!

~Daily Inspiration by Lisa Harris, MS, RD, Fitness Pro

18.

Manifest Your True Desire

"Within all of us is a divine capacity to manifest and attract all that we need and desire."
WAYNE DYER

I did not know the power of manifesting until my maternal clock was ticking. I always knew that I wanted to have children but kept engaging and focusing on my career. Then, one day I realized it was time. After trying for 18 months, I was panic-stricken. Through divine intervention I met a fertility doctor and from the moment we were introduced the world started to sync for me. The doctor asked me a very powerful question: "Do you want to find out why you cannot get pregnant or do you just want to have a baby?" With complete certainty, I answered, "I just want to have a baby" and within 4 weeks I was pregnant, though a combination of modern medicine and my powerful commitment to be a mom.

I remember the feeling of wanting something so much that nothing was going to interfere with the outcome and to this day, I try to duplicate that intense feeling of desire and manifest other things into my life. This includes manifesting love, money and good health. I even created a mantra for my son on the very day I was confirmed pregnant. Through the manifestation of that mantra, my son has turned into a caring, compassionate, wonderful contribution to this world. Till today, he continues to be a manifestation of my original mantra. **You too have the power within to bring your ultimate desires to life. Dedicate the month of May to manifesting at least one true desire.**

~Daily Inspiration by Bonnie Bonadeo, The Connection Coach

19.

Thought for the Day

"It doesn't matter who you are, where you come from. The ability to triumph begins with you. Always."
– OPRAH WINFREY

20.

Prompts for Your Writing … and for Life

In my work helping clients write for their business, I'm often asked about "writer's block." While experts offer plenty of well-intentioned tips, the one that really matters? Clarity of self and purpose.

When you come from this place, your voice - and your words - flow powerfully and purposefully. **There's no substitute for your unique and authentic voice,** whether it's in your writing or in your life. So, how do you reach down inside and express clearly the YOU that is meant to show up in this world?

I recommend (and use myself!) three "writing prompts" which, taken together, help me feel MORE myself, and in turn clarify my expression of my truth and purpose to the world. Try this: Write down each of the following prompts, then complete the sentence with at least 5 thoughts for each – whatever comes into your head with the most open of hearts!

Is it possible that…? 'Possibility' to me is **the perpetual potential promise of something even better!** Invite in what's possible for you to be and to have. "Is it possible that I am MEANT TO do xxx in my business this year?"

I'm willing to… Promising we'll do - or try to do - something just adds pressure on ourselves to *not fail*. This prompt means I'm **willing to open myself to the possibility** of another way of doing things or a better choice to make. "I'm willing to see myself as THE expert in ___."

I'm so grateful now that I…. *Gratitude is the key to self-love and acceptance.* I hereby give you carte blanche to list all the fabulous things about who you are, what you've accomplished, and what you're going to do next! Even, "I'm grateful that I had a crappy day yesterday, because I've chosen to go full force today!"

~Daily Inspiration by: Bettyanne Green, Content Marketing Strategist

21.

Thought for the Day

"In the middle of difficulty lies opportunity."
– ALBERT EINSTEIN

22.

There's Always Tomorrow

As you know, life does not come with a manual. Everyone has a battle they are facing and have to figure out how they can be overcomers and walk in victory. Life comes in cycles; it can be draining, joyous, and sometimes unbearable. When you find yourself overwhelmed with today, be encouraged and know that there's ALWAYS tomorrow!

Here are some ways you can remain encouraged while you deal with 'Today':

1. **To Everything there is a Time and a Season**
   There's a saying which states that "seasons come and go." When you are facing hardships that have you stuck in the 'rut' of today, it is essential to remember, that everything has a set time and a season. If life is throwing you hard punches, choose to buckle up against the wind, and soar forward!
2. **You Will Come OUT Better!**
   I know you might be 'down and out'; just remember that this trial and season is not the end of you! There is life to you after this! You will come out better, so endure!
3. **The Only Place after Going Down....is UP!**
   If you find yourself at 'rock bottom', look up! The days ahead must be glorious! You did not die in your situation! You've gained strength and momentum! So, it's time to pursue your purpose and to proclaim that your latter years will be greater than your former years! You're coming UP!!

Remember, there's always TOMORROW! Rejoice now and prepare for your tomorrow!

~Daily Inspiration by India White, Author and Inspirational Speaker

23.

Thought for the Day

"Embrace uncertainty. Some of the most beautiful chapters in our lives won't have a title until much later."
– BOB GOFF

24.

A Time for Birthday Celebrations

May is a full month for birthday celebrations. We begin with 3 generations, Mother, Daughter and Granddaughter. May 3 is Natalee's birthday, age 1 year; the 6th myself age 60 and May 28th, Vanessa age 30.

My first great-grandchild was born on May 21st and is also a year old. We had a big celebration for Natalee's first birthday then the next day was a party for my 60th. It was great spending time with everyone together.

Although May is our biggest month for birthdays we have many throughout the year. With a family as large as ours we don't skip many months. Tony and I are parents of seven adult children, his, hers and mine. We have fifteen grandchildren and one on the way, and two great-grandchildren with one more on the way.

December is another big month for us. Whatever month you celebrate birthdays, make sure you take the time to truly be with each other and enjoy everyone's company. It's these big celebrations which bring us closer together.

I believe birthdays are a wonderful opportunity to stop, pause, and celebrate the gift that person is in our life. In fact, we can bring that appreciation of the gift of each other into our life every day. Reach out today and celebrate someone in your life by sharing with them the gift that they are to you.

~Daily Inspiration by Catherine M Laub, Advocate for Mental Health

25.

The Other Side of Fear

"Everything you ever wanted is on the other side of fear."
– GEORGE ADDAIR

What exactly are you afraid of? Do you worry about what other people will think? Do you fear rejection or failure? Does the thought of putting yourself out there leave you feeling vulnerable?
In order to overcome fear and move past it, you need to know what the root of the problem is.

For example, if you're nervous about putting yourself out there to promote a service or product, you may be scared of rejection or failure. While no one wants to fail, remember that this is something we all experience.

If you let that fear hold you back, you will never have the opportunity to succeed.

~Daily Inspiration by Carmell Pelly, Empowerment Leader

26.

Permission Slip

"Permission Slip?" Most of us might defiantly say, "I don't need permission, I'm a grown-up!" The thing is, we do. We need it from ourselves. Whether we like it or not, we live with rules, regulations, and expectations in this life. As we learn to navigate within those rules, regulations, and expectations, we often find ourselves pushing our own personal needs aside. We either forget who we are because we've been listening too long to the labels of the outside world, or we feel guilty about needing things that are basic to being human. **We forget to give ourselves grace and end up being our own worst critic.**

I'm going to let you in on a little secret... you are an incredible creation with needs, and you are still learning. **It's okay to give yourself grace.** When you give yourself grace, you give yourself a permission slip to be you, meet your needs, and shine in your own way. Doing this enables yourself to be strengthened, revived, and ready.

I use my permission slip! When the hall monitor of life is shoving its expectations of how I "need" to fit into its box, causing self-doubt, feelings of failure, and frustration start to sink in... I remind myself that I get to have grace too. That's when I whip out my permission slip. Whether it's allowing myself to pursue after a dream of becoming an inspirational speaker and writing, or just no longer having to wear high-heals... because that pain is just not worth it to me... learning to give myself permission frees me up to, not only learn who I am, but also to be whom I am meant to be.

Use your permission slip every day. Allow yourself to take care of yourself. You are allowed to relax, grow, make mistakes and learn from them, have fun, travel, be true to yourself, not EVER wear high-heals again, and most of all, SHINE!

~*Daily Inspiration by Julz DeFant, RDH*

27.

"YES" Now - Figure Out the "How" Later

In saying "yes" and being willing to be seen and to serve, I have discovered a very rich and dynamic life that uses all of me, not just part of me. I keep growing, stretching, and discovering new ways to serve, come out of hiding and touch lives. I'm so grateful for the opportunity to do the work I do, to touch the lives of others as they richly touch and bless mine.

I actually love most of the things I was trying to stay safe from by saying "no" to them in advance. I celebrate moving beyond my comfort zone and into my destiny step by step, heart by heart, choice by choice.

I have learned to say "YES" and figure out the "how" later. We can get too caught up in the "how" and let fear take over and stop us.

I promise, if you are saying "yes" to your purpose and your "Why," the "how" will come! Sometimes it involves learning something new or building some new muscles in a new area, but the "how" frequently comes after you say "yes"...not before. Be willing to step out of your comfort zone and release the need to know how to do things first. Be willing to lean in, say yes, and figure it out as you are in action and bringing your "yes" forward.

What are you saying "YES" to today?

~Daily Inspiration by Rebecca Hall Gruyter, Influencer & Empowerment Leader

28.

How Are You Feeling?

You are not your feelings. You don't even have to trust your feelings. I woke up this morning feeling a bit down. That pervasive unhappiness sat with me as I prepared my daughters' lunches for school and drove them across town.

But wait a minute! Every moment I get the chance to decide how I want to react. I am not my past moments. I do not have to stay feeling any particular feelings. I have free will; I have a choice. I thought, "I am not going to stay in this lull. I am moving forward, and I want to feel content, worthy and loving." As soon as I committed to this new reality, my pervasive heavy feelings lifted and I began to feel upbeat and positive. I was now ready to take on the day!

I understand that issues like depression are an entirely different thing and are not as easy to ignore and refocus. But with your average run of the mill emotional slump, you don't have to believe your feelings. Use the moment to create the emotional reality that you want.

I know it is not in my best interest to focus so closely on my emotions. Further, I don't believe that every emotion is worthy of devoting my time or energy. **I know that when it comes to my emotions, I can be like a surfer catching waves. I can choose which feelings I am going to pay attention to, and which ones I am going to let pass by me.** From now on, I plan to float on top of the waves of emotion and only follow the troughs downward when I really intend to.

"I AM... two of the most powerful words. For what you put after them shapes your reality." -Bevan Lee

~*Daily Inspiration by Dr. Ruth Anderson, Spiritual Counselor*

29.

Plan B

"The three things that are most essential to achievement are common sense, hard work and stick-to-it-iv-ness..."
– THOMAS EDISON

Do you have a plan B? At one time, I thought having a plan B was a great idea. Working in the corporate world, my team would have a "just in case" plan when the first one didn't work. I hear it now with people I speak with about their vision. "I want my current business ... that which I love to do ... to thrive. I'm also doing this other thing on the side (essential oils, skin care) just in case." Is there anything wrong with this?

It depends upon where you place your focus and in what way you place your focus. Here's what I know – **what you focus on the most grows.** When you have a vision/goal for your project whether in the corporate world, entrepreneurial world or your personal world, stick to plan A. This is the key to it succeeding quicker. Notice my words here ... "quicker". Can your plan succeed? Yes, given enough time and enough attention to that plan.

If you have a plan A and a plan B, two things can happen. First, you can become fractured – your mind doesn't really believe that you can make plan A work since you already have a plan B in place. Then there is failure – you have created a clear intent with having a plan B since you are already preparing for plan A to fail. Having a plan B is not the end of the world. Understanding how to implement plan B is key. Clarify plan A and your success ... move from this point.

Thomas Edison completed over 3000 filament tests. He had one vision in mind, believing in the outcome.

~Daily Inspiration by Denise Hansard, Empowerment Expert

30.

Choose Your Focus

Within you lies the keys to your purposeful life. Do you believe it? Your friendships, chance encounters, successes, challenges, and defeats have worked to help you to remember who and what you are. Sometimes along your journey you will encounter people who are in your life specifically to awaken you, to have you take the next step to your highest good. However, these deceivers aren't aware of the role they play in your higher life. What was meant for evil, God has a way of turning it to good. Though their actions were mean spirited and painful, they proved to be ultimately purposeful. Choose to respond with love, find the silver lining, and focus on who you choose to be and are becoming.

Your main goal in life should be one in which you stay true to who you are. Do not concern yourself with your friend(s) successes in their careers, how much money they make, what neighborhood they live in, the big 5-bedroom house they live in, the nice luxury car they both drive, their lifestyle, the vacations they take to exotic places, their marriage, their children. **Focus on you by staying in your lane**. You get to choose what you focus on, how you respond, and who you choose to be. Choose with great purpose.

~Daily Inspiration by Cassandra Garabedian, Stylist

31.

Thought for the Day

"Let us always meet each other with a smile, for the smile is the beginning of love."
– MOTHER THERESA

June

1.

You Were Made for Such a Time as this, Therefore SHINE!

"If not now, when?"
- HILLEL THE ELDER

Things happen in our lives that we don't expect and certainly didn't choose - a car accident, a divorce, a job loss or illness. "Such a time as this" could be an opportunity. We may not have chosen the event, but **we can choose how we are going to respond - to suffer or to SHINE!**

These times may have us answering questions we don't often answer until we're faced with the possible end of ourselves. These are times when we get to ask...**What matters most to us? And how to we make that move forward and serve us?**

Life events challenge us to respond from an empowered place, to rethink things, and to realize that time is precious.

Wherever you are in your journey, wherever you're being called, remember, it's now, it's today. Tomorrow isn't guaranteed. We have now.

What action can you take today to help you move forward that which matters most to you?

~Daily Inspiration by Rebecca Hall Gruyter, Influencer & Empowerment Leader

2.

Thought for the Day

*"All our dreams can come true,
if we have the courage to pursue them."*
– WALT DISNEY

3.

Be the Light

As the sun grows hotter and daylight longer, we have time to reflect and soak up all the possibilities. You have an opportunity to shine daily. **Take the chance every day to be the light. You must choose. It does not happen by chance or happenstance.** It is a choice. So, today make the decision to be the light in the darkness.

Look daily for opportunities to be a blessing and help to others. As you walk through your day take time to smile and greet those you meet. Be the light in their day and spark to their flame. You will be blessed and repaid by the universe. So, choose to light the flames of others and fan the light. Someone is waiting on you to shine!

~Daily Inspiration by Teresa Hawley Howard, Empowerment Leader

4.

Thought for the Day

*"Stop limiting your potential.
Realize that there's an unlimited amount
of things that you can do with your life."*
– SONYA PARKER

5.

Practicing Success

"You have to practice success. Success doesn't just show up. If you aren't practicing success today, you won't wake up in 20 years and be successful, because you won't have developed the habits of success, which are small things like finishing what you start, putting a lot of effort into everything you do, being on time, treating people well."
– MICHELLE OBAMA

Unfortunately, many people do not take time to celebrate their successes or even recognize their value. Do you?

Success doesn't have to be a big endeavor. We congratulate you on every little step you take to take charge of or change whatever isn't helpful for you or your family anymore!

Our question for you is this: "What small step or new behavior can you initiate today in order to change an area that you are not fully satisfied with?" For instance, is there an area in your home, your emotional life, your activities, etc.? Develop your habits for success one step at a time!

~Daily Inspiration by Mooniek Seebregts and Martina Caviezel, The Parent Empowerment Coaches

6.

Message from My Father

My father, Michael Luciano, passed December 2012 and is always helping guide my journey. I am thrilled because he guided me to find this message to share with you.

My father shared with me: "*Cathy, I heard this a long time ago but don't remember when. I have to tell you a story about what happened to me. It was the night before I left to go in the army. In Astoria (NY) there is a big nice park across the street. I was feeling a little down so my mother said why don't you go for a walk in the park. So as I was walking across the street, you know how you kick rocks. There was a piece of paper on the street and I kicked it. I saw a picture on it. I picked it up and it was a picture of the Patron Saint and I felt much better. I still have the picture of the Patron Saint of Soldiers, Saint Rocco.*"

When we need guidance from God it is sent to us at just the right moment. Listen and look for those messages and follow through by incorporating them into your daily life and especially those times you need extra support.

~Daily Inspiration by Catherine M Laub, Advocate for Mental Health

7.

Feed Your Soul Spiritual Empowerment

Commit to a daily Self Love and Spiritual Empowerment practice that nourishes your Soul and fortifies you as you navigate along your Path. Everything you experience and desire feeds on the nourishment you give your Soul. Begin by starting to feed your Soul in the same way that you feed your other appetites, with affirming spiritual practices and a positive perspective on the things that matters most to you. Arrange your life around your lifestyle and make your outside obligations fit into your Spiritual Lifestyle. Give your Soul what it truly desires, full control of your life and trust the guidance received. Treat yourself better than The Most Important Person in Your Life.

Affirmation:
I AM Devoted to Self-Love and Spiritual Empowerment. I AM Treating MySelf Better Than the Most Important Person in My Life. I AM Committed to My Daily Spiritual Practices that Nourishes My Soul as I Navigate My Current Path.

~Daily Inspiration by Mark Edward Pyle, Manifestation Expert

8.

Thought for the Day

"You were designed for accomplishment, engineered for success, and endowed with the seeds of greatness!"
– ZIG ZIGLAR

9.

Forgiveness is a Gift

To the degree you hold onto the past through feelings of anger, guilt, shame and resentment, you filter your present time experiences through your unhappy memories. These emotional chains of your history condemn you to recreate it and ensure that your love will be conditional.

Do not judge yourself or others knowing we all do the best we can, given what we know at the time. This is the basis for forgiveness, which is the basis of healing all disharmony within. You can now forgive because you realize that holding onto past injustices hurts you and not those whom you believe have wronged you. Acknowledging there is Divine Order and Perfect Timing in the Universe helps you open up to the possibility of forgiving.

From a perspective of conscious awareness you can see that all of your behavior, positive and negative, has been motivated by your need to be loved, accepted and emotionally safe. With compassion for your inner child, embrace and nurture that part of yourself, knowing you were doing the best you knew how to do to be loved. When you forgive, it means that you release the negative emotions of your ego, shifting to neutrality, which activates your deepest Spiritual feelings, along with opening a direct channel to your Higher Self.

You can now transcend your old viewpoint of right/wrong illusions and redeem your Innocence in the Light of Truth. Taking this step will release your fear, revealing the presence of Love; release your pain, revealing the experience of Joy; and release your anxiety, revealing the Peace of God.

Today forgive all and set yourself Free.

~Daily Inspiration by Kathleen E. Sims, D.D., C.H.T.

10.

Stop. Pause. Listen. Then Choose.

I believe the ability to live on purpose and with purpose is tied closely to stopping, pausing, and listening. June is the perfect month to pause, sit in your garden or yard or a field with a nice cold beverage, shoes kicked off and legs outstretched…aaaah!

Feel the breeze, smell the flowers, listen to the buzz of the flies and tree frogs and locusts…And listen within. Living a life on purpose and with purpose means listening for the wisdom your heart has to tell you. Take a deep breath and lean in a little more to the reminder of who you are and what you are called to bring forth.

Then choose your next steps on purpose and in alignment with what matters most to you to bring forward…one breath, step and choice at a time.

~Daily Inspiration by Rebecca Hall Gruyter, Influencer & Empowerment Leader

11.

Thought for the Day

"The question isn't who is going to let me; it's who is going to stop me."
– AYN RAND

12.

A Tribute to Fathers!

As a young girl at twelve, I had so many emotions swirling in my pre-teen self when my father left our family. Even at that age, I understood that parents had a tough time agreeing on issues as well as just getting along with each other. My parents owned a business, and though they were not home very often, they always arrived by at least midnight.

Once I got past being devastated, angry, sad, and abandoned, the one thought I held tightly to was my memory of the unconditional love he had given me, especially years after he left. I am not even sure how I knew it was unconditional love, or even that what I felt from him was named that. I just always knew that whatever happened in my young life, he never asked anything of me beyond the basic parenting expectations. Though a man of few words, I understood the hugs, love in his eyes, and tenderness of his punishments. It was so hard to say goodbye four years later when he died.

I never thought I would feel that unconditional love again until I got to know my step-father in my adult life. Though very different from my father, my step-dad had the same heart as my father. What I loved the most about my step-dad was the way he loved and cared for my mother. Not only did I have a special respect for him, but I also appreciated that unconditional love that he offered me. I'm so fortunate that he gave me an example of what a marriage should look and feel like.

The real bonus for me today is that I am celebrating twenty years of a happy marriage with my Harvey who has given me that same very special unconditional love. Thank you Dad and Pops. I love you both so much. Happy Father's Day.

~Daily Inspiration by Syndee Hendricks, Certified Business Consultant and Intuitive Coach

13.

You Are Blooming Amazing!

Have you ever noticed how flowers boldly show off their amazing beauty each Spring**? As flowers of the Universe, we are all meant to do the same!** So how do we embrace and celebrate the beauty of our unique gifts?

When it comes to sharing our unique gifts with the world, many of us have feelings that lie somewhere between discomfort and pure terror. As Marianne Williamson says, "It is our light, not our darkness that most frightens us."

I invite you to spend a few minutes imagining the experience of sharing your unique gifts with the world. Imagine this experience in the grandest way possible. How do you feel? Are you exhilarated? Do you feel at ease? Or does the whole image terrify you?

Preparing ourselves to express our unique gifts is the greatest journey of our lives. For many of us, it unveils our deepest wounds and invites us to heal and love ourselves even more. Know that like the Spring flower that grows more beautiful each year, you are more amazing each time you bloom. Be willing to share the gift of you...bloom and SHINE!

~Daily Inspiration by Olivia Parr-Rud, Corporate Love Ambassador

14.

Thought for the Day

*"In order to carry a positive action
we must develop here a positive vision."*
– DALAI LAMA

15.

Who is Writing Your Story?

We all have goals and dreams...that we take action on creating our story. When creating your story, it's important to keep these four elements in mind: Expectation, Emotion, Encouragement, and Hope. And as we bring our story forward remember *"Do not conform to the present world but be transformed by the renewing of your mind. In this way, you will be able to verify what God's will is, good, pleasant and perfect."* If we do not renew our mind and spirit when difficult times and failures come, we are likely to repeat the same behaviors and keep thinking negative thoughts stored in your subconscious.

Our subconscious is where the ghostwriter of your life lives, he is the one that holds your innermost dreams and can often differ from your goals. Remember that your beliefs affect how you see things, that's why you see things not as they are, but as you think they are. You see what you believe, that's why you can assume you are always in the right. Pay attention to what you are feeding into your mind and spirit on a daily basis. Is it helping you write your story? One that holds beautiful expectations, great emotion, encouragement and hope for all you seek to bring forward?

~Daily Inspiration by Pastor Nicolas C Pacheco

16.

Exercise Your Curiosity Muscle

*"To build the life that matters to you, lean in
and get the results that you want."*
- REBECCA HALL GRUYTER

Leaning into life means building in practices that are supportive of us so we can keep that pace and keep having that impact. Helping ourselves go farther, faster!

This often means stretching ourselves to using new muscles, expanding ourselves in new ways, going in directions that are unfamiliar. It's just like when your body uses new muscles when learning a new sport - but it doesn't have to be painful!

What if you choose to open yourself up to be coachable? You lean into it with curiosity, knowing you'll be invigorated, inspired and better able to be out there in the world.

I encourage you to make that choice to open your heart and your mind - wide open! Be willing to receive. And be willing to share your amazing expertise and gifts as well. It's really important to have a balance of both. Invite opportunities to show up, and soak up like a sponge what serves you. There is always something new to learn and reasons to expand your impact. Be willing to grow new muscles and lean into what matters most to you.

Because you're absolutely needed in this world!

~Daily Inspiration by Rebecca Hall Gruyter, Influencer & Empowerment Leader

17.

Thought for the Day

"Start where you are. Use what you have. Do what you can."

– Arthur Ashe

18.

You Are Enough

Loving yourself is the most important first step to transforming your life. I once read that all emotions really boil down two emotions: Love and Fear. If you are not feeling Love, then you're feeling some form of Fear. Fear takes many forms: anger, resistance, resentment and the one that is very common to many of us, the fear of not being enough.

We all have that internal dialogue we listen to. You know the one---the voice inside us that tells us what we are or are not; the voice that says yes or no to the fear of change, or trying something new; a new relationship, a new career, a new experience.

The person we become or think we are starts very early in life with the internal dialogue we create as a young child. It's important to pay attention to our internal dialogue between the "internal parent" and "internal child." That internal dialogue comes from many sources but generally starts early in life with what we heard or thought we heard as a young child from our parents. Paying attention to your self-dialogue is the single most important thing you can do to help you get what you want in your life. Many of us go through life not feeling like we are enough, like the unique contribution we have to offer the universe is not going to be of value to others. If there is one truth I know...It is that **you are enough!** We are all on this Earth at this time for a reason. When you can say "I am enough!" and really know in your heart that the gifts you have to offer are of value, life begins to open up like a flower in Spring. WE are all anxiously awaiting the gifts you have to share!

~Daily Inspiration by Carmen M. Bryant, Business Coach

19.

In Celebration of All Fathers

Happy Father's Day. Dear Father, the love I have for you is indescribable. No words can express the love and admiration I feel for you. You are/were a great husband, father, and provider for your family, you gave with your heart so tenderly. You accomplished many things in your life, purchase your homes, and sent your children to college.

In celebration of Father's Day how would you like to honor your father or a man who has impacted you powerfully? How would you preserve his memory and legacy for future generations? What would you say about the man you call father? How would you describe his character and values? How did he make you feel? Was he a man of many words or did he keep his feelings to himself? What, if anything, would you like to carry forward you're your father to honor him?

It's not unusual to hear parents tell their children how proud they make them feel but this day especially, the table has turned. Although we don't always say it, today we say "We are proud to call you Father," and we will say it again and again. Happy Father's Day!!!

Take a moment today to celebrate your Father and his legacy in your life.

~Daily Inspiration by Cassandra Garabedian, Stylist

20.

Choose Love

One of my spiritual teachers, Reverend Joan Steadman, often said:

"Every situation is an opportunity to be more loving."

What a beautiful practice this is!
In each moment you have a choice of how you will respond to every circumstance, person and situation. Will you choose to be more loving?

Being loving starts with loving yourself. Try asking yourself:
- What is one loving thing I can do for myself today? Or
- How can I be more loving to myself?

In regard to others, ask yourself:
- To whom can I be more loving?
- What is one loving action I can do for another today?
- How can I be even more loving?

Love grows love. Today, choose love.

Some Essential Oils to connect you with Love:

Rose - *The Oil of Divine Love*
Invites you to experience the unconditional love of the Divine.

Geranium - *The Oil of Love & Trust*
Encourages emotional honesty, love and forgiveness.

~Daily Inspiration by Tish Reese, Health + Wellness Mentor

21.

Thought for the Day

"Act as if what you do makes a difference. It does."
– WILLIAM JAMES

22.

Learn to Dance with Fear

Have you ever noticed that the more you try to avoid fear, the more it seems to grow and take you over? I have learned to "dance" with fear - move with it and through it...not avoid or run from it.

Think of fear as an indicator of stepping out of your familiar comfort zone into a new place. If you want to go where you haven't been before and serve in new ways, then you're choosing to move out of your comfort zone.

It is your choice to move forward or stay where you are.

Be willing to be a little uncomfortable (for a while) to build what you're called to build and be what you're called to be. What helps me through my fear is remembering my "Why" and that my choice is voluntary. I just take one step at a time, pulled forward by my purpose of bringing truth, empowerment, choice and value into someone's life.

Fear is temporary - the rewards of the dance last a lifetime!

~Daily Inspiration by Rebecca Hall Gruyter, Influencer & Empowerment Leader

23.

Flamingo Flamboyance

I will freely admit to being prejudiced. I can't stand those tacky pink flamingos people put in their yards. That means, of course, that my family delights in giving me flamingo cards, toy flamingos, and pointing them out whenever possible. I apologize if that hurts your feelings, Don Featherstone. I know you invented them, but did you know there are now more plastic flamingos in the United States than real ones? (https://www.thespruce.com/fun-facts-about-flamingos-385519. There is something very wrong about that).

Real flamingos, however, are rather amazing. They get their eye-popping red, orange or pink color because of their diet. They can even be yellow, blue or green! If they don't get enough of the pigments from their diet they aren't colorful. So what? Well, if you as a person really want to stand out, you need to fill your life with things that will enhance and advance you. Bring more color and vibrancy into your life.

Flamingos love to be in the company of other flamingos. They feel much safer in a big crowd. Can you imagine the spectacle of one million flamingos flying? Isolation, even in a crowd of people, can be a very dangerous thing. Having a solid group of friends, maybe not a million, increases your feelings of safety and success. Don't you think flamingos look awkward standing on one leg? When the flamingo is resting on one leg, it is a position of strength. We can securely rest in our own space until the choice is clear.

Flamingos are strong flyers and swimmers, but are most often seen wading on those long legs. That should remind us to stay firmly grounded. They also don't like other birds to invade their space. That should remind us to respect personal boundaries. Guess what a group of flamingos are called. Yes, a, flamboyance! **So, put on some colorful clothes, get together with friends and be flamboyant! No plastic, imitation flamingos allowed.**

~Daily Inspiration by Elda Robinson, Teacher

24.

Thought for the Day

"Problems are not stop signs, they are guidelines."
— ROBERT SCHULLER

25.

You Are Exactly Where You Are Meant to Be

I remember a time not long ago when I had a dream to build a new business. There were so many moving pieces that had to be learned to get the business off the ground and I was overwhelmed. Add a baby on top of the mix and most days I walked away not only overwhelmed but feeling defeated and wondering what I was even doing. I used Journaling as a way to pull me back to feeling grounded. **Journaling can help you shift from overwhelm to being on** purpose.

So the next time you start to feel overwhelmed, I invite you to: Sit down, set a timer for 3min and just write. WHY?

Journaling brings you into that state of mindfulness. Frustrations and anxieties lose their intensity when you are present to the moment. Journaling is an outlet for processing emotions and increases your self-awareness. Studies have shown that the emotional release from journaling lowers anxiety, stress, and induces better sleep.

~Daily Inspiration by Carmell Pelly, Empowerment Leader

26.

A Mini-Vacation: Seeing Money Differently

"...freedom is sometimes just simply another perspective away; who could you be if your lens was changed for a moment, would you still be the same?"
- Perspectives by KUTLESS

When we find ourselves stuck in our relationship to money, I have learned that the reason is almost always due to what I call "invisible baggage" weighing us down. By this, I mean the hidden, subconscious money-beliefs we carry in our money story that often sabotages our financial success. It is therefore so important to invest time in learning what you really believe about money, in order for your money dream to come true.

There are many different types of self-limiting money beliefs. Here are some of the most common:

- "It's not safe to have money."
- "It's not spiritual to have money."
- "You have to work hard for money."
- "Rich people are greedy and dishonest."
- "I can only make good money working for someone else."
- "I have enough to get by."
- "If I make more money than my family, they won't love me."

All of us hold limiting money beliefs. Consider what limiting belief may be holding you back from your financial goals. Write down the belief, then phrase it in an opposite statement. Gently spend time today seeing life through the lens of the new, opposite belief. Notice the thoughts, feelings and a-ha's you experience.

- Daily Inspiration by Marlene Elizabeth, Author of MONEYWINGS™

27.

Thought for the Day

*"Be patient with yourself.
Self-growth is tender; it's holy ground.
There's no greater investment."*
– STEPHEN COVEY

28.

Joy

"Spring being a tough act to follow, God created June."
– AL BERNSTEIN

June is awesome - it starts out with Dare Day and ends with Meteor Day, and in between there is Best Friend's Day, Ice Cream and Pop-Goes-the-Weasel Day. June is my birthday month, and I relish in the budding, beautiful landscape, as well as, the smells and memories of being a kid and running outside to play and swim until sundown. The word that represents June for me is joy!

Although joy is a simple word, it can be misunderstood and is often compared to the definition of happy, but the definitions of these words are different. Joy comes from deep within you and represents the spiritual core value that no matter what is going on in your life, you can find your joy in any moment. Happiness represents an external and fleeting emotion which is dependent on outside factors. Joy can be easily achieved by taking actions that bring you excitement, peace and gratitude.

Let June be your month of joy – engage in activities that fill you up and make you feel like a child who is about to go out and enjoy a beautiful summer day again!

~*Daily Inspiration by Bonnie Bonadeo, The Connection Coach*

29.

Pete Rose

(A.K.A CHARLIE HUSTLE)

Pete Rose is a legendary baseball icon who primarily played during the 1970s. Many of his records still stand today (some considered to be unbreakable).

Importantly, Pete earned his nickname of "Charlie Hustle" because of his habit of charging all out toward first base EVERY time his bat touched the ball. Even though he was never a particularly fast runner, Pete knew that every once in a while, against the odds, a player would bobble the ball, or overthrow First Base. Pete Rose knew that **all-out** *effort* was a more effective tool than speed!

When the dust settled, there stood Pete with that silly grin standing safely on First, or quite frequently, sliding successfully into Second Base. Most other ball players just assumed the odds were so stacked toward an easy throw-out that they just headed back toward the dugout. They **dismissed the opportunity** to take a <u>*chance*</u> on beating the odds.

Did all of this "Charlie Hustle" effort pay off? **Absolutely!** He holds the title of "Hit King", with the Major League record for the **most hits ever** (4,256) (only *two* players in the history of baseball have achieved over 4,000 hits!). His records for getting on base with most career Singles and National League career Doubles still stand today!

Interestingly, Pete Rose also holds the record for the most career **outs**!! He was "out" over 1 out of 3 times he came to the plate! What made Charlie Hustle so successful while being out so many times? **SHOWING UP** to try!! He holds the record for coming to the plate **15,890 times**! He was willing to take the **opportunity** to make a difference, even if it meant being thrown out. He was not afraid of failure, which led to record breaking success!!

So I encourage us to "**show up**", **not be afraid of failing**, and **run as hard as we can** toward First Base *no matter what the odds are against us*. Then we too might find ourselves making our own Major League records of success!

~*Daily Inspiration by John F. Hall, MBA, Author, Business Owner*

30.

Choose to Live Your Purpose

How do you make the choices that will take you on the path of a purposeful life?

Pause and listen. Often you need to pause and listen the most when you think you can least afford to do so! When you are feeling confused, stressed, empty or emotional, stop, take a breath, and listen. **You will then have the clarity to make empowered choices with every breath.** *(Stopping, pausing, and breathing for 1-2 minutes lowers your stress levels, brings oxygen to every cell in your body, and helps bring you to the present moment.)*

Don't wait for permission. If you see something that no one else does, part of your purpose may be to bring that vision forward. It means you are there first and get to bring it forward. Step out in faith no matter what people say. Be willing to create it, lead it, and build the bridge to it eventually others can see it too.

Realize you might never "feel" ready. "I'm not ready" is a place to hide when we are fearful. The question is: "Am I willing to make the choice to live my purpose?" When we say "YES" we step forward in the right direction.

Celebrate, don't criticize. Remember to treat yourself like your best friend in the highs and lows of life. As you are making choices to embrace your purpose, it is important to always speak to yourself with kindness. It's about connection, not perfection!

Step into your power and purpose - one choice at a time!

~Daily Inspiration by Rebecca Hall Gruyter, Influencer & Empowerment Leader

July

1.

Summer is a Great Time to SHINE!

We are halfway through the year, approaching Q3. I toast you with my fresh, minty, lemony iced tea - Here's to you!

And it's the perfect opportunity to take a look at where we are. Are we doing the things that matter most to us? Are we purposefully doing those things that bring us forward? Are we choosing to SHINE and echo out those things into our families, business, community, and world?

Between the delicious summer moments of absorbing sunshine, eating barbeque, taking long walks, sitting with our summer reading books, also take some moments of reflection...Do a "check-in" on:

What is important for you to build into my life that nourishes you, that is positive, and that helps you grow?

In what ways can you stay mindful of the types of things that get poured into you, and to make sure they include practices that will uplift, feed, encourage, and empower you?

This type of insight can come into your consciousness, become part of you, just like your wonderful memories of long summer evenings with loved ones and ice cream with friends on a hot day. Just remember to take time to stop, pause, listen and choose with purpose.

~Daily Inspiration by Rebecca Hall Gruyter, Influencer & Empowerment Leader

2.

Meant to Shine

"You are the light of the world. A city on a hill cannot be hidden. Neither do people light a lamp and put it under a bowl. Instead they put it on its stand, and it gives light to everyone in the house. In the same way, let your light shine..."
– MATT 5:14-16 (NIV)

This passage, is very significant to me. For the longest time I had no idea that I even had a "light", let alone that I was supposed to let it shine. I grew up feeling very insignificant, just another piece of dust in the undesirable dirt pile of poor society.

I was the stinky kid. The kid you might feel sorry for but keep your distance from. I didn't get new flashy toys or clothing, the ones I got came from thrift stores, clothing banks, or hand-me-downs. My parents were addicts, drug-dealers, more concerned about where their next "high" would come from, or when the welfare check would show up, than what I wanted, needed, or felt like. By the time I was eleven, I was homeless. I found myself sleeping wherever I could find a dry place to crawl into. The world was determined to label me as "forgotten", "powerless", and "insignificant".

Despite it all, I didn't give up. Through a love greater than this world, I had been given a gift. I had been told that I was significant, that I wasn't meant for this... and I listened. I held onto the light of hope. It was so hard, especially as a lonely child without parents to help guide and protect me. I worked hard to make decisions that would keep me out of trouble. I CHOSE to be responsible, caring, helpful... daily I pushed myself past my comfort zone and insecurities. I chose not to believe the lies and **I CHOSE my own labels. By doing this I gave myself permission to shine.**

Too often we've learned to "dim" our lights or be threatened by the lights of others... to that I say, STOP BELIEVING THOSE LIES! Instead, **give yourself permission to shine, AND be inspired by the lights of others.**

~*Daily Inspiration by Julz DeFant, RDH*

3.

Thought for the Day

"The only person you are destined to become is the person you decide to be."
– RALPH WALDO EMERSON

4.

Claim Freedom in Your Life

In the US, on July 4th, we celebrate our country's freedoms, it is a great time to see how we are each claiming freedom in our own lives.

Are you taking steps proactively to share more of who you are, claim more of who you are, live more of whom you want to be? Or, are you sometimes feeling trapped, hemmed-in, fenced-in, or limited?

If you are feeling trapped, it's really important to look at what is limiting you so that you can shift it and become better able to live in all your talents and abilities! To shine in a way that's meaningful to you!

We get a little caught up sometimes in telling ourselves, someday I'll have freedom. Someday I'll have balance. Someday this will happen…And it doesn't.

Part of the reason is that we are not taking proactive action to get there. We're doing more of the same. If we shift the steps in the dance, away from what is limiting us and toward what will free us, then we will shift our results.

Think about your own part in your path to freedom. In a quiet space, contemplate:

- What is it that you need and are willing to receive?
- How will you know you are free? What does it look like, feel like, sound like?
- What step can you take today to move you closer to that freedom in all areas of your life?

~Daily Inspiration by Rebecca Hall Gruyter, Influencer & Empowerment Leader

5.

Thought for the Day

*"Don't be pushed around by the fears in your mind.
Be led by the dreams in your heart."*
– ROY T. BENNETT, The Light in the Heart

6.

Celebrate You!

My birthday is one of my favorite days of the year. For as far back as I can remember, I have celebrated my birthdays as my personal celebration of self. Every July 5th, I stay awake and reflect on the past year of my life. I wonder if I am continuing to become the person I want to be when my time on the planet is finished. I then consider my desires and goals for the coming year. My thoughts go to my mother and what she might have been thinking all those years ago as she welcomed her 4th child into the world. When the clock hits 12:15 a.m. on my birthday, July 6, I drift off to sleep with the excitement of a young child for the upcoming day.

I don't expect anyone else to plan a birthday celebration for me. Each year I envision how I want to celebrate my special day, and then I make it happen. Sometimes my personal celebration is being surrounded by my favorite people for dinner at a restaurant of my choosing followed by my favorite German chocolate birthday cake, which, yes, I order from the nearby bakery.

So why not make your birthday your celebration of self? **Don't wait for someone else to tell you that you are special. Tell yourself, because it's true.**

So, today isn't your birthday? That's OK. Why wait? Who says that we can only celebrate our existence in the world one day a year? Find a day that you would like to celebrate you. And go enjoy!

"Life should not only be lived, it should be celebrated."
– OSHO

~Daily Inspiration by Dr. Ruth Anderson, Spiritual Counselor

7.

The 6 Pathways to Radiance

Underneath your fears, your self judgement, and your worries lies the most powerful energy that can transform your life. When you uncover this radiant part of you, you unleash your true power, your unique gifts, and your greatest potential in life. To connect to this radiant source of joy, love and power, you must open the six pathways to Radiance.

Open the pathway of **Presence** by cultivating deep awareness and acceptance of yourself and life. Invite and accept the sensations of life as a way to guide you on your powerful journey.

Open the pathway of **Peace** by cultivating the practice of getting closure. Learn to resolve the stories and emotions of the past to free yourself to live in a state of clarity and peace.

Open the pathway of **Perspective** by cultivating the practice of gratitude. Through the act of gratitude, your perspective expands to see the love, the joy, and the beauty in the life around you. Choose to see that every experience, no matter how challenging, is an invitation and an opportunity to uncover more joy, love and radiance in your life.

Open the pathway of **Possibility** by cultivating the practice of wonder. Wonder allows you to effortlessly open the field of infinite possibility. Allow your inner sense of wonder to dissolve your worries and reveal new possibilities that expand your potential for more joy and fulfillment in your life.

Open the pathway of **Purpose** by cultivating the practice of unconditional self-love. When you love yourself unconditionally, you open yourself up to your deepest purpose, your most powerful gifts, and a vision that inspires you to live with passion.

Open the pathway of **Power** by cultivating the practice of leadership in all aspects of your life. Leadership is the act of making conscious choices in alignment with your radiant being and taking empowered action.

When you open the 6 pathways to unleash your authentic Radiance, you no longer see the world as a means to an end, but as an opportunity to live each moment with love, joy and deep fulfillment.

~Daily Inspiration by Ron Coquia, Radiance Coach

8.

Thought for the Day

*"Hard times don't create heroes.
It is during the hard times
when the 'hero' within us is revealed."*
– BOB RILEY

9.

It is a Courageous Act to Say 'YES' to YOU

From a childhood of abuse, I know a lot about being disempowered and how to overcome that in order to step into my passion, power, and gifts. The gift I have found is my passion to help other women step forward and into their courageous and empowered selves no matter what.

Today I celebrate you for saying 'yes' to your journey. I know you have your own stories or messages you have received that have disempowered you in some way. I also know that you are taking the journey to stand up, focus on your purpose and joy, and **SHINE**!

I encourage you not to take this journey alone. **It is also a courageous act to be willing to let others walk beside you** to support and cheer you on in life. I invite you to pause, take a deep breath, and be ready to receive the inspiration and wisdom of others who are on this journey with you. We need others to encourage us, to speak wisdom and truth into us, to love us and cheer us on, and to help us stand up again when we fall. To help us stay courageous and continue to say 'YES' to ourselves.

Take that in, along with the magical, beautiful warmth of a June day...

~Daily Inspiration by Rebecca Hall Gruyter, Influencer & Empowerment Leader

10.

Backyard Adventures

The summer flies by too quickly. There are always gatherings that we usually spend every weekend with family and friends.

The gatherings at our home were lots of fun. Our property is large with a built in pool. You could find a volleyball net set up and horseshoes were played. When I met Tony he had his annual "Attitude Adjustment "party. It was to let go of the daily stress and have fun with family and friends. From the Sweet Sixteen party, to an engagement party, and to a wedding celebration, we have enjoyed many adventures in our backyard.

We miss those days of partying at our house but it is much more fun going to someone else's house now. (We don't have all the set up then clean up.) Last year was a baby shower and a Sweet Sixteen, both for granddaughters. Tony and I passed the baton to the next generation and only help by providing some of the food. I love to make spinach dip and "dirt", a mixture of pudding and Oreo crumbs.

The summer still flies by but we don't do as much work anymore which furthered it. Take time to smell the roses, as they say, because it flies by during the planning. **Don't wait until there are grandchildren's celebrations to enjoy yourself. Make time today.**

~Daily Inspiration by Catherine M Laub, Advocate for Mental Health

11.

Declare Your Independence!

Declare your independence from your past and promise that you will never give up on creating a new story for yourself.

Spend fifteen minutes reflecting on where you are in your life right now. **Whatever challenges you have faced thus far, you are here now and stronger because of the wisdom garnered from those life lessons.** I view my breast cancer as a gift because it has given me a new perspective on life so that I now pursue my dreams instead of waiting for someone else to permit me to dream. Give yourself a little breathing space by making a list of all you are proud of in your life. Now, make a list of where you'd like to be at this time next year. Your words have the power to bring you from where you are to where you want to be.

~Daily Inspiration by Mary E. Knippel, Your Writing Mentor

12.

Thought for the Day

"If you set your goals and go after them with all the determination you can muster, your gifts will take you places that will amaze you."
– LES BROWN

13.

In The Now You Access True Choice

Your pivotal point of power is only available in present time and experienced by making conscious choices. Only you have the power to change your perceptions, beliefs and feelings. You can repeat your old pattern of reacting from fear, ego and your history, or you can choose to create from your Soul's present time resource of Love. All True answers come from the heart, are always in present time, and come in the form of "Yes"! Your intellect is the structure to activate those choices. Acknowledging your own free will in all your thoughts and actions reminds you that the choices you make are what will determine the results you manifest.

You, therefore, respect and honor your own and each individual's free will and timing, knowing everything is a part of the Divine Plan. You acknowledge your Spirit as the Creative Life Force within you, your Heart as the Master of your desires, and your intellect as the perfect servant through which you carry out your actions to manifest your Visions. Only from a place of conscious awareness and responsibility can you truly own your personal power in the creation of your life as you desire it to be.

Today practice the power of being in the NOW, and creating the Life of your dreams by making Conscious Choices moment by moment.

~Daily Inspiration by Kathleen E. Sims, D.D., C.H.T.

14.

The Choices We Make

Even the choices we don't get to make can be stepping stones on the path that leads us to our purpose. Some of those choices that were made for us have been disempowering, abusive, and even dangerous. So, how can they be stepping stones to good things? **I have discovered we can't always choose what happens to us, but we can choose our response.**

As a teenager, the seed of what my purpose would be was planted at a Women of Faith Conference, where I was inspired by the powerful women sharing their stories of hardship, tragedy, and struggle - and how they chose to use their experiences to help and encourage other women. In that moment I knew I wanted to be a motivational speaker, even though I was SO fearful of being visible in any way, shape or form. I wanted my story and life to be used for good. The seed planted in my heart was that maybe…just maybe, my story could help another. That seed pulled me forward to overcome my fears, and today I have bloomed from the seeds of my purpose planted so long ago!

Perhaps you can relate to not feeling like you have a choice, that others are controlling your life and your destiny, that it's better to hide? **You still have a choice.**

Despite everything that may happen TO you in your life, you do have at least one choice that is always yours to make. You can STILL be empowered and choose your response - today and going forward! Your choices - your responses - can change the path of your life.

All of the things that happen to us can become the fuel that propels us toward our purpose.

~Daily Inspiration by Rebecca Hall Gruyter, Influencer & Empowerment Leader

15.

Are you in a Pit?

Have you ever felt trapped in a dark place? If you are anything like me, negative circumstances make you feel like you are in a pit, hurt, isolated and trapped. One of my favorite Bible passages is found in Psalm 40:1-2 (NIV) "I waited patiently for the Lord; He turned to me and heard my cry. He lifted me out of the slimy pit, out of the mud and mire; He set my feet on a rock and gave me a firm place to stand."

Allow these verses to paint a picture for you. First, God hears your cries, even though you may *feel* alone in your pain, He hears you. Second, He will pull out you by providing whatever you need, whether it's love, healing or peace. Last, He will steady you. After facing a difficult situation, it may take time to feel secure and steady, but He'll be right by your side until you're strong enough to stand on your own.

Next time you find yourself in a pit of darkness imagine yourself in these verses. Close your eyes, picture yourself in a dark hole, imagine your Heavenly Father hearing you cry and reaching down to pull you out. He brings light into darkness and healing to pain - **He is your rescuer.**

~Daily Inspiration by Sunday Burquest, Women's Empowerment Speaker & Author

16.

Thought for the Day

"When someone tells me "no," it doesn't mean I can't do it, it simply means I can't do it with them."
– KAREN E. QUINONES MILLER

17.

Big Love

"When you identify what makes you cry, and you tap into it, you receive a major piece of the puzzle for your purpose, your why, and begin seeing your pathway to a life that matters."
- JOHN MAXWELL

It takes big love to break through big fears that threaten our pursuit of happy-ever-after.

But human beings show up with that big love, again and again. And miracles happen.

My financial happy-ever-dream is to raise a money-smart girl and positively influence future generations of our family tree. My love for my daughter gave me strength and courage to unfold my financial potential beyond my comfort zone, one brave feather at a time.

I persisted through the many challenges of mama-preneurship, in my devotion to empower her to live *her* financial happy-ever-after, whatever she decides for it to be. As it turns out, my success is not about me at all. It's about my daughter's well-being. This is so often the case for heart-centered leaders, that their dreams arise to serve a greater purpose, than for personal gain alone.

Ironically, when it's no longer just about us, it becomes all about us.

The universe begins to support our dream in more ways than we imagined possible, helping us to make our vision a reality. Doors that were once firmly closed, start to open. The right people begin to arrive. We discover a check in the mail that we never expected. A positive opportunity arrives out of the blue and changes our lives forever. The rest is history.

What fuels your strength and courage to keep on loving and growing? What keeps you from giving up, throwing in the towel, walking away from your dream that's meant to come true, for a purpose? Whatever it is, it's your time to embrace your financial dream and create a plan of mini-habits to transform your dream into reality!

~Daily Inspiration by Marlene Elizabeth, Author of MONEYWINGS™

18.

Thought for the Day

"Setting goals is the first step into turning the invisible into the visible."
– TONY ROBBINS

19.

Life is Not a Solo Journey

I'm not sure where this myth got started that we have do it all on our own. **In truth, we are not meant to do everything on our own because "Life is not a solo journey!"**

As you are stepping into your goals and forward into that place of visibility and influence, you may be facing some things that are making your uncomfortable. It may be something new that you've never done before, some expertise that you need but can't do yourself, or simply just a feeling that you're in this whole journey on your own.

It's not true! You get to be supported so you can go out into the world and share your gifts. There are people out there waiting to support you with their unique gifts and talents. But you do need to be willing to reach out for help.

How find and build in the support you need? Start here: Identify it. Get very specific about what you need. Step a little bit outside of your comfort zone and imagination to think even further about what you really want help with. When you do that, you allow space for it to appear.

Identify it. Ask for it. And then listen. And know that it is a courageous act to say "yes" to you and be willing to let others walk beside you to support and cheer you on. Not only will the make the journey richer, but I find we can go further with others walking beside us.

~Daily Inspiration by Rebecca Hall Gruyter, Influencer & Empowerment Leader

20.

Thought for the Day

"You cannot afford to live in potential for the rest of your life; at some point, you have to unleash the potential and make your move."
– ERIC THOMAS

21.

Declare Your Freedom from Dieting!

It's summer and we all want to look great while enjoying our favorite pastimes. But while you're getting ready for your outdoor fun, there might be a little nag in the back of your mind: you'd like to drop a few pounds, but you know that dieting hasn't worked in the past.

Well here's some news that will make us all feel better: Dieting doesn't work for anybody! So shake that old paradigm. It's July, time to make your own wellness declaration of independence--to think and eat in a way that's just right for *your* body!

Instead of counting calories and watching portion sizes, a new study reveals that focusing on the *quality of foods* produces significant weight loss. An article published in the February 2018 edition of *Journal of the American Medical Association* concluded that, whether participants consumed a low-fat or low-carb diet, as long as they concentrated on healthy, minimally processed whole foods, they shed pounds over a year. Imagine eating foods directly from your garden or kitchen--fresh and wholesome--and losing weight following the food plan you enjoy most.

The key is to fill up on fruits, vegetables, and whole grains, while minimizing processed, high-sugar foods. And it's also important to cook with whole foods at home whenever possible.

So skip the coffee drink and low-fat cookies; reach instead for water and whole-grain crackers with natural peanut butter! Not only will this help you lose weight, but eating a nutrient-dense food pattern while cutting back on added sugar, refined grains, and highly processed foods can also decrease your risk of chronic diseases such as diabetes and heart disease.

~Daily Inspiration by Lisa Harris, MS, RD, Fitness Pro

22.

Vision Checkup

I am old enough to remember when I sat in the optometrist's chair with a big metal contraption in front of my eyes. "Is this better, or this?" I couldn't tell because they both seemed about the same. Helen Keller said "The only thing worse than being blind is having sight but no vision". What a profound statement. **When was your last vision checkup?**

Sometimes our vision is cloudy. It might be because we have listened to the "shouldn't, couldn't, wouldn't, and can't" voices, those strident loud voices that can cloud our judgement and drown out our dreams. Turn them off! Sometimes our vision is double. This happens when we haven't taken the time to fully realize the possibilities. How do we correct this? **By gaining a clear focus on what we are called to do.** Joel A. Barker is quoted as saying "Vision without action is merely a dream. Action without vision just passes the time. Vision with action can change the world." (www.brainyquote.com)

Sometimes we are near-sighted. What is right in front of us can block out possibilities. **Clear out the underbrush, the daily weeds that grow and obstruct our view of what truly is important.** It may not be comfortable, like that big metal device, but it is necessary.

Sometimes we are far-sighted. The goal is so enticing yet we cannot comprehend the way or the work that it takes to get there. I have taught my students a chorus written by Ron Hamilton, called "Little by Little". It goes like this: "Little by little, inch by inch, by the yard it's hard, by the inch what a cinch! Never stare up the stairs just step up the steps, little by little, inch by inch." Do the work! **Dreamers must be doers to accomplish the vision.**

Do you need a vision checkup today? Just think what you could achieve with a clear vision of who you are and what you want to accomplish. Then make it happen!

~*Daily Inspiration by Elda Robinson, Teacher*

23.

Thought for the Day

*"It's not whether you get knocked down.
It's whether you get up."*
– VINCE LOMBARD

24.

Free to Create Your Reality

As we celebrate freedom, remember that our greatest freedom is the freedom to choose our thoughts.

Quantum physics reveals that our world is not as it appears. It is not a solid object. Rather, the world is made up of energy that is continuously being created by our individual and collective thoughts.

The practice of meditation encourages us to observe our thoughts. With consistent practice, our thoughts disappear. From this state, we can access our deepest wisdom.

I invite you to spend a few minutes each day in meditation. Enjoy the peace it brings and the insights that emerge. These insights are powerful seeds for your conscious thoughts that enable your deepest wisdom to create your reality. Create with freedom, choice and love.

~Daily Inspiration by Olivia Parr-Rud, Corporate Love Ambassador

25.

Thought for the Day

"More smiling, less worrying.
More compassion, less judgment.
More blessed, less stressed. More love, less hate."
– ROY T. BENNETT, *The Light In the Heart*

26.

We Are Unlimited

"You are immortal; you exist for billions of years in different manifestations because you are Life, and Life cannot die. You are in the trees, the butterflies, the fish, the moon, the sun. Wherever you go, you are there, waiting for yourself."
– DON MIGUEL RUIZ

Take a moment to look around you, to experience yourself in the universe. Look with your heart and see yourself in the flowers in your garden, in the mountains, lakes and streams, the birds that fly across the morning sunlit sky. Look to the night sky and know that you are a part of the moon and the stars that glitter and shine down from above, illuminating the path. In each of these moments, if we are able to still ourselves and listen, we can hear our own self saying, "Yes, here I am, and there I am. All is one and all are a part of the whole of the cosmos." And, if we listen even more carefully, we will be blessed to hear Spirit asking us to "Be still and know that I AM." To hold the thought that Spirit is all around, in, and through each and every particle of the universe is to welcome in an almost overwhelming but all encompassing experience of love beyond measure. And, it is in that moment, that we are made aware of our limitless nature.

Yes, we are unlimited and each of us a part of something larger than our own individual selves. In taking care of ourselves, we are taking care of others and our created world...and vice versa. It promotes awareness that we are all an integral, necessary, and constant participant in the whole of the universe. Look at tonight's sky...listen to yourself asking you to be gentle with yourself and to let love the way. Remember, you are unlimited—an integral, necessary, and constant participant in the workings of the whole of the universe.

~Daily Inspiration by Dr. Nancy Tarr Hart

27.

Thought for the Day

*"The pessimist sees difficulty in every opportunity.
The optimist sees opportunity in every difficulty."*
– WINSTON CHURCHILL

28.

Efficient Production Maximizes Results

Maximum productivity starts with you being and living at your Maximum Efficiency. Mastering ones' efficiency starts with recognizing and enriching and encouraging your strengths and limiting your exposure to things that are negative and toxic and drain on your energy. Passionately pursue those positive outlets and maximize those opportunities that present themselves, as a result. Persistently search for and align with Equal Exchange of Energy endeavors, associations and people, as these will add value to your journey and provide an energy balance, which is a Soul Booster. Analyze every process in your daily life and look for the gaps of time that are not lining up with your Highest Good and fill them with positive and progressive action steps towards manifesting your Highest Good Goals and Desires.

Eliminate wasteful appetites that add anything unwanted to you or causes an interruption to your lifestyle and embrace the realness of who you truly desire to be and positively progress towards your goals, efficiently.

Affirmation:
I AM Recognizing and Encouraging My Strengths. I AM consistently aligning with Equal Exchange of Energy Opportunities. I AM Living at My Maximum Productive Efficiency. I AM Positive and Progressive in My Action Steps Towards Manifesting My Highest Good Goals and Desires.

~Daily Inspiration by Mark Edward Pyle, Manifestation Expert

29.

Thunderstorms

"Every great change is preceded by chaos."
– DEEPAK CHOPRA

One of my fondest memories growing up in the country were the thunderstorms. First, the stillness... no wind, no birds chirping... so deathly quiet the hairs on the back of your neck stood up. You could feel it in the air ... a storm was coming.

The wind would pick up, the dark clouds would roll in turning day into night. My mom would call to us to help her take the laundry in. Big fat drops of rain would start falling getting us wet before we got into the comfort of the house. BOOM came the thunder ... so loud you jumped right out of your skin. Finally, the lightening, so blindingly bright you saw stars.

When we had these storms, my Dad would sit on the carport and watch. I loved being there with him as it was exciting to ride out the storm. For my Dad, he was thinking about the damage the storm would leave ... would the garden be flooded, would we be without power. As the rains continued to come down fast and furious, the carport would begin to flood and the wind would be so strong you could hear the trees creaking. This was when my Dad would send me inside to safety.

Do you feel as if you are going through thunderstorms in life? Storms, of any kind, feel chaotic and can have you fearing what will be left after the storm. In the midst of any storm, there will be changes ... changes that you can choose to allow to destroy you or changes that you can choose to ride it out ... to see the rainbow ... a promise of better times. **Choose to see the rainbow.**

~Daily Inspiration by Denise Hansard, Empowerment Expert

30.

The Joy of Being Visible

"We must be willing to be seen on the same level we want to serve."
- REBECCA HALL GRUYTER

For a long time, I resisted being visible. I wanted to disappear. I wanted to make a difference in the world without being seen, hoping people would just find me by osmosis!

Then I realized that staying inside accepted boundaries - acting a certain way, hiding parts of myself, following other people's rules - was not moving me forward to what I was being called to do. In fact, it was taking a lot of energy and getting me nowhere. People couldn't really connect with me because I was not fully showing up as myself.

It wasn't always an easy path to change. But do you know what I discovered about being willing to be seen, being vulnerable, stripping away some of the layers I'd been hiding behind, and finally really being seen as I am?

It is actually freeing and joyful! The "old way" was literally draining my life away. When we are willing to strip all that away and say, "This is me!" our energy increases and people really lean in and connect. What joy that brings to everyone!

~Daily Inspiration by Rebecca Hall Gruyter, Influencer & Empowerment Leader

31.

Thought for the Day

"It only takes one person to make you happy and change your life: YOU."
– CHARLES ORLANDO

August

1.

Choose to Share the Gift of You with the World

"Insanity: doing the same thing over and over again and expecting different results."
- UNKNOWN

The world is waiting for the gift of more of you! I know you are sharing what you're called forth to bring to the world in your life and business. And I encourage and support you to share even more of you!

Let's check in on how you're doing: What actions are you taking, that you'll be practicing or implementing, that are different from last year (further expanding and helping you grow) - and will bring you different results that you want?

Often, we can be doing the same things – just pushing harder! – and be expecting different results. You have choices in everything that you're doing, and can make different choices that better serve you. Think about what you can choose to echo out, the things that will allow you to be seen and heard even more. To be visible!

Visibility is simply how you are showing up in the world. It could be on stage, on the radio, or on the grocery line! I believe so much that **visibility is how you best share the gift of you with the world.**

Today, think about how you are showing up in your life for yourself, and for others. **You are called to be visible, to show up exactly as you are made.** Be willing to build new practices and take new actions - today - that might be different from what you did last year, so that you can be even more visible or in a different way, that lets you SHINE even brighter.

~Daily Inspiration by Rebecca Hall Gruyter, Influencer & Empowerment Leader

2.

Inner Work Matters

"Dis-ease can be reversed by reversing mental patterns."
-LOUISE HAY, Heal Your Body

While doctors may be able to help you heal your body from the outside, only *you* can do the inner work necessary to heal from the inside. Mental patterns of resentment, anger and stubbornness can show up in your body as all kinds of symptoms of pain or illness. You can get your symptoms treated, but they may easily return if you don't pay attention to and clear up the mental patterns underneath. Release negative energy, forgive yourself and others.

You have the power to change your "dis-ease" into radiant health.

~Daily Inspiration by Dr. Liz Lyster

3.

Thought for the Day

"The heart of human excellence often begins to beat when you discover a pursuit that absorbs you, frees you, challenges you, or gives you a sense of meaning, joy, or passion."
– TERRY ORLICK

4.

The Comfort of Home

Tony and I celebrate our anniversary August 22nd. We are married twenty years and together twenty-six. When we met, we were both recovering from marital separations A **knight in shining armor slowly became the love of my life and I still call him my Prince Charming.** Tony opens doors for me, does most of our shopping, housekeeping and cooking. He takes care of me in every way possible. I tell people he is a Saint because of how much we have been through and he still stands by me.

When we met Tony received a large salary and thought his career would never end. The company closed in 1994 and Tony found himself unemployed. Since I never had much money it was easy not to need dinners out and some of the many things we enjoyed with his large salary. He had a position in another company for a few years but it wasn't the same.

It took Tony a long time to adjust to this, but now it gives us a sense of togetherness. This sounds strange, but we both work hard to bring the necessary income to survive. We do this because we love each other so deeply. We do not have to go out to enjoy each other's company. We watch movies in the comfort of our home and sit to talk throughout the day.

The time spent together doesn't have to be at a lavish restaurant or a movie theater. The moments spent alone in your own home can be just as great.

~Daily Inspiration by Catherine M Laub, Advocate for Mental Health

5.

Thought for the Day

"The mystery of human existence lies not in just staying alive, but in finding something to live for."
– FYODOR DOSTOYEVSKY

6.

Simply Fabulous

You're fabulous. You're fabulous with. You're fabulous without. **God made you fabulous.** Your personality has already attracted a multitude of unique individuals, who would've passed you by, had you not been declared, "fabulous." Each morning declare how fabulous you are. **"I'm fabulous. I'm fabulous with. I'm fabulous without."** Then stretch and reach for greatness. Enjoy and celebrate your fabulous self!

~Daily Inspiration by Kri' Shawn Terrell, Motivational Speaker

7.

Let the Freedom of the Outdoors Take Your Spirit

"To me a lush carpet of pine needles or spongy grass is more welcome than the most luxurious Persian rug."
– HELEN KELLER

What I love about summer is nature's lush display, from the flowers to the trees to the grasses to the birds and other wildlife that abound. It is clear that nature wants us to enjoy the pleasure of all of these sights, sounds, tastes, smells, and luscious feeling!

How often do you take the time to get up from whatever you're doing, at home or work, and step outside to take in some really great fresh air? To draw some deep, cleansing breaths? To just let go of the stress and tension you've been holding in your body?

I often will do just that, especially if I am working on a complex problem or the flow of a new program. By removing the boundaries of the building and letting the freedom of the outdoors take my spirit, I find that creative ideas and clear solutions come up – about my business as well as other aspects of my life.

I do take my phone, but not to answer email, troll social media, or even talk to anybody. I use it to capture anything that might bubble up on my nature walk. These moments are golden. There are times when I have gotten the "answer," when I strike my "Easy" button – why was I making this so difficult?

Taking these moments gives you an opportunity to let go of what is tying you down, keeping you chained to the chair, the same idea, and the past. Take that chance to break free and let your ideas flow and fly free.

What are you working on that might benefit from a pleasurable walk in nature?

~Daily Inspiration by Linda Patten, Leadership Expert

8.

Thought for the Day

*"Definiteness of purpose is
the starting point of all achievement."*
– W. CLEMENT STONE

9.

Life is Not a Dress Rehearsal

I believe sometimes we treat life like it's a dress rehearsal - NEXT time I'll do this, SOMEDAY I'll do that. **I want you to know TODAY IS THE DAY!** This is the stage, this is the time you are being called to step forward and SHINE, to share all of who you are powerfully in the world.

Things are going on in our lives or in our community that can feel unsettling or difficult, and I'm seeing more and more that people are stepping up to make a positive difference. This is when we need to be visible, on stage, even if we are uncomfortable.

I once felt called in this way, with a big heart to serve. But I wanted people to pick up on (somehow) what I wanted to share, that they could just come to me and I could stay behind the curtain! I wanted the change without the vulnerability. What I've discovered is that it doesn't work that way! We have to be willing to be seen, to be visible, to step on center stage so that people can find us.

I encourage you to listen in to what others have to say, as well as what your inner spirit has to tell you, about what will empower you to take that step, climb those stairs to center stage to be more visible. **Lean into what you need to do to bring that impact you're wanting to see in the world.**

~Daily Inspiration by Rebecca Hall Gruyter, Influencer & Empowerment Leader

10.

Thought for the Day

"It's not enough to have lived.
We should be determined to live for something."
– WINSTON S. CHURCHILL

11.

Friendship Pie

When I was young, I had a book that I loved called "Honey". Honey, a teenage girl, doesn't get what she needs from her home life so as she makes friends, and "adopts" them as her family. They fill her life with love and happiness and they become a part of her "pie".

I always think of this book when I think of my close circle of friends. I left home at an early age and they became my family in a sense, each one teaching me different life lessons and providing support where I needed. They taught me so much: how to drive, how to live on my own, how to wrap presents, and so on. I managed to get by on what I learned through them and from them. Their support was, and still is, immeasurable.

Your family will always be your family. They will (hopefully!) support you and stand by you no matter what differences you may have. However, you can't possibly get everything you need from your parents, or even a partner, but friends are the family we get to choose. In doing so, we bring in what we need. They fill us up, they encourage us, they put us back together, and they hold our hands. Even new friends can become part of our Tribe.

Honor your friends today. Get in touch with old friends and new. Phone calls, emails, E-cards, even texts are great ways to reach out. See if you can make plans for lunch, or a cup of coffee with a friend, or even a phone date.

~Daily Inspiration by Jaimie Harnagel, Certified Reiki Master and Shamanic Practitioner

12.

Build Your Reputation

*"You can't build a reputation on what you
are going **to do**"* (emphasis mine)
-HENRY FORD

Have you ever encountered people who sound so believable that you don't question their capabilities? Have they convinced you of their expertise with their credentials and name dropping *only* to discover that they aren't able to actually perform (As former President George W. Bush would say, "All hat and no cattle")?

I have come to believe that it isn't so much important what is **said** as it is what is **done!**

A **built reputation** is much better than a **professed reputation.** You do the **work**, and let *others* do the **talking**...you will *build* a much stronger reputation.

~Daily Inspiration by John F. Hall, MBA, Author, Business Owner

13.

Thought for the Day

"Hardships often prepare ordinary people for an extraordinary destiny."
– C.S. LEWIS

14.

You Have the Power to make your own Happy Ending

Who doesn't want to be happy? Sadly, if you speak with most people, they will tell you that they are not happy. Why? I have noticed that most people are waiting for what they consider an ideal situation to happen so that they can be happy. Do we find ourselves complaining about the house not being clean enough, not being able to lose ten pounds, or not being able to afford the fancy car? When we could be profoundly grateful that we have a roof over our heads, have relatively good health, and a reliable vehicle to get us where we need to go. It is possible that you are currently navigating through a difficult situation in your life and happiness seems to be eluding you.

Just remember three things

1. it may be grievous in the moment, but the storm always passes, and you will be wiser
2. as long as you are breathing, you are living, and if you are living that means you are already winning
3. if you are living, then you have choices.

You can choose to be happy. *Ask yourself what choices do you plan to make today? Will you choose to be grateful? Will you choose to focus on the positive? Will you choose to make a positive impact on the world around you, for example a random act of kindness in word or deed?*

It is not the big life decisions that will make us happy, it is finding joy in the daily activity of living and being grateful for the time we are here and the differences we can make. Go live and be happy!

~Daily Inspiration by Adrian Jefferson Chofor, Global Personal Transformation Strategist

15.

Today

Today is your lucky day. Today you will clear a path for any success you desire in your life. What I want you to do is get some sticky notes. Then start writing on them your goals, dreams, desires like: "Take a spin class", "clean my desk", "save 10% from every paycheck", "want new shoes", or "Christmas vacation." Write as many you like.

Then stick them on your bathroom mirror, car, refrigerator, or any place where you can see them every day. Once you start seeing them every day the universe opens your mind and your mind starts working towards that goal. When you work without a dream or a goal it becomes just a wish. There is so much power in paper and pen. Once you have practiced this for some time, I want you to let me know how it's going. Wishing you great success starting today!

~Daily Inspiration by Inguss

16.

Thought for the Day

"The best way to lengthen out our days is to walk steadily and with a purpose."
– CHARLES DICKENS

17.

Prioritize to Monetize

Fall is coming soon, the time when your garden is beginning to blossom and flourish and bear fruit for your life and business! This means lots of activity to make your harvest successful. And it brings up questions: What do you need to do now? What are your priorities for spending your time, energy - and money? Your financial investment is an important part of bringing forth what you are called to do, and deserves your attention.

The key to balancing all of your goals, dreams, current needs, and financial priorities is a practical approach that is personalized to YOU. Every person's strategy is going to be different and unique, just like you are. An expert can guide you through the process to understand where you are, where you want to go, and the decisions and steps to empower you to get there.

Here are some signs that it is time to lean in to getting help with prioritizing and inviting money in:

- You don't really know where your money is going.
- You feel like you can't seem to grow and SHINE like you want to.
- You want money to interact in your life differently.
- You want to feel empowered around money

If any of these make you feel that pull at your heart - that urgency to get help in this area - honor it! You and all that you are called to do are too important to settle for less in this area of your life!

~Daily Inspiration by Rebecca Hall Gruyter, Influencer & Empowerment Leader

18.

Encourage Others

Today is a good day to talk to someone and encourage them. Remember that a leader acquires greater credibility when he shows interest in those whom he leads. During the 40-year exodus, the word "encourage" is mentioned only twice in the Scriptures.

In each case, it was Moses who encouraged the people. Not once did the people he led encourage him to be a leader. Remember, when addressing yourself use your head; when addressing others, use your heart. And never underestimate the importance of building bridges, which begins with reaching out to others.

~Daily Inspiration by Pastor Nicolas C Pacheco

19.

Nil By Mouth

You can learn a lot about systems when you visit friends and family in hospital.

Arriving one day with a tub of yogurt for my Dad, it was only by accident that I found out he wasn't to have anything to eat. Not being a medical person I didn't understand why. There was a risk that the food could go into his respiratory system and he could end up with all sorts of complications.

There was no instruction or sign to tell me this. In fact, his name wasn't even written on the white board above his head. He was bed number 14. Being a systems person, I couldn't help myself. I suggested to the nurse that she write "Nil By Mouth" on the board so others wouldn't make the same mistake. So she wrote "NBM." That works! Who knows what "NBM" means?

Eventually she wrote "Nil By Mouth", and I noticed nurses and visitors and the orderlies actually read it and took notice of it; avoiding a near catastrophe.

Looking at your business or life, are there things you or your staff or family are doing that are "obvious" to you, critical to your business and yet something that an outsider or new recruit would not understand?

We need systems, but more importantly we need them to work. Their purpose is to take the guesswork out of the equation. Could it be time to have a little review of yours? Have you got systems and are they relevant?

~Daily Inspiration by Shirley Dalton, Business Expert

20.

Thought for the Day

*"You must first be who you really are,
then do what you need to do,
in order to have what you want."*
– MARGARET YOUNG

21.

Memory Boxes

It's an old shoe box that is tattered around the edges and maybe a little stained. Or maybe it is a scrapbook that has been artistically arranged. We all have them – that container of old photographs. They are probably a mix of black and white, Polaroid, color photos, or even slides. Some of the pictures are out of focus, some have an index finger blocking part of the shot, and some have the head cut off. But, we can't seem to throw them away.

Photographs are memories. They can transport us to a different time and place. We can laugh at the clothes and hairstyles. We are astonished that we ever looked that young. As Andy Warhol said, "The best thing about a picture is that it never changes, even when the people in it do." (https://petapixel.com/2014/05/29/70-inspirational-quotes-photographers/). They can bring a tear to our eyes as we look at loved ones we can no longer see. Pictures can also make us laugh as we recall the great time we were having when they were taken.

When my family packed up the homestead there were boxes and boxes of slides. The next year we got together at my sister's. One night we sat outside relaxing in lawn chairs and went through every slide. We had such fun looking at the old photos, yelling out "Yes" when we wanted to take one. It's such a fond memory because it was one of the last times our mom was with us.

It is possible, at the right moment, for any of us to create a masterpiece.

Sometimes, cameras aren't available. **Don't let those inspiring, funny, unexpected moments slip away without being recorded firmly in our minds. Then they can be enjoyed at our leisure again and again.** And, you don't have to hunt for the old memory box.

~Daily Inspiration by Elda Robinson, Teacher

22.

Bring in Support to Bring Your Gifts Forward

"I'm doing everything myself and I don't think I'll ever be able to afford to bring in help! How are you able to grow your team?" someone asked me recently.

We cannot bring our gifts and talents forward without help from others. One of the myths out there is that you have to have a certain amount of money to start hiring and building your team - it's all-or-nothing. I want you to know that it's not the truth. You can do it one step at a time, starting from exactly where you are!

I have grown my team size to 30+ within the groups and organizations we've created. Here is what I did...

When I first started out, I really needed help but I couldn't afford to hire a full-time person. So, **I started setting aside $50 or $100 a month, then getting that amount worth of support.** Then I'd set aside more, get more help, and so on. Eventually, I was able to get ongoing support.

I built my team one person at a time. Even today I don't have any full-time employees; I work with contractors that specialize in that area and in different ways - doing the things they really love.

This way, you get to work in the gifts you love and expand your impact, while allowing others to bring their own gifts forward!

~Daily Inspiration by Rebecca Hall Gruyter, Influencer & Empowerment Leader

23.

Thought for the Day

*"Efforts and courage are not enough
without purpose and direction."*
– JOHN F. KENNEDY

24.

Taking a Moment to Embrace Humanity

It's hot, I'm crabby, problems and worries are crowding my mind. I decide to take refuge in the cool halls of my neighborhood gem, the Oakland Museum of California. Wandering randomly through the interactive exhibits, I find myself in the Natural Science section, a lovely room whose walls are covered in little tacked-up notes from visitors. All have been invited by a bright sign to answer the question: HOW DO YOU INTERACT WITH NATURE?

My blocked-up brain doesn't even comprehend the question. I begin to circle the room to read the hundreds of slips of paper on which people have shared their thoughts. The handwriting reflects a variety of ages and writing ability; some have added their names or where they are from - Ohio, Sierra Leone, England. I begin to feel like I'm part of a silent, intimate conversation with Humanity on the common subject of Nature. My heart lifts as I stop at each response...

- By remembering that sometimes it's okay to stop and smell the roses
- I lift my face to the sun, close my eyes and breathe deeply.
- W/respect to those that came before me, to the indigenous peoples who's land we are on <3.
- Respetate y Respeta la Madre Naturaleza [Respect Yourself and Respect Mother Nature]
- By tapping into my inner stillness & allowing my intuition to do the guiding
- Letting the wind unwind my thoughts
- I take walks and feel what the plants are telling me.
- I bark Back at Dogs
- Kissing the Earth with my steps
- Via the five senses that all humans & animals have in common.
- I get my grubby lil paws all over it! love, a gardener
- Stand still ... Listen ... Take a breath ... Relax and soak it in.

My worries slip away as I feel the embrace of these words. With a realigned and expanded perspective, I step out into the beautiful, sunny day. Thank you, Humanity!

~Daily Inspiration by Bettyanne Green, Content Marketing Strategist

25.

Refresh

Over the years I have had the privilege of working with many types of people facing the difficulties of daily life and threat of burn-out. Often, I am told how positive I am and asked how I do it. After considering this question, **I have found that it isn't just one thing, one method that I can "nail down." Instead it is a constant, continuous, purposeful set of actions that comprise what I like to call, my "Refresh" button.**

I would venture to say that pretty much all of us are familiar with the "refresh" button. We push "refresh" in order to update the display of our computer screens when things start to lag. When we push our personal "Refresh" button, we take a quick moment to be reinvigorated.

Remember to "refresh" throughout your day:

- **Breathe:** Allow your cells to be refreshed, use breathing techniques for relaxation, healing, meditation, praying, energy, etc.
- **Let go:** We may not be able to immediately change our circumstances, but we are able to decide upon how we operate within them.
- **Listen to your heart:** Decide who you are, decide what kind of day, relationships, life-style, or team member you are going to be.
- **Be productive:** Make a difference, get things done.
- **F-U-N:** This is one of the most important things in your day - Have some fun!
- **Give:** Give your time and efforts, this will fill you up!
- **Appreciate:** Being appreciated gives confidence and inspires. Ask yourself, "how can I better appreciate others". Purposefully discover what to appreciate about one-another.
- **Gratefulness, "Thank You":** Take time to allow yourself to **FEEL** *grateful*, you will allow an inner joy and love to truly fill you up and refresh your soul.

It is important that we take time throughout our day to "refresh", that is my secret. I printed off an image of a refresh button and hung it up in places where it catches my eye throughout the day, this way I am reminded to "refresh" often. I encourage you to do the same.

~Daily Inspiration by Julz DeFant, RDH

26.

Thought for the Day

"If you can tune into your purpose and really align with it, setting goals so that your vision is an expression of that purpose, then life flows much more easily."
– JACK CANFIELD

27.

Exercise Your "Go For It" Muscle

Jumping, Running or Swimming? What is your form of exercise?

While I was visiting family over a 4th of July holiday, someone made a statement about my older sister. It was such a profound statement that I wanted to share it with you.

"There she goes again, getting her exercise in by *jumping* to conclusions."

How often do you find yourself...

Jumping to conclusions

Running on empty

Swimming upstream

These phrases are your mental exercises. And there is magic in your words. **Your words are powerful having tremendous energy behind them.** The words that you speak ... to yourself and to others ... become a part of you in the actions you take and the behaviors you exhibit.

I can hear you now ... 'Denise, how do I do this?' Awareness of each and every word that is thought or said is the key. Along with stop being stuck in the how. When you become stuck in the how, it means you are really trying to decide on IF you can do this ... become aware, change your words to change your behavior. The real question becomes ... 'am I ready to change?' Don't you owe it to yourself to at least try? I say you are and instead of just trying, go for it ... full out ... do an experiment for a day become aware of all the words and phrases you use. Are they limiting you or are they inspiring you? From this experiment, you can decide if you are willing to go further, to really make changes in who you are. **Empower your words and your actions.**

~Daily Inspiration by Denise Hansard, Empowerment Expert

28.

Thought for the Day

"Everyone has been made for some particular work and the desire for that work has been put in every heart."
- JALALUDDIN RUMI

29.

You Are a Duplication & Multiply Source

You are made in the image of God and your function is to allow the *essence* and Will of God to duplicate Itself in the world through you. The yearning you have felt is your Divinity wanting to experience Itself. When you recognize you are created in the Image of God with the potential of Pure Consciousness, you know your function is to duplicate the Creator in the world. When you consciously choose to extend Love with reverence from a Pure Heart, you experience All Is One. Thus, the Image of God is expressed and multiplied through you with others, extending Light into the world.

Today know the life you live is God's Life.

~Daily Inspiration by Kathleen E. Sims, D.D., C.H.T.

30.

Thought for the Day

"Let all that you do be done in love."
− 1 CORINTHIANS 16:14

31.

You Are Beautifully Made

*"You are beautifully and wonderfully made,
on purpose and for a purpose."*
– REBECCA HALL GRUYTER

Let's talk about you for a moment…Here is the truth about you: YOU are beautifully and wonderfully made. You have unique gifts, talents, abilities, stories, journeys, and perspectives that you alone can bring forward. **You matter and are needed just as you are. It is safe to be seen, heard, and SHINE!** The more you **SHINE**, the more you pave the way for others while sharing the amazing gift of you with the world.

So, I invite and encourage you to really step forward fully in your life because you have so much to give. Bring it all, authentically and powerfully! Complete all that you are called to complete.

Are you ready? Are you willing to share the gift of you with those around you? Are you willing to be seen on the same level you are wanting to serve? Are you ready for a great adventure when you do these things?

Then let's go!

~Daily Inspiration by Rebecca Hall Gruyter, Influencer & Empowerment Leader

September

1.

Thought for the Day

"The best and most beautiful things in this world cannot be seen or even heard, but must be felt with the heart."
– HELEN KELLER

2.

Be Happy in the Moment of Now

Remember Ralph Waldo saying, **"Life is a journey not a destination?"** What if we shift our thinking just a bit and say: **"Life is about the journey AND the destination?"** Attracting what you want into your life is about creating a vibrational energy that brings what you want to you. How do we do that? **By being happy in the NOW.**

Most of us think that if we have the next-- you name it-- job, relationship, car, whatever it is that we think will make us happy—then we will be happy. **What if you shifted your thinking to – I am happy now—even if I have not attained my vision of what I want yet?** What if that energy shift started to attract more of what you wanted into your life?

Have a clear vision for your future and create a force. This clarity and energy of expectation starts to not only attract what you want into your life—but the energy actually pulls the opportunities, ideas, and the people that can help you make it happen. Take back your power! When we believe that we will only be happy if something outside of us happens for us, then we give the power of our happiness to outside forces. We don't need to do things to be happy—we need to be happy so that we can do things!

~Daily Inspiration by Carmen M. Bryant, Business Coach

3.

Thought for the Day

"No matter what you look like or think you look like, you're special and loved and perfect just the way you are."
– ARIEL WINTER

4.

You Can Overcome ANYTHING!

To overcome is defined as "to prevail over" (Dictionary.com: http://www.dictionary.com/browse/overcome?s=ts)

When I think of the world 'Overcome', I tend to imagine a pearl from the bottom of the ocean, a diamond, which transformed from being a piece of coal deep within the earth, an eagle and even Mohammed Ali with his 'Rope –A- Dope' boxing technique.

In order to overcome, an individual must be determined that no matter the circumstance, they will walk in victory when it's all said and done!

So, here are some tools to help you overcome:
- Stay determined
- Establish solid goals and accomplish them one at a time
- Never give up
- Love yourself by doing your best
- Ask for help when needed
- Have faith in God and trust Him!

Remember, if you want to overcome bad enough, you will...

Here are some things to remember while you are overcoming:
- Eliminate excuses!
- Choose to win!
- Don't Doubt YOURSELF!
- Make it Happen!
- Be a believer!

Be encouraged and KNOW that you can overcome ANYTHING!

This is your season to overcome! So, dust yourself off, and by the grace of God, make it happen! You are an overcomer!!

~Daily Inspiration by India White, Author and Inspirational Speaker

5.

What is Love?

"The beginning of love is the will to let those we love be perfectly themselves, the resolution not to twist them to fit our own image. If in loving them, we do not love what they are, but only their potential likeness to ourselves, then we do not love them: we only love the reflection of ourselves we find in them."
- THOMAS MERTON, *No Man Is an Island*

As parents, it can be a challenge to let our kids be who they are, since we are very invested in their future. We want them to be successful; we think that we know what is good for them. Yet we need to remember that we don't know everything about them, ever.

Instead of continually pushing our kids--telling them what to do, always knowing what is best for them--can we try to stay curious and, instead, explore who they are? Can we observe what their talents are, help them discover what their own ideas look like, what they need to grow at that very moment? Life would be inspiring if we did.

Our question to you: What can you do this month to discover who that kid is that is in front of you? Can you rediscover them day after day, week after week?

Our gift to you: greatparentsempower.com/3-questions-free-booklet/

~Daily Inspiration by Mooniek Seebregts and Martina Caviezel, The Parent Empowerment Coaches

6.

Thought for the Day

"Love the giver more than the gift."
– BRIGHAM YOUNG

7.

Reset

We can choose the attitude we bring forward. **Our attitude is a powerful trait. Make sure your attitude matches your values.** Here's a true example, a school teacher with a bad attitude towards a certain kid will treat that kid badly. Then what happens? That kid gets a bad attitude toward the teacher and he will not perform up to his potential. That's overt and there's no doubt what the teacher is thinking.

Then there is our subconscious that controls our behaviors in ways we don't realize. I experienced this many times. I had to be told about my behaviors. Then I had to reset. I needed a new perspective and I found it by looking up. The best we can do is acknowledge the behavior and work to reset our thinking. We need to pray for guidance and understanding so we can totally reset when your attitude is out of alignment. Now we have our new sparkling attitude that spreads like wildfire.

~Daily Inspiration by Tresté Loving, Racial Equity Expert

8.

The Gift of Grandmothers

I was blessed to have four grandmothers in my life...all unique, powerful and wonderfully made women who greatly impacted my life and who have inspired the shape and form of the empowerment work I now get to do in the world.

I learned from one of my grandmothers how to give myself the grace, love and understanding just like I would for my very best friend. Another taught me to not wait for permission but to step into who I am authentically and powerfully. From another I learned to work hard for what truly matters to me, and always to walk with honor and integrity. And another taught me the importance of lifting others up, and how we can all make a positive difference heart-by-heart and life-by-life.

They each walked in great love, and in deep respect of others and of God. I'm thankful for their legacy and the gift of having them in my life.

Who in your life has influenced and inspired you along your journey? Take a moment now to think about them, celebrate them, and send your love and gratitude their way. We don't walk alone on this journey, and the more we open ourselves up to remembering those who walked beside us, the more we bring out their powerful gifts to guide us. Who can you walk beside and encourage today? What is your legacy message to give and share with the world?

~Daily Inspiration by Rebecca Hall Gruyter, Influencer & Empowerment Leader

9.

Thought for the Day

"To begin to think with purpose, is to enter the ranks of those strong ones who only recognize failure as one of the pathways to attainment."
– JAMES ALLEN

10.

You Gave Your All. Now Let Go

Fall is such a wonderful time to celebrate the rewards of all our efforts. And yet many of us feel disappointed that we didn't accomplish everything we had hoped. Or perhaps we didn't get the results we expected. Our greatest challenge is letting go of our attachment to the outcome.

If we allow our hearts to guide us and make every effort to do our best, we can feel good about whatever happens. It doesn't serve us to cling to any particular outcome. Our success is determined by our depth of presence throughout the experience.

"There is no way to happiness, happiness is the way."
- THICH NHAT HANH

Each day, I invite you to fill your heart with love, do the best you can, be present with every experience, and let go of any attachments to the outcome. Know that the Universe is conspiring in your favor.

~Daily Inspiration by Olivia Parr-Rud, Corporate Love Ambassador

11.

Belief + Action = Manifestation

Invest in yourself (BELIEF) and inject ambition (ACTION) and you will achieve your desired results (MANIFESTATION). Your thoughts and dreams only manifest after you take the necessary steps towards your goals. Make the investment (BELIEF) of your time, talent and treasury, into your Highest Good Goals and Desires, and add your own committed ambition (ACTION) and you will produce (MANIFESTATION) your Highest Desired Results.

Give to yourself, the same as you have given to others, wholeheartedly and completely. Tap into the Belief Center of Your Soul and bring forth the Well of Assurance that bubbles deep inside you. Be Positive. Be Productive. BE COMMITTED. Seek out the most efficient way to manifest your goals and trust the steps you take towards manifestation. However and Forever Passionate, BE INFORMED when making decisions. Become Resourceful and Resilient while you process through obstacles and progress towards goal manifestation. Belief + Action = Manifestation. Apply this principle to every association, situation and endeavor, for maximum returns.

Affirmation:
I AM Believing, Acting and Manifesting My Highest Good Goals and Desires. I AM Positive. I AM Productive. I AM Committed. I AM Informed when making All Decisions. I AM Resourceful and Resilient as I progress towards Manifesting My Highest Good Goals and Desires.

~Daily Inspiration by Mark Edward Pyle, Manifestation Expert

12.

Thought for the Day

"I never dreamed about success. I worked for it."
— ESTÉE LAUDER

13.

Be Willing to Learn

The Celestial Spoon Radio Podcast is new in the sense of the name, but the show has been running since March 2017. When I made the decision to do my own podcast it was at the asking of a producer. I was excited because the idea of bringing spirituality to the world in this manner was thrilling. My background is working in an office but once my spiritual soul awakened it was time to help make the world a better place. By utilizing the podcast to do this we are spreading the love throughout the world. There are many variations of guests and they all share their personal journey with spirituality and self-help.

The name change is recent because the producer wasn't following through airing my shows. **I could choose to stay frustrated and stuck or learn another way. I decided to learn how to produce my own show and am proud to say I learned this and the show continues.**

Although the show is already running for a year, this felt like a new venture. In changing the direction there were many aspects to be learned on setting up every portion of internet links and pages. I was up to the challenge because I love learning how things run and then follow through with those lessons.

I want to encourage you to be willing to learn new things. When you allow yourself this gift you will feel very accomplished. Possibly journal some ideas you have had and create a plan for new things.

This willingness can open new doors and provide you a feeling of accomplishment which giving you great freedom in life. What is in your heart today to learn? Are you willing?

~Daily Inspiration by Catherine M Laub, Advocate for Mental Health

14.

Where Fashion Meets Style

Fashion Week's womenswear shows happen in the fashion capitals of Milan, Paris, New York and London twice a year in February and September. The fashion industry takes its cue from what is being shown on the runway of these fashion capitals, and you as a consumer get to try to make sense of it all, and get to develop a style that works for you.

Are you looking to take your image to the next level? Do you desire a look that captures the true essences of who you are? Do you want to a "signature style" that is unique to you yet identifiable by others? Making Statements N Style™, a Premier Fashion and Image consulting company, was created to transform the lives of women in the achievement of their goals and aspirations. **It is a place where all women are celebrated for their true beauty and are encouraged to become a better version of themselves.**

Here is the truth about style. Style is someone's personal preference, it's a signature look that is as unique and personal to the individual as her DNA or finger prints. I want to encourage you to discover your own style in life. Not one that is set by outside forces and the fashion industry. Rather, a look that helps you shine from the inside out, so you can have a style that helps you have the impact you want to have on the world!

We must learn how to honor the woman/man within, before we can start exhibiting true expressions of who we present to the world. Celebrate who you truly are, share and shine YOU out into the world!

~Daily Inspiration by Cassandra Garabedian, Stylist

15.

Thought for the Day

"Remember who you are. Don't compromise for anyone, for any reason. You are a child of the Almighty God. Live that truth."
— LYSA TERKEURST

16.

The Process of Change

"Change is the law of life, and those who look only to the past or present are certain to miss the future."
– JOHN F. KENNEDY

I love FALL! I love the cooler nights where I can leave the windows open and throw a quilt upon my bed having the heaviness of comfort it brings. I love the changing colors of the leaves … all the beautiful colors of burnt orange, fiery red, buttery yellow and the beautiful purples that sometimes pop in the leaves. And, let's not forget the wonderful root vegetables that become available … golden beets, butternut squash, plums, and pumpkin (in everything).

Change in the weather is inevitable. Change in you is a choice.
Why Change? I say, Why Not! Someone told me the other day, "you really love change, don't you?" I didn't hesitate when I said 'Yes'. And, then it got me to thinking … why do I love change? Could it be because I find it exhilarating? Perhaps it is because I have a passion for learning and growing wanting to constantly see myself and the world I am in as different.

Most people find change daunting and scary. I know people I work with have this fear of making change. They fear not knowing what the change will bring.

When you find yourself going through any kind of change in your live, learn to embrace the change by changing your perspective, see it as exhilarating and easy. **Look for the good that is on its way to you.** Sometimes the shift from denial to acceptance is all that is needed to ease your anxiety, allowing you to move through nervousness to joyful excitement about the good to come.

~Daily Inspiration by Denise Hansard, Empowerment Expert

17.

Thought for the Day

"Life shrinks or expands in proportion to one's courage."
– ANAIS NIN

18.

Full Plate Syndrome

Ever been in a buffet line? I like to try different things, so I put many little helpings and pieces on my plate - because my eye is on the chocolate cake at the end of the buffet! And it's not polite to skip to the end. It's quite a mystery, because no matter how careful I am with the choosing, there's always more that could fill up the plate before I get to the chocolate cake.

We do that in life. We keep adding and adding, and the plate gets so full that things begin to roll and fall off. The results of adding more things and trying to keep the other things on our plate in a heroic juggling act? We get too busy, too stressed, and we drop off things that we promised to other people or ourselves that never get done. **The secret is...you can. You can take things off your plate and make room for the things that really matter to you.**

Here are some tips for Full Plate Syndrome:
- It's your choice to take something off on purpose, or to let things roll off.
- Check in, evaluate everything that's on your plate, and be willing to take things off to make room for those things you are saying "yes" to.
- Guard your plate and say "no" to those things that no longer serve.

Bon appetit!

~Daily Inspiration by Rebecca Hall Gruyter, Influencer & Empowerment Leader

19.

Thought for the Day

"Success breeds confidence."
– BERYL MARKHAM

20.

Just Take One Step

"You do not have to see the whole staircase, just take the first step"
-MARTIN LUTHER KING JR

Being sober and recovering from any type of addiction, whether it be drugs, alcohol, food, TV, anger, a habit of always being late, an abusive relationship or any kind of self-sabotage. It can be very lonely and isolating.

When you are all alone in those moments, what do you do with them? Do you allow yourself to be paralyzed with fear and sabotage more? Or do you use those moments to step into your power and listen?

Listen to what plans God, Universe, Mother Earth, spirit (whatever your higher power may be) has for you.

Rest in the knowledge that what is coming is greater than you could have ever imagined and be willing to take one step.

~Daily Inspiration by Carmell Pelly, Empowerment Leader

21.

Feel More

Tears are a sign of empowerment...they demonstrate your vulnerability and your strength.

I used to be embarrassed that I am so easily moved to tears. Now I embrace my tears as my superpower of being able to express myself in such an intimate way. Have you ever found yourself feeling foolish because you melted into a puddle, or sputtered gibberish in the face of an emotional situation? Have you ever had a wave of inner knowing, or had inkling you should turn left instead of right with splendid results? The world has become so disconnected from human connection because we seem to be plugged in to gadgets instead of people. First and foremost, **I urge you to feel more. Yes, thinking is part of who you are. Embrace your emotions as lightning rods to your intuition and inner wisdom.** Spend fifteen minutes reflecting on a time when you felt vulnerable. How did you reconcile that feeling and turn it into a source of strength? Record in your journal where you are now and give voice to the person you want to be. Your words have the power to bring you from where you are to where you want to be.

~Daily Inspiration by Mary E. Knippel, Your Writing Mentor

22.

Thought for the Day

"If you look at what you have in life, you'll always have more. If you look at what you don't have in life, you'll never have enough."
– OPRAH WINFREY

23.

Where We Belong

*"Home is not where you are from, it is where you belong.
Some of us travel the whole world to find it."*
~ BEAU TAPLIN

Having the sense of belonging is a powerful and deep need of most all humans. When we know we belong, we are free to feel secure. We are accepted and a part of something that is greater than ourselves. Knowing we belong tells us we are right where we are supposed to be, and there is such a peace in that.

Having the peace of belonging is important, however, so is the unsettling feeling of not belonging. Do you ever find yourself searching? Not knowing where you quite fit in? Sometimes it's like the square peg in a round hole scenario, and no matter how you try to shimmy it just doesn't feel right. When that happens that may just be a sign that maybe you are not where you are supposed to be, and sometimes, that's okay because now you know. It may also be a prompting for some growth to happen... yay!

Maybe it's a change of perspective or attitude that is needed. Maybe it's a whole new change of position or relocation. Maybe it's just your time to grow out of where you've been in relationships, career, life-style, etc., and into the next chapter of your purpose.

As you grow, it is so important to keep an open heart and mind. Allow yourself to realize the opportunities around you and accept the blessings that are in store. Know that you may not be at the checkpoint yet, but you are transitioning into it... and that is also exactly where you belong at that point in time.

You are priceless part of this world, take courage to find where you belong and allow yourself to be there.

~Daily Inspiration by Julz DeFant, RDH

24.

Follow Your Calling

My father was an avid research scientist. If he was not actively doing research, he was writing or thinking about it, seeking inspired thought that would lead to another hypothesis or yet one more answer. A brilliant student in high school and throughout his college career, his desire to understand and challenge scientific principles lasted throughout his 80s until cancer insisted that he stop.

I remember as a teenager not wanting to bring boyfriends home. I knew their time with my father would evoke the "big talk." Not the talk about respecting his daughter or adhering to curfew, but the one about atmospheric wind shear, aerodynamics, and theories of lift and flight. No one understood his passion or his desire to continue with his calling. In reality, none of us were smart enough to understand his long drawn-out descriptions of his latest theories and how they contradict commonly held beliefs.

Following one's calling is not always popular or appreciated by others. It is not possible for someone else to understand why something is your calling because they do not hear the same call themselves. That's why it's your calling and not theirs. Even if you don't feel the support of loved ones or experts in your field, **stay true to your calling. The world needs you to step into your brilliance and share the gifts that only you can give.**

> *"There is no greater gift you can give or receive*
> *than to honor your calling. It's why you were born.*
> *And how you become most truly alive."*
> - OPRAH

~Daily Inspiration by Dr. Ruth Anderson, Spiritual Counselor

25.

You Are a Co-Creator

The Essence of true Creation, by its very nature, means creating from no-thing. Therefore, you must create from your Highest thoughts and deepest Spiritual feelings. When you create from the limitlessness of your Higher Self your life will become the perfect manifestation of Harmony and All Good. You now let go of measuring the possibilities for your life against your history or the way things are currently. Your power comes from the clarity of telling yourself the real truth about what you want, including how you most deeply want to feel as a result of those desires becoming realities.

Therefore, to the extent you are not satisfied with the things you have, you must release your judgments and ask your limitless Higher Self and heart to assist you in defining the Vision of what your heart wants and deserves. Since the seed of everything you have came from a thought that you originally generated, you know you can only manifest those things that you are capable of imagining and embracing as already being your own. You recognize that whatever you can imagine in your mind and fuel with your deepest feelings, will be manifested, therefore, it is essential to co-create a partnership between your Higher Self and the depth of your heart. Life-Energy of God's Creation is 'seen' as Universal Light and 'felt' as unconditional Love. This is your Spiritual Nature — to Co-Create. Be willing to yield to the co-creative experience with your Higher Self, remove all obstacles to the Presence of Love — and experience the Truth of Who You Are.

Today realize you are a Conscious Creator with Spirit, making your life experience one of inspiration, power, contribution and grace.

~*Daily Inspiration by Kathleen E. Sims, D.D., C.H.T.*

26.

Thought for the Day

"Continuous effort — not strength nor intelligence — is the key to unlocking our potential."
– WINSTON CHURCHILL

27.

Success

"The real measure of our wealth is how much we'd be worth, if we lost all our money."
- JOHN HENRY JOWETT

One of my favorite money stories is about a determined woman who turned her love for cookies into a $450 million-dollar empire. Of course, most of us would relish having such an extraordinary sum of money, especially doing what we love! Her financial success is awe-inspiring. Yet what deeply moves me beyond the money she created is the extraordinary *choice* Debbi Fields, founder of Mrs. Fields Cookies, made despite attempts of being shamed.

During dinner one night, at the beautiful, but intimidating home of one of her husband's clients, the man asked her "What do you do? "Oh," she replied, "I'm just trying to get orientated." The man got up, pulled an enormous, leather-bound dictionary off the shelf, put it in her lap and said, "The word is **oriented**. If you can't speak the English language, you shouldn't speak at all." Incredibly embarrassed, Debbi Fields sat there in his library with tears streaming down her cheek. ("How Debbi Fields Built An Empire From Scratch", Libby Kane, LearnVest).

The man's shaming words and actions hurt terribly. In that moment, she could have let doubt reign and allow herself to remain feeling small and insignificant. Instead, she heard her father's voice, who taught her "that **true wealth is found in family, friends and doing what you love."** That night, she gathered herself together and set out to live her purpose, grow to meet her maximum potential and sow seeds that benefit others. With the internal, emotionally healthy, landscape she inherited from her family, she chose to love, trust her gifts and believe in herself. **The wealth she manifested on the outside reflects the wealth she already owned on the inside.**

Success certainly means different things to different people. John C. Maxwell beautifully and simply captures the way I view it. Mr. Maxwell defines success as *"knowing your purpose in life, growing to meet your maximum potential and sowing seeds that benefit others."*

How do you define success?

~Daily Inspiration by Marlene Elizabeth, Author of MONEYWINGS™

28.

Thought for the Day

"One of the most courageous things you can do is identify yourself, know who you are, what you believe in, and where you want to go."
– SHEILA MURRAY BETHAL

29.

Put Yourself in Ink

As our lives are busy and scheduled to the max, we must take time for us. In the fall the colors are beautiful and brilliant. We can take some time to enjoy these moments. We can reflect on the year so far. Set goals for the last quarters and our year end. We can take the time for family and friends and to just breathe. It is so important to make sure we are scheduling for our personal life and goals as much as we are for business ones. So, make yourself a priority in your planner. **Put yourself on your schedule in INK not pencil! And live your life to the fullest.**

~Daily Inspiration by Teresa Hawley Howard, Empowerment Leader

30.

Thought for the Day

"Let all that you do be done in love."
– 1 CORINTHIANS 16:14

October

1.

Perfect in Our Imperfections

"People aren't looking for "perfect" people...they are looking for real people to walk alongside them and show them the way."
- REBECCA HALL GRUYTER

I resisted speaking in front of people even as I knew I was being called to do it. I had all sorts of reasons why I wasn't "ready," why my message wouldn't be "perfect" or "good enough" Things that I felt like need to change before I could really lean into speaking in front of others.

My weird laugh was one of those things - I had to do something about that laugh! So, I hired a really powerful coach to help me get rid of it. He gave me a powerful truth: "Rebecca, I think you are confused about assets and liabilities as a speaker. When you have something that is contagious in a good way, that people lean into, that they associate with you, it becomes part of your brand, they like it and it makes them smile? That's a good thing! That's not the thing you want to get rid of! If anything, you want to do that more. You want to have things that are distinctive about you to bring forth. The liabilities are the things that interfere with your message, that make it so that people can't hear what you're saying and wanting to share."

"Imperfection" is a relative term. Your assets are often the things that are unique about you. Don't let what you may see as imperfections stop you from SHINING. Celebrate them!

~Daily Inspiration by Rebecca Hall Gruyter, Influencer & Empowerment Leader

2.

You Are Already Fulfilled

Fulfillment isn't something to strive towards - in Present Time it exists through all time. A personal commitment to your Higher Self will open the door to a relationship with your Source that generates, nurtures and sustains you. By maintaining a strong connection to your Higher Self you endow this part of yourself with the power to create loving relationships with everyone equal to their Divinity. Embodying this Principle allows you to experience the reality of your wholeness and realize you are already fulfilled. God expresses through you and uniquely as you. From the inner knowledge of this, you can now live a Spirit-filled life.

Today feel the reality of the Eternal world made manifest as Inner Peace and Fulfillment within you.

~Daily Inspiration by Kathleen E. Sims, D.D., C.H.T.

3.

Thought for the Day

"The most effective way to do it, is to do it."
— AMELIA EARHART

4.

Freedom From Fear To Thrive

"Ring the bells, that still can ring.
Forget your perfect offering.
There is a crack in everything.
That's how the light gets in."
– LEONARD COHEN

Experiencing freedom from fear, takes time. And new fears surface, just as soon as old ones fade away.

So be very gentle and kind with yourself.

Love has a way of persistently showing up, tugging at you, like a child, encouraging you to choose life beyond your fears, again and again and again.

Let love ease the sorrow, anxiety and suffering that fear brings.

Because the world needs your financial dream to come true, with its purpose.

Where is love tugging you to grow beyond your financial comfort zone today?

What support do you need to start unfolding your financial potential?

~Daily Inspiration by Marlene Elizabeth, Author of MONEYWINGS™

5.

Your Voice Matters

Your voice matters because you matter. Give yourself permission to let your voice be heard.

It took me getting breast cancer…twice…for me to give myself permission to let my voice be heard. **Don't wait until you have a health crisis to speak up!** Your voice matters and no one else can tell your story from your perspective. Someone is waiting to hear from you! Spend fifteen minutes listening to that still small voice whispering from your soul. What do you long to accomplish with this one wild and beautiful life of yours? Make a list and then mark on the calendar when you will do them. Record in your journal the first small step you will take to accomplish one of those things on your list. If writing a book is in the mix, one small beginning step would be to get a notebook and pen your working title on the first page. That's all you'd have to do to let the world know your intension. Your words have the power to bring you from where you are to where you want to be.

~Daily Inspiration by Mary E. Knippel, Your Writing Mentor

6.

Thought for the Day

"Our greatest fear should not be of failure but of succeeding at things in life that don't really matter."
– FRANCIS CHAN

7.

Kindness Ninja

I heard of a teaching strategy that encourages kids to be kind and more importantly, the impact it has. It is creatively called "Kindness Ninja". This is a sneaky way of doing random acts of kindness without the recipient knowing who did the kind deed. What kid doesn't love to be sneaky?! So, my question is, why should the kids get to have all the fun?

During the month of October, let's wear the mask of the Kindness Ninja and see how stealthy we can be with random and unabridged acts of kindness.

Buy a cup of coffee or tea for the next person in the line or bring in a neighbor's trashcans.

A Kindness Ninja can sneak unsuspecting friends trinkets or treasures they want without them knowing it was you. An unsigned card in the mail can brighten anybody's day immeasurably. In this day and age, I think perhaps it's the gesture that someone took the time to do something so personal.

Let's see how many ways we can spread kindness. For that matter, why can't we don this Kindness Ninja warrior costume year-round?

~Daily Inspiration by Jaimie Harnagel

8.

Why Visibility is Important

"If they cannot see you, if then they cannot hear you, then you cannot help them."
- REBECCA HALL GRUYTER

Visibility is about being seen so that we can shine our light to help others along their path. Let's be easy to find.

I was once VERY resistant to being seen - staying invisible was part of my DNA on a cellular level it was so programmed into me. When I had to be in front of people I would shake, turn purple, lose my words and barely be able to say my name! So it was a really long journey to be able to come through that to live and serve in the way that I do today.

I learned that any of the discomfort I might be experiencing was so worth it. If I could make a difference for one other person, to somehow make the path a little bit easier for someone else, then I was willing to be uncomfortable, to stretch outside of my comfort zone - to be vulnerable and imperfect.

To this day that is still what pulls me forward. I believe that if we tap into our 'why' - to know our purpose, our passion, what we are called to do - it will pull us forward to stretch and succeed on a higher level and SHINE our unique light on the world! What is your why? Will you choose to **SHINE**?

~Daily Inspiration by Rebecca Hall Gruyter, Influencer & Empowerment Leader

9.

Thought for the Day

"The power you have is to be the best version of yourself you can be, so you can create a better world."
– ASHLEY RICKARDS

10.

Dear Stress, Let's Break Up

When the holidays come around, I begin to make lists of all the things that need to be done lamenting as the lists grows into pages of things to do instead of the hopeful couple of items that I thought would be there. Overwhelm takes the reins of my life. Stress begins to rear its ugly head. STOP! **This year, I've decided to break up with this stress and move forward with calm intentional daily actions.** How about you? Do you find yourself suddenly with a massive list of daily activities taking over and stressing you out?

Pause and breathe ... this is the key to becoming present in the moment allowing yourself to make a choice for you. The toxic relationship you have with stress (the drama that has held you captive for so long) is affecting your health, your relationships and you. Let's kick this toxic relationship to the curb and decide for you. Release the stress.

Every day, wake up in gratitude. **Decide for no more than three intentional action items for the day.** If there are more things to do, ask for help. Delegate those things that you don't want to do or can't get around to doing. For the items that are on your daily list, do them with ease and clear intention. **Then celebrate your success in accomplishing them.** You are so worth the time of stress free living.

~Daily Inspiration by Denise Hansard, Empowerment Expert

11.

Thought for the Day

"May your walls know joy, may every room hold laughter, and every window open to great possibility."
– MARY ANNE RADMACHER

12.

Your Most Precious Resource is... YOU

When you're looking at what you want to have and what you want to build, it's really important to be careful of how you're spending your time and your energy. We all have 24 hours a day - nobody has 36, they're not taking your time and stockpiling it somewhere!

We all have the same 24 hours - How are we choosing to use it? Are we letting other people put things on our place of commitment, Are we adding and forgetting to take something off? Are we paying attention or is time just passing us by?

Every single day...Choose on purpose how you're going to spend your day, how you're going to spend your time, and how you spend what you're called to do - your **YOUness**. You're a precious gift. Your time is really precious! Be mindful of how you're going to spend your 24 hours, what you're thinking, what you're building, what you're echoing out there in the world. **Spend your time on purpose and with great purpose.**

~Daily Inspiration by Rebecca Hall Gruyter, Influencer & Empowerment Leader

13.

Live Your Truth

Speaking and Knowing Your Truth will absolutely liberate you. Anxiety and Stress can be alleviated. Nervous Conditions and Anger Issues can be greatly diminished. Personal Dispositions definitely improve. **Speaking and Knowing Your Truth will align you with your Highest Good Goals and Desires and serve as your greatest promoter.** Old Doors Close and New Doors Open. Unhealthy alliances dissolve and profitable partnerships organically form. Speaking and Knowing Your **Truth allows you to experience Highest Good Expansion.** Trusting and Living (BEING) Your Truth will elevate your standard of living and deliver the lifestyle you desire. Trusting and Living (BEING) Your Truth affords you many opportunities to Plant Self-Empowerment Seeds in Your Highest Good Ground. Trusting and Living (BEING) Your Truth places you on the Path of Ascension. Abandon and Avoid all endeavors, associations and people that are unwilling or unable to align with the Speaking and Knowing, Trusting and Living (BEING) of Your Truth.

Affirmation:
I AM Liberated by Speaking and Knowing My Truth. I AM Aligning with My Highest Good Goals and Desires. I AM Elevating My Lifestyle by Trusting and Living My Truth. I AM Speaking and Knowing, Trusting and Living My Truth.

~Daily Inspiration by Mark Edward Pyle, Manifestation Expert

14.

I've Got You

*"If you want others to be happy, practice compassion.
If you want to be happy, practice compassion."*
~DALAI LAMA

Do you feel like some days you are just counting down the minutes to do whatever you can to get through the day? You scramble to finish tasks, respond to emails and phone calls, and do whatever you can to just-stay-on-time... ugh! All the while watching others around you go about their day seeming to accomplish things with ease with smiles on their faces? What the heck??! Ever want to scream, "what about me?"

The truth is, no matter how professional, accomplished, independent, or strong we are – we are still human, and we need to have each other's backs. Think about it, when you are someone who knows they are not alone, supported, backed up, and believed in... that breeds confidence. When you have confidence you are strong, you are peaceful because you are not standing on the shaky ground of doubt. How about within our groups; be it family, friends, or workplace teams? Think about a group of people who KNOW they have each other's backs! What a force!

Compassion is a huge element that goes beyond sympathy or empathy. With sympathy we feel sorry for someone, realizing what they're going through is tough. Empathy is when we "feel their pain," we find ourselves commiserating with them. The thing is, neither of these requires any real action. Although we do show we care through sympathy and empathy, either of these elements can be felt from the privacy of your own space without any contact at all.

Compassion, however, compels us to step forward and take action. Compassion is going beyond our "self" and wanting the best for another person, "getting their back." When you go forward choosing to "have the backs" of those around you, it empowers you to step into your purpose of being meant for something greater than just "self," it also sets an example, plants seeds, and builds trust for others to do the same.

~Daily Inspiration by Julz DeFant, RDH

15.

Thought for the Day

*"The most common way people give up
their power is by thinking they don't have any."*
- ALICE WALKER

16.

Inspiration In Life & Business

We hear about businesses coming and going all the time. When I attend small business conferences it is stressed how important it is that small business owners get out and network, get to know and support one another through the trials and errors of being first time business owners.

I remember the first time I was asked to identify myself in the dynamic world of business, as a business owner. I was intimidated, stumbled a bit, but found the courage to share by remembering those who have come before me. Always remember the trailblazers who came before you, some famous and others not so well known, but their work equally as important.

Whether you're a business owner, in business, or not,we all have moments where we get to stand up, be seen and heard. I want you to remember that you are not alone. As you stand up and share in your life, know that many trailblazers have gone before you, and now you get to blaze a trail for those that come after you.

~Daily Inspiration by Cassandra Garabedian, Stylist

17.

If You Have to Force it, Leave it

Sometimes we get caught up in the "doing" and because we have not taken time for ourselves, everything becomes hard. Create space for yourself to go inward and allow your creativity to flow. Set aside time do nothing and just be. Slow down, be still and just listen. A lot of emotion can come up and be cleared during this time, allow it to flow out.

Make this time special. A great way to do this is by creating an area just for you. Make it beautiful. For example: buy Fresh flowers, add essential oils, soft music, candles and, choose colors you love. When you feel like things are difficult, take a step back by retreating to that special space and allow.

~Daily Inspiration by Carmell Pelly, Empowerment Leader

18.

Aspire to Your Greatness Each Day!

To aspire to our greatness means we have to live with purpose and be authentic. Trailblazers are rarely conformists because they dance to the beat of their own drum. They are not seeking paths, rather they create paths for others to follow in places no one thought possible. They champion new ideas that drive creativity and usher in change in the world.

Trailblazers, like all of us, have a comfort zone, but as nice as that place is, they seldom stay in that zone because they know nothing can grow there. They have learned to be comfortable outside of their comfort zone to reach all of their aspirations. These non-conformists think outside of the box, wholeheartedly embracing the characteristics people might consider *'different'* or *'weird'* and turning them into strengths that work for them and not against them.

The very thing that you might be trying to hide from others because of guilt, shame, or embarrassment might the very thing that could take you to the next level. Liberate yourself from being enslaved to the feelings of guilt and shame by taking back your power and be your authentic self. **Get outside of your comfort zone, grow and thrive becoming the person you were meant to be! You will then be able to move forward powerfully, making all of your aspirations come true, and bring your greatness forth each day.**

~Daily Inspiration by Adrian Jefferson Chofor, Global Personal Transformation Strategist

19.

Thought for the Day

"A friend is a gift you give yourself."
– ROBERT LOUIS STEVENSON

20.

Season of Reflection and Inner Peace

> *"We don't realize that, somewhere within us all, there does exist a supreme self who is eternally at peace."*
> – ELIZABETH GILBERT

Autumn is the season to reap the benefits of the harvest, a time of completion, and the doorway into the quiet and peace of winter. This is a time for you to "reap your harvest," to look at what you have sown and grown so far this year.

Take stock of what you have accomplished, from the projects and launches, to the prosperity you have realized, to the relationships you have begun and fostered. Celebrate the successes and reflect on areas that will need attention next year, just as farmers would their fields at the end of the growing season.

Autumn is also the right time to reflect on ourselves and the broader picture. In the busyness that swirls around this season, take time to stop, consider your "supreme self" and what would make you feel more aligned and at peace.

I love the colorful autumn leaves. Watching them flutter to the ground reminds me of nature's cycles, of releasing burdens and of endings. I also love to kick through a pile of leaves like a kid, which feels playful and hopeful! Nature gives us so many opportunities to get over ourselves, open to the bigger space and flow, and to be in communion with our inner selves.

What are you proud of this season and this year so far? What aspects bring you in closer connection with your supreme self? What changes do you want to make and new projects to embrace that will nourish you?

~Daily Inspiration by Linda Patten, Leadership Expert

21.

Surrender to Radiance

I am not here to be who I'm not. I am not here to live a life that is not my own.

I am not here to be driven by pain. I am not here to live in suffering.

I am not here to hide my gifts. I am not here to hide my joy.

I am not here to hide my love. I am not here to hide anymore.

It's time to let go, to fall into the depths, beneath all my masks, and into the place in my soul.

I surrender my fears. I surrender my expectations.

I surrender my attachments. I surrender my creations.

I surrender my pain. I surrender my suffering.

I surrender all that I think I am, all that I think I own, and all that I think is my life.

Into the emptiness I go, where all that surrounds me is darkness.

For, in this space I can finally see the light that is my own.

In the darkness we can uncover the beautiful radiance of the light that we shine.

~Daily Inspiration by Ron Coquia, Radiance Coach

22.

Color Blind

If someone can't see color then they are color blind. But about 99.7% of people who say they don't see color do see color. People believe that if they make that statement it proves they are not racist. It's not that simple. I'm sure the person who states they don't see color is saying it with no malice. We see the color of the person we are speaking with no doubt about it. You see different facial features that are different than yours. The construct of race is man-made but God gave us these wonderful colors and different features that make us all beautiful.

Speaking for self, I want you to see that I am a Black female. I'm not truly me without my color and I love that. Most of my friends say they want people to see their color too. So when someone says "I don't see color," then inquire if they are color blind. **I encourage all of you to embrace all of the beautiful colors, textures and powerful difference we each bring to the world.**

~Daily Inspiration by Tresté Loving, Racial Equity Expert

23.

Thought for the Day

"The best thing about the future is that it comes only one day at a time."
- ABRAHAM LINCOLN

24.

You are a Survivor

If you've never thought of yourself as a survivor, I challenge you to change your thinking. Prior to 2012, if you would have asked me if I was a survivor, my answer would have been no. Up until this point, my focus had always been on challenge rather than the fact I that I survived it. Over the past few years I earned the actual title 'survivor' after beating breast cancer in 2012 and then four years later competing in the reality television series, Survivor Millennials vs Gen-x. I do not consider myself a survivor based on my experiences, I am a survivor because I survived.

You are a survivor because you survived.

Instead of thinking about the negative situations that earned you the title, survivor, concentrate on the simple fact that you survived. Choosing to focus on what you *have* survived, will give you the courage to face the next situation you **need** to survive. Viewing negative life experiences in light of what went right, rather than what went wrong, will give you the courage to confidently face your next challenge knowing **you are a survivor**.

~Daily Inspiration by Sunday Burquest, Women's Empowerment Speaker & Author

25.

What Are Your Fears?

This time of year, kids like to talk about things that spook them: goblins, witches, and black cats! Fortunately, we grown-ups have long since outlived those fears. Unfortunately, those scary things have been replaced with dreads that are far more dire: heart disease, diabetes, cancer, Alzheimer's. These diseases cause millions of deaths each year, and lead to countless dollars spent on healthcare and disability.

If one of these conditions tops your list of "spooky" items, here's one simple thing you can do to help decrease the risk of developing all of them-move! That's right, sedentary behavior (sitting for three or more consecutive hours at a time) has now been identified as a new public health problem, and movement is the antidote.

In fact:

> *"If exercise could be packed in a pill, it would be the single most widely prescribed and beneficial medicine in the nation."*
> - ROBERT N. BUTLER, MD, *former director,* National Institute of Aging

So never pass up a chance to move! Look for opportunities to move! Stand every 30 - 60 minutes (during commercials, at break time, or to throw away trash) and move the big muscles in your legs with brisk walks or mini-squats. And while you enjoy moving these big muscles, celebrate the way it feels and thank yourself for bestowing these benefits on your body. You'll decrease your risk of diabetes, obesity, some cancers, other chronic diseases, and even an early death while embracing movement, celebration, and empowerment!

~Daily Inspiration by Lisa Harris, MS, RD, Fitness Pro

26.

Thought for the Day

"It takes a great deal of courage to stand up to your enemies, but even more to stand up to your friends."
- J. K. ROWLING

27.

Stop. Oxygenate. Search.

"Breathe. Let go. And remind yourself that this very moment is the only one you know you have for sure."
– OPRAH WINFREY

When all your senses are on high, you know it is October! While some anticipate the month of October, others feel despair as it approaches. We have all said this at least once in our life: Where did the year go? This statement is usually said in October, as we realize the year is coming to a close soon. At this time, we need to reflect and appreciate where we are the current moment and notice the transformation that can happen in October. **So, in this moment, Stop, Oxygenate, and Search for successes that you have accomplished up to this point of the year. Take this moment and remind yourself of all that you have accomplished in this moment without stressing over the next few months.**

This is your S.O.S. signal and it will allow you to reflect, relax and enjoy the beauty of October without feeling anxious and rushed. Enjoy the changing leaves, the chill in the air, and the smells of the season transitioning and remember that each day, you can still take steps to accomplish your goals.

~Daily Inspiration by Bonnie Bonadeo, The Connection Coach

28.

Thought for the Day

"True happiness...is not attained through self-gratification, but through fidelity to a worthy purpose."
– HELEN KELLER

29.

Fun for the Holidays

We come into the season of stress for some people. It doesn't have to be that way. You can choose to enjoy your days regardless of the season. Think about developing a plan that includes fun events. This can be daily for just fifteen minutes, once a week, or once a month until the holidays are past.

- Invite friends or family over to help decorate then have a buffet dinner where everyone brings a dish.
- Attend a play or two, or go to a concert with your children or other family neighbors
- Make a play list of your favorite Christmas music and play it often to lift your spirits
- Watch Christmas movies on the Hallmark channel
- Make homemade decorations
- Plan a baking day with family or friends to make various cookies
- Display the cards you receive to remind you of all the people who love you
- Read a book a chapter each night before bed for relaxation
- Create your own fun and share your creations with others

A plan can help you look forward to the upcoming fun holiday activities. It can support you to have a smooth flow and takes the stress away.

~Daily Inspiration by Catherine M Laub, Advocate for Mental Health

30.

Thought for the Day

"Power is not given to you. You have to take it."
– BEYONCE KOWLES

31.

Come Out of Hiding and SHINE!

Why is empowerment so important to me? It is because I grew up from a very **DISempowered** place, where it was not safe to be seen or heard, where I could not SHINE. Once I was rescued from that environment and could live in a place that allowed me to heal and bloom, I realized that those old messages I believed...were lies. That I actually AM beautifully and wonderfully made, that I DO matter.

And that it's safe to come out of hiding and SHINE.

Have you had a calling in your life, a pull to do something that you can feel mind-body-spirit-soul? I did, but at first I said, No, I can't do it! No, that's impossible! What helped me step into it is was that I discovered that a calling doesn't go away....it just sometimes we just need to grow and evolve a little bit to become more fully what we're called to be, to be ready to step forward. As I began to take those baby steps, "surviving" a step and becoming braver for the next step, moving ever forward - so much changed for me. Surviving shifted to serving others and thriving.

Be ready for those opportunities and trust that you'll be ready to say yes and SHINE! Recognize that every step prepares you for the next. **We don't always know our potential, all of what we're called to be because we only look at what we are right now** - and we never will until we choose to come out of hiding and take those steps. Be ready! It is so worth the journey! Take a step today and choose to SHINE!

~Daily Inspiration by Rebecca Hall Gruyter, Influencer & Empowerment Leader

November

1.

What Matters Most to You?

As we head into the holidays that will soon lead us into another new and exciting year, it's a perfect time to look at where we are. Are you purposely bringing forward the things that matter to you? Are you choosing to shine (share your gifts and talents)?

I encourage you to look at those things that matter most to you. This is a powerful practice to incorporate into your life - checking in to make sure that you are doing those things that are in alignment with what you are called to bring forth.

Where I find life can change most is in these moments of reflection followed by purposeful action.

When we remember what is most important to us, then we can build into our lives those things that support it, nourish us, uplift us and help us grow and that are positive as they feed into us. **We have to be mindful of the types of things that we let pour into us, especially in a hectic holiday season.** It's important to make sure to be mindful of what we watch and listen to. Are these things that uplift, feed, encourage and empower us? This is because all of this information you take in becomes part of your DNA.

Be mindful of what you are taking in, making it only what is in alignment with what truly matters to you most. You are valuable and precious. Only let in that which supports and serves you to become all that you are called to be.

~Daily Inspiration by Rebecca Hall Gruyter, Influencer & Empowerment Leader

2.

Friendsgiving

Enduring the holidays after the loss of a loved one can be excruciating. Walking through my favorite department store, I was visually bombarded with Thanksgiving and Christmas decorations. My eyes were drawn to a Thanksgiving serving platter that simply read "Friendsgiving" written in a beautiful script. Tears came to my eyes, and I was plunged into grief over the loss of Thanksgiving traditions with Sylvia's passing. My best friend of 23 years passed away of cancer five years earlier, and I still missed her dearly.

Thanksgiving was always a special holiday for us as Sylvia and I would cook together for 20+ friends and family members. Sylvia encouraged and helped me to be at my best. She represented unconditional love, adventure, and not taking the Universe's "no" for an answer. There was no task too difficult or time consuming for us to tackle. How lucky I was to have a Sylvia.

Rather than wallow in my grief of what I was lacking, maybe I could turn that around and provide someone else with those same gifts of unconditional love, excitement, and adventure. **Rather than waiting to receive, I could give. If I couldn't have a Sylvia of my own, maybe I could be a Sylvia for someone else.**

By creating love-filled moments with others, I don't diminish or replace that which I shared with Sylvia. By allowing myself to bring someone else love, fun, and adventure, it could forge our own deep connections, strengthen our relationship, and create future memories. And maybe, without realizing it, I will have allowed myself the opportunity to feel joy again. Perhaps, selfishly, by creating stronger relationships with others, I will be giving myself an opportunity to heal.

"A single rose can be my garden... a single friend, my world."
-LEO BUSCAGLIA

~Daily Inspiration by Dr. Ruth Anderson, Spiritual Counselor

3.

The Gift of Be-Ing

So much has been written on the subject of **Be-ing**, but the reality is that we often fail to seize the opportunities offered us to actually experience the joys associated with the practice. This is due, in part, to the level of our engagement with our lives and the world around us—how focused we are on our family life, or on our work, school, or other outside activities. We lose sight of the fact that we are a part of something much larger than ourselves. And, while most of us are tuned into the reality that it's necessary to pay attention to our surroundings as we negotiate life, we often fail to take that to the next step—the larger act or practice of **Be-ing**.

Just be-ing.

It involves full on spiritual, physical, mental, and emotional presence; it embraces and resonates in our heads, our bodies, our energies, and our hearts. We are filled with an awareness that transcends the mundane aspects of earthly living while anchoring us firmly in the here and now with a heightened sense of who we are, who others are, and how we are connected to all of creation. **We are gifted with a deep knowing that goes beyond the traditional boundaries of understanding, taking us to our most spiritual self . . . our divine selves.** This is the reason for which we are here – our purpose – to fully know, love, create, and, most of all, be. In those moments of true be-ing, we are able to realize our own divine selves.

I urge you to take a moment to just be... let Spirit enter your heart and fill your being. Step into the fullness of who you are intended to be as you walk in the knowledge that all of creation is sacred and a blessing for which to be grateful as you walk with Grace and with Blessings.

~Daily Inspiration by Dr. Nancy Tarr Hart

4.

Thought for the Day

*"I'm not afraid of storms,
for I'm learning to sail my ship."*
– LOUISA MAY ALCOTT

5.

What's Your Dream?

I am feeling happy this morning. I have this joyous feeling about me, last night while I was asleep, I dreamed of angels watching over me. I can feel the power of love stirring and enfolding deep inside of me. There is nothing in this world that I can't do in this moment, space and time with faith in God and Him walking by my side guiding my footsteps in a purposeful way.

A new day has dawned, and I am awake, I give glory to God for allowing me another day. As I begin to step into another day of bringing my dreams forward, to a brand new clean slate.

What's on your heart today? Has something or someone inspired you to act on your own life- long dream(s)? What does this day hold for you? Are you interested in unveiling today's: Who? What? Where? When? Why? How? Are you willing to take the steps to bring your dream forward?

Say hello to your new way of thinking and being. Be kind and gentle with yourself because old habits are hard to break. Give yourself time, it will surely come for it is Truth. With faith we can overcome anything, we can remove all obstacles in our path with God walking by our side. "If at first you don't succeed try again." Continue to be open and loving, absorbing the currents of life's energy that is flowing through you.

You have been chosen for such a time as this and are absolutely needed. Learn to meditate and ask for wisdom and discernment, for that will serve you well through every life challenge you may encounter. **Be willing to bring forth your dreams one day and one choice at a time.**

~Daily Inspiration by Cassandra Garabedian, Stylist

6.

Thought for the Day

"If I were a medical man, I should prescribe a holiday to any patient who considered his work important."
– BERTRAND RUSSELL

7.

Commit to SHINE!

As we watch the cold creep in and we are indoors more, it is the perfect time to take out our journals and write. To pick up our pen and paper and start that book we have been talking about. The project, the vision, and the dream you want to bring forth. You just have to begin. To start the project and see it through to the end. But it all starts with you. So choose to write it! Stand in it! Build it! There are millions waiting on your words, you and your shine! So stop making them wait! Step into your destiny and your shine today and share it with the world!

~Daily Inspiration by Teresa Hawley Howard, Empowerment Leader

8.

Your Essence is the Vibration of Gratitude

When you give thanks for everything that led you to this place in your Spiritual growth, including life's challenges, you can acknowledge you chose everything that happened. All of it has been for your fulfillment or essential for your Spiritual evolution, and is therefore perfect. Thankfulness is a key transforming power that allows you to feel deserving of unconditional love. Negative thoughts cannot co-exist in the same moment you feel Gratitude. Your conscious connection with Source is your supply, producing its own image and likeness in the form of things that support your well-being.

To the extent you focus on the things in life that are working perfectly – the more the Good increases in your life. You are already filled with the positive energy of Gratitude… it is your innate nature. Knowing this increases your ability to manifest more goodness by opening your heart to the Divine influences of Spirit. This begins to infuse you with the Spiritual feelings of Love, giving you the power and energy to fuel manifestations of All That Is Good. Since you can have whatever you want and whatever you focus on and feel, you can now choose the best. You know the Universe will provide you with all of its energy and support to effortlessly transform your Highest Thoughts and deepest Spiritualized Feelings into realities. When you feel Blessed you are filled with gratitude and contentment, and thereby feel worthy of the Highest Good to which you can aspire.

Today acknowledge Source as your Supply, accept Infinite Abundance as natural, and share the feeling of Gratitude for All Life.

~Daily Inspiration by Kathleen E. Sims, D.D., C.H.T.

9.

Thought for the Day

*"Greater love has no one than this,
that someone lay down his life for his friends."*
– JOHN 15:13

10.

Thank You

Let the words "Thank You," not only flow from your mouth, but also fill your soul. **Let the words "thank you" remind you of what you DO have and open your eyes to the blessings all around you.**

In my early twenties, I allowed myself to pause and consider what "Thank You" has meant to me. I looked at my life, and how far I had come. All of the people who had encouraged and helped me, the opportunities that I eagerly pursued, the love that I had been given. **All of the sudden, the intent of those words in my life became so much deeper. I was so overtaken by gratitude.** I went out and got some huge pieces of paper, painted "thank you" all over them, and hung them up. I wanted to be surrounded by those words and reminded of what they meant to me.

This was also during a time I had been accepted to host international students in my home. I was excited for this because it was not only a way to help pay my mortgage, but also an awesome opportunity to get to welcome people from other cultures into my home.

When my first students arrived, I didn't even think about the "thank you" posters covering my walls. After a couple of weeks, the students asked me about the posters. I shared my story and why I was thankful. I had no idea the impact this would have on them. After a while, I noticed other writings on the posters. My students told me that after hearing my reasoning for the posters, they had begun to think about the words "thank you" in their own lives. They were also compelled to write their stories and the words/meanings of "thank you" in their languages.

Sometimes in life we forget to allow ourselves to **BE** grateful. **When you take the time to allow yourself to FEEL grateful, you will allow in inner joy and love to truly fill you up and refresh your soul.**

~Daily Inspiration by Julz DeFant, RDH

11.

Bravery

"Promise me, you will always remember: you're braver than you believe, and stronger than you seem, and smarter than you think"
- Christopher Robin to Winnie the Pooh, as written by A.A. MILNE

You may have heard the horror stories from returning prisoners of war about the conditions and inhumane treatment they had to endure while being held captive. These were conditions that no one, including themselves, could possibly imagine enduring; **yet** these brave people did. They were braver than they believed… **as is each of us!**

So no matter how brave you *feel* about something, just **know** that you are indeed braver (and can be more confident) than you believe. The way we *feel* about things is **NOT** a good indicator of our capabilities. As those brave prisoners of war came to understand: **You can do *much more* than you believe!**

However, upon reflection, you may find that you knew all of this because, after all, "**…you are smarter than you think**"!!!

~Daily Inspiration by John F. Hall, MBA, Author, Business Owner

12.

Thought for the Day

"You have to have confidence in your ability, and then be tough enough to follow through."
– ROSALYNN CARTER

13.

Gratitude is Not Just for the Holidays!

Thanksgiving has always been a very special time for me as a child and adult, and not just because of the fabulous cooks in my family! Since my parents and grandparents both owned businesses we rarely had a meal together, except for holidays. My last memory of that in youth was at age 16 at a table rambling on to fit over twenty people. Our times with all of us together at one table would not ever happen again.

Today the tradition continues at my home with my own family, though we are a much smaller group, with one added piece. We go around the table with everyone sharing what they are most grateful for in their life. It is a wonderful reflection, and a proud moment for us as parents, to hear what our children and our granddaughter are most grateful for. It is also a time of reflection within ourselves to give thanks and gratitude for our own reflections.

In daily life, it is important for everyone to release all that no longer serves them, and give gratitude at least in the beginning and end of the day. There are many meditations that I wrote and recorded that can be life changing. I offer them to those who want them, and many are available free of charge at www.YouTube.com under Meditate Me Now. If you subscribe, you will be informed of more to come.

The question becomes "How can you receive more if you are not grateful for what you already have?" Gratitude is not only for holidays, but it is also for daily life so that you can be open to receive more. When you have more and you appreciate it, you are able to give and receive more. Choose gratitude.

To help you to enjoy more gratitude and empowerment, visit the free meditations and be blessed with gratitude and many blessings!

~Daily Inspiration by Syndee Hendricks, Certified Business Consultant and Intuitive Coach

14.

Be Extra Kind to Yourself

"My grandmothers (all four of them) richly blessed and impacted me and have inspired the shape and form of the empowerment work that I do."
- REBECCA HALL GRUYTER

I've always been a really good "to-doer!" Getting things done, crossing things off my list, and (for a looong time) just pushing through life - push and push and push, getting things done and not even giving myself time to rest, process, or celebrate what had been accomplished!

My Grandma Quinn was the one who taught me to be present and to be mindful. After I had shared yet another accomplishment, she would say to me, "Honey, that's wonderful! I'm so proud of you. But, remember to pause, remember to take a breath, give yourself time to process it on a cellular level."

When something difficult would happen to me that I couldn't push, push, push, through, I would call Grandma. She would say, "**Be extra kind to yourself now - treat yourself like your best friend.**"

I was a little better at pausing and listening in those moments with her voice in my ear and her wisdom in my heart. In her later years as illness and death were ever near, she would say on our calls, "So, Rebecca, I want you to make me a promise. I want you to promise me to take care of my granddaughter"...which, of course...was me. I made this promise, in every single call.

Later, when I was a financial adviser, I got to sit across from people as they were having the highs and lows in life – at those times I would share Grandma Quinn's advice: **Be extra kind to yourself, especially in those times. Treat yourself like your best friend. Allow yourself to be. You don't need to push, push, push. Give yourself the opportunity to stop, pause, be mindful, and breathe. Sometimes that is absolutely enough.**

As you enter the busy holiday season, I invite you to be mindful, pause, and be extra kind to yourself.

~Daily Inspiration by Rebecca Hall Gruyter, Influencer & Empowerment Leader

15.

Awaken the Very Best of You

Self-Determination begins with establishing the value that you add to every situation, endeavor and association. Your Value is determined by what you give, how you give it and the intentions that motivated you into service, along with what someone else determines is beneficial, therapeutic or satisfying, in some way. Make it your practice to always live in a way that is truly giving the best of you, truly sharing your gifts, and your value. Connect with and Embrace and Trust the Magic that resides inside of your Soul. Entertain and Appreciate and Attract, to yourself, all of Your Highest Good Goals and Finest Tastes and Desires that reside inside of your Soul. Give Yourself every Highest Good "thing" practically possible. Believe Your Own Most Humble Hype and Begin to Quench Your Highest Good Thirsts. **Awakening the Very Best of You will allow you to start Taking Care of the Rest of You!**

Affirmation:
I AM Establishing My Value. I AM Living a Beneficial, Therapeutic or Satisfying Lifestyle as an Example to Others. I AM Embracing and Trusting the Magic that Resides in My Soul. I AM Attracting Every Highest Good Opportunity to Me.

~Daily Inspiration by Mark Edward Pyle, Manifestation Expert

16.

Thankful for Everything

Have you had a few setbacks this year? Or maybe you've experienced a few cosmic lessons? I hear you. I've had my share.

Now is the time to release any feelings of victimhood. No matter what happens to us, no matter how bad it gets, our only failure is our failure to learn and grow from our experiences. And the best way to respond to failure is with gratitude. Yes, actually be thankful for each experience.

I have personally survived many setbacks and failures throughout my life. When I began my healing journey, I was encouraged to find the gift in every negative experience. As I became grateful for each and every one, I started to sense my true power. In my most difficult moments, I found solace in the following quote by Emerson.

> *"We need not fear that we can lose anything by the progress of the soul. The soul may be trusted to the end."*
> – RALPH WALDO EMERSON, *Love*

I invite you to trust your soul on this amazing journey. And find true gratitude for all of your life experiences. This simple practice allow you to access your inner wisdom and step into your greatest soul expression.

I encourage you to go deep within yourself. Consider every experience, both positive and negative, and say "Thank you." It will free you from your sense of being a victim and empower you to step into the highest expression of yourself.

~Daily Inspiration by Olivia Parr-Rud, Corporate Love Ambassador

17.

Thought for the Day

"When one door of happiness closes, another opens; but often we look so long at the closed door that we do not see the one which has opened for us."
— HELEN KELLER

18.

She Won't Change

Sometimes when we're dealing with people, either working with them or managing and leading them, it's really easy to blame them and make them wrong.

We call this "living below the line."

This week I was talking to a marriage counsellor. The counsellor was at a loss as to what to do for two of her clients. The husband and wife had been seeing the counsellor for a couple of months. The husband decided not to continue any more. The wife was still happy to come. When asked why he wouldn't be coming back, and referring to his wife, he replied "She won't change."

It's a timely reminder to look at ourselves first if we find we are in conflict with another.

The interesting thing is, that when we change ourselves; our attitude, belief, perception or behavior, by default the other person changes as well.

If there's something you want; a better relationship; a better career; better health; more money, look to what you can change. This is where your power lies.

~Daily Inspiration by Shirley Dalton, Business Expert

19.

Let go, Lean in.

I am very happily married to Tony for twenty years, plus together for six years prior. Tony helped me get through the tough times of my divorce and child custody/support issues. Those times were rough because of the bitterness and horror in the battle.

I fought hard through the court system and never felt any satisfaction with the outcomes. It took many years to let it go and enjoy the life I have with Tony. In fact, I only released the whole situation in December 2012 at my father's funeral. I hugged a man thanking him for attending, but until later didn't realize it was my ex-husband. I recognized at that time I am happy and focused on the life I currently have and consciously let go of the bitterness of my past.

Today we spend many times together as a family as they respect me and Tony because we are always there for them. Recently we had Christmas Eve together and included our extended families, including my former in-laws. We had lots of fun playing a funny game that amused us all, including my mother too.

It is important to recognize when we are allowing situations to overpower and consume us. When we do we realize there is so much more to life that we actually begin to live it again with a joy filled heart. **Allow yourself to let go of what no longer serves you and lean into the new life of happiness.**

~*Daily Inspiration by Catherine M Laub, Advocate for Mental Health*

20.

The Holidays are Coming – Get Creative!

For me, November rings in the most creative season of the year. My childhood memories of the holiday season, starting with making our own Halloween costumes to watching the Rose Bowl Parade on New Year's Day, are filled with delicious dinners, colored lights, family games, special desserts, magical music, brightly wrapped packages, building snowmen, and beloved traditions.

However you experience "the holidays," it's the perfect time to call in creative expression – music, art, dance, theater, literature, poetry, comedy – that bring you joy and closer connection to each other and to your deeper purpose.

I love that we have in our lives these tools, whether created by ourselves or by others, to move us along the path of a joyful, purposeful life. Has a dance or movie or words in a book ever brought a tear to your eye, or bubbled up a chuckle? Or maybe churned up feelings of anger or discomfort? All these responses are gifts to us, lessons to learn or warning signals of things we need to deal with so we can better live our purpose.

The creative arts are tools we can use to create the lives we want to live.

"But I'm not an artist!" you say. Mary Morrissey shares: "What a wonder, then…when we discover that the highest form of creative expression is simply this: 'Be yourself.' Each human life, we thrill to find, is the canvas upon which the soul paints the scenes of its unique pattern of unfoldment."

This, of course, makes us ALL ARTISTS! I invite you to see creative experiences in this way, never to take them for granted, to bring them into your life in conscious intention so you can appreciate the ways that creative expression can lift you up. Oh … and don't forget to have fun!

~Daily Inspiration by: Bettyanne Green, Content Marketing Strategist

21.

GRATITUDE

"Gratitude unlocks the fullness of life. It turns what we have into enough, and more."
~ MELODIE BEATTIE

Gratitude is the antidote for "less than" feelings.

If at times you feel you're not good enough, lovable enough, *whatever* enough, focus your attention on what in your life you feel grateful for. Gratitude has the ability to shift your energy to a higher place and perspective.

A wonderful practice is to ask yourself daily, "What am I grateful for?"

Really feel into the things for which you are grateful, giving thanks for each one. These things can be as simple as, "My breath," or "My good health," or "Another day of living."

As you practice, notice what unfolds, what is different, what improves in your life and mood. Watch how this practice of gratitude shifts your energy as you begin to notice more and more in your life you appreciate.

Some Essential Oils to inspire more Gratitude:

Bergamot - *The Oil of Self-Acceptance*
Invites you to see life with more optimism and has a cleansing effect on stagnant feelings and limiting beliefs.

Spikenard - *The Oil of Gratitude*
Encourages you to find appreciation in all of life's experiences.

~Daily Inspiration by Tish Reese, Health + Wellness Mentor

22.

Thought for the Day

"Stop wearing your wishbone where your backbone ought to be."
– ELIZABETH GILBERT

23.

Let Go

*"The best way to navigate through life is
to give up all of our controls."*
- GERALD JAMPOLSKY

As winter approaches, the trees use their internal intelligence to release their leaves and go into dormancy to protect themselves from the cold. Trees and other plants know how to give up control and let Mother Nature dictate what needs to happen. However, if we as individuals give up our control, our fear responses would be activated. How can we have the lives we want and without being in control of each step?

When we look at everything around us, we realize that we really don't have control – and that's ok. As we enter this month of gratitude, look for areas that add stress to your life, like preparing for the holidays, family gatherings and year-end expectations and relinquish some control of planning, preparing and expecting the perfect outcome. **Allow yourself to let go and surrender while the season navigates you to witness miracles.**

~Daily Inspiration by Bonnie Bonadeo, The Connection Coach

24.

Be Present to Enjoy the Holiday Magic

"It's not something outside you; YOU bring the magic."
- REBECCA HALL GRUYTER

Sometimes we get caught up in the busyness of the season, and it starts to feel heavy as we're pulled in a lot of different directions. In those times, I encourage you to use these simple techniques to help you realign and bring yourself back into the moment so you can be fully present to all the magic the holidays bring!

When you feel out of alignment or in a stressful situation: Stop. Pause. Breathe. Make each breath a deep belly one, expanding your waist as you do. Deep belly breathing lowers your cortisol levels, which reduces your stress. If you like, put both your hands over your heart. Listen to and feel your heartbeat. Take your time, until you feel more aligned and present.

When your mind is filled with distractions, worries and concerns: Do the above, then close your eyes. Think about all those things that have taken you away from being in this moment. Imagine a heart-shaped box - choose a color for it, make it shimmery and bling-y! Gather all those things up and place them lovingly in the box. Place your lid securely on the box. Deep breath! Then lift that heavy box and, in your imagination, take it out the door. Let it go and come back into the room. A couple more deep breaths, then open your eyes.

And feel yourself free and present to fully enjoy your time! (You can always pick that box up later if you decide to do so.) Don't let the "to-do" list take you away from the joy, purpose, and magic of now.

~Daily Inspiration by Rebecca Hall Gruyter, Influencer & Empowerment Leader

25.

Thought for the Day

*"Blessed is the season which engages
the whole world in a conspiracy of love."*
– HAMILTON WRIGHT MABIE

26.

Give You!

The gift of giving in today's world can be hard, confusing, and expensive. You could go out of your way to buy things and gifts that are not only unnecessary, but too expensive. These gifts could end up being impersonal and unappreciated. With all the holidays' stress, and work deadlines, **we can forget that the best gift to give our loved ones is time with you.**

Instead of swiping your credit card, take them on adventure and build memories you can laugh and enjoy for a lifetime. **The best gift you can give someone is your time and love.** Schedule some time today with someone you love.

~Daily Inspiration by Inguss

27.

Challenge or Gift?

View life challenges as gifts from the Universe.

Growing up as a small-town farm girl, I never imagined I'd be living on the beautiful California coast. Here I am and loving it. It's all because the company my husband worked for closed and his new job brought us to California. **All of our life stressors have taught us valuable lessons.** Each unique situation is intimately connected with the others to bring you to where you are and made you who you are today. Spend fifteen minutes reflecting on where you are in your life right now. Did you have plans that never quite worked out, yet something magnificent came along instead? Record in your journal where you are now and give voice to the person you want to be. Your words have the power to bring you from where you are to where you want to be.

~Daily Inspiration by Mary E. Knippel, Your Writing Mentor

28.

Thought for the Day

"If you can't fly, then run, If you can't run, then walk, If you can't walk, then crawl, but whatever you do, you have to keep moving forward."
- MARTIN LUTHER KING JR.

29.

Oxygen Masks

"Put your own oxygen mask on first, then help others."
- The pilot of every flight you have ever been on

Women often have a bad habit of putting themselves at the bottom of their own to-do list. They are "human *doings*", who run around doing stuff, instead of human *beings* who schedule the time they need for self-care so they can truly *be* there for their friends, families and loved ones. **What happens on a flight if you don't put on your oxygen mask first? You might actually lose your ability to help others. This is indeed what happens when you don't take care of yourself.**

It might happen so slowly that you don't even notice until you have a true health crisis. Don't wait for your body to *require* care. Take care of your body, mind, and spirit; get your needs met. Today, what are some ways you can put on your own oxygen mask on first?

~Daily Inspiration by Dr. Liz Lyster

30.

Thought for the Day

"We must believe that we are gifted for something, and that this thing, at whatever cost, must be attained."
– MARIE CURIE

December

1.

Make Magic During the Holidays

Have you ever experienced this? You host a holiday dinner or party with a lot of people. Your head is filled with all the distractions around the event - the planning, cooking, gifts, attending to guests, family drama, excitement and laughter ... Then, it's over. And you hardly remember any part of it!

An event that was supposed to be memorable instead is a blur. Yes, it's happened to me too - I wasn't fully present in the moment, and those precious moments never had a chance to embed in a cellular level.

My holiday gift to you is this: Before you start something or go to an event, take some moments to stop, breathe, and ask:

"What is it that I need to know or to have today?"

"What is it that will encourage me, equip me, and empower me to bring in my magic?"

"What can I appreciate and celebrate in this moment?"

There is real power in stopping and checking in with yourself this way, a strength about it that you can feel, that helps keep you grounded, no matter what.

Taking this a powerful step further, ask yourself: **"What is it that I'm willing to receive [today in general, or in regard to the activity or event you are about to experience]?"** Then open yourself up to connect with the answers. You may be surprised by the magic that happens!

~Daily Inspiration by Rebecca Hall Gruyter, Influencer & Empowerment Leader

2.

Christmas Season

The holidays begin early in my house. It is my favorite time of year. We start with the decorations mid-November. There is the Christmas village that is spread throughout the house. A firehouse with a label from a town I visited often growing up. Then we have a church with my parish name, and the Montauk Lighthouse which is local to my home. Filled in with people, animals, a town square and a schoolhouse with a playground filled with children and snowmen.

The tree goes up the day after Thanksgiving when we formally welcome the Christmas season. That weekend we celebrate with a turkey dinner.

My adult children come over with their young children early December and we make cookies; Pfeffernuesse, Sugar, Peanut Butter, plus various with Chocolate Chip and M&M candies.

By then the house is decorated throughout and most nooks and crannies are beautiful. We spend a lot of time with family which makes it extra special.

When the holidays approach be sure to take it all in. It is the beauty in the season that sparks the happiness in all of us.

~Daily Inspiration by Catherine M Laub, Advocate for Mental Health

3.

Thought for the Day

"Forget about the fast lane. If you really want to fly, just harness your power to your passion."
– OPRAH WINFREY

4.

Believe

"Doubt kills more dreams than failure ever will."
- SUZY KASSEM

An amusing image I often use during my workshop to illustrate moneywings™ is a cartoon of two little birds sitting high atop a branch. One of them, worrisomely peers straight down at the ground with a parachute securely tied to her back. The other bird perched natural and free, looks at her anxious friend and casually says, *"maybe we should try jumping without the parachute this time."*

Even with every bit of preparation, you may never truly feel ready to leap, but I'm here to gently and positively remind you that **you are equipped to fly and soar!**

Believe in yourself.

Believe in your financial dream.

Believe in your strengths and talents.

Believe you can transform your relationship to money,

one brave feather at a time.

Believe in your wonderfulness.

Surround yourself with others who believe in you.

Believe and your faith will increase! Believe ♥

~Daily Inspiration by Marlene Elizabeth, Author of MONEYWINGS™

5.

Thought for the Day

"Don't be afraid to speak up for yourself. Keep fighting for your dreams!"
– GABBY DOUGLAS

6.

Joy Was Delivered

Every Christmas I spend hours painstakingly decorating sugar cookies, my favorites are the snow-globes, flooded with white and blue icing, hand piped snow and small Christmas tree candies. Why do I spend hours baking cookies and mixing icing? I do it for my family, especially the kids. I find great joy in watching my young nieces and nephews excitedly pick a sugar cookie of their choice; seeing their tiny hands and big smiles as they take their first bite is **priceless.**

The Bible refers to God as our Father and like most dads, He was excited to share His most valued gift. Thousands of years earlier He put a plan into place to restore His broken relationship with man; **He wanted a relationship with you.** Waiting for the right time must have been difficult as He prepared a way to send His son to earth. Jesus' birth marked the beginning of the joy and peace that would be the result of His great sacrifice. When the angels sang, "Glory to God in the highest and on earth peace among men" in Luke 2:14, it was a declaration of things to come. Peace had finally made its appearance, joy was delivered, and we were given hope. If you are blessed enough to enjoy the magic of the holidays through the eyes of a child, remember God has the same feelings when He sees you experience the joy He sacrificed so much to give.

~Daily Inspiration by Sunday Burquest, Women's Empowerment Speaker & Author

7.

Thought for the Day

"Don't let the past steal the present. This is the message of Christmas: We are never alone."
– TAYLOR CALDWELL

8.

Thought for the Day

"In order to succeed you must fail, so that you know what not to do the next time."
– ANTHONY J. D'ANGELO

9.

The Whisperings of Our Souls

Sometimes we are so busy doing all that we are told to do, feeling all that we are told we should feel, that we can forget how to listen to the whisperings of our souls. We get separated from our feelings and our heart. We forget or don't know what our purpose in life is. We may think finding our purpose is harder than it has to be, that we have to go on a long journey or have a big epiphany.

The truth is that you can start right where you are today... Just pause... and listen.

You will find that your soul is whispering to you in-between the chatter and busyness of your everyday life. When you pause and listen - as many times as you can - you will begin to uncover those things that make you feel fulfilled, that point you to your purpose. You will become aware of who you are and how you impact others around you.

If you feel you need a little guidance, find two or three people you trust to be both honest and real with you. Ask them to share with you three things they see in you that are unusual, unique, or special in some way. This can give you information and perspective that will help you dig into and uncover what you are good at. **When you consistently hear the same thing... know that these are truly some of your gifts and a reflection of the special light you share with the world.**

You can then make those choices, moment by moment, that will take you on your unique path of living on purpose, with purpose! **Share your gifts and choose to SHINE!**

~Daily Inspiration by Rebecca Hall Gruyter, Influencer & Empowerment Leader

10.

Thought for the Day

"Christmas gift suggestion: To your enemy, forgiveness. To an opponent, tolerance. To a friend, your heart. To a customer, service. To all, charity. To every child, a good example. To yourself, respect."
– OREN ARNOLD

11.

Choose Joy

"We have to choose Joy and keep choosing it every day."
~HENRI NOUWEN

Joy is a choice, just like everything else in your life. If you are not feeling particularly joyful right now, try asking yourself:

"What can I do to bring some joy into my day?"

Even just one small thing can quickly shift your energy toward feeling more joyful. For example:

- Think of three things or people for whom you are grateful.
- Move your body and dance like no one is watching.
- Go outside in nature and feel the sun and wind on your face.

Focus on things that bring you joy and watch your joy expand. Where you choose to put your attention determines how you feel. Today, choose joy.

Some Essential Oils to help you feel more joyful:

Wild Orange - *The Oil of Abundance*
Invites you to reconnect with your inner child and brings spontaneity, fun, joy and playfulness into your life.

Ylang Ylang - *The Oil of the Inner Child*
Encourages play and restores a childlike nature and innocence.

~Daily Inspiration by Tish Reese, Health + Wellness Mentor

12.

Finding your Bliss/Choosing Bliss

One of my mentors and life coaches, Vishen Lahkiani, from Mindvalley, has a term I love to use to inspire others for living with bliss. He calls it Blissipline. Blissipline starts with creating a daily practice for yourself that will allow you to live in a state of bliss. It can be anything from having a morning meditation ritual to an exercise routine that incorporates nature into your routine.

Long walks in the forest or on the beach watching the waves, doing something creative, or a yoga practice. **Finding your bliss even for just a few moments every day is a gift that you can give yourself.** How does happiness and bliss happen anyway? From my experience, **happiness and bliss happen when you live in the NOW.** If in the present moment, you are actively experiencing a feeling of gratefulness, growth, meaning, or consciousness you are probably also experiencing happiness.

Blissipline is the art or practice of living in a state of happiness all the time. When things get out of balance—do you have the tools in your toolbox to bring yourself back to bliss?

Here are three tools you can use to help get in a state of happiness when you're not. **Gratitude:** Find something to be grateful for in this moment—change your focus there. **Forgiveness:** Ask yourself, "In the plan for the Universe, how significant is what I am focusing on that is making me so un-happy?" It is almost always infinitesimally small! Choose to forgive yourself and others. Third, is **Giving:** When we are giving to others, our happiness increases. Think of all the unique gifts we each have to give the Universe—there is only one you! Giving something of yourself to another is the ultimate gift because it gives to both of you. Find your bliss.

~Daily Inspiration by Carmen M. Bryant, Business Coach

13.

Thought for the Day

"Success is getting what you want, happiness is wanting what you get."
– INGRID BERGMAN

14.

Woman Stand Up Straight in Your Eminence of Truth

Created in His image, magnificently crafted, look not just with *your physical* eye. **I urge you to take a moment to see "life" from a spiritual perspective; using your spiritual eye. Look within, see what lies within you. All that your body and mind is equipped to do, see what is awaiting your command. Become aware of how great you are.** In power and in truth you are the chosen one, the one that would hold in her womb another life for generations to come. Accept who and what you are, you are "woman". Never let anyone make you feel that you are "less than" or irrelevant, you can never be taken out of the life force equation. **Therefore, focus on that which you desire, direct all your energy towards the achievement of your goals. Claim them, move forward with the assistance of the Universe.** Associate with people of like minds, go places where you can continue your growth by engaging in subjects that are relevant in today's climate as it relates to you as a woman. Join organizations and associations as a means for networking and keep up to date and relevant.

Woman stand up straight in your eminence of Truth. Take time to discover your true Being. Become acquainted with the beauty of being a "woman" and all the possibilities: sister, wife, aunt, niece, grandmother, mother, godmother, womanhood, sisterhood. You are a "woman".

~Daily Inspiration by Cassandra Garabedian, Stylist

15.

Thought for the Day

"God's work done in God's way will never lack God's supplies."
– HUDSON TAYLOR

16.

What Light Are You Sharing?

An old children's song starts with these words, "This little light of mine, I'm going to let it shine..." (song attributed to Hary Dixon Loes) Light stimulates life. However, the word luminosity hints at something more. It is defined as "the relative brightness of something." That suggests that the light is shining through the object. The light is not coming from another source, but it actually coming from the object.

Some of us, I fear, are not projecting much light! Some of us are wearing shades that dim and diffuse that light. John Steinbeck described a woman in his book *Travels with Charley: In Search of America*, like this. "Strange how one person can saturate a room with vitality, with excitement. Then there are others, and this dame was one of them, who can drain off energy and joy, can suck pleasure dry and get no sustenance from it. Such people spread a grayness in the air around them." Does that sound like anyone you know? Does that sound like you?

We can be opaque. Not much light, if any, comes through. We are closed off to others. We can be translucent. The light that comes through is dimmed. Or we can be transparent. Truly sharing authentically our beauty and imperfections. This means others see our weaknesses. What a challenge that is. **But if we are not projecting light to others, then we are projecting darkness.** If others aren't energized and sustained by us, we are increasing the lifelessness in the world! So, let's make a choice to SHINE and share out light, joy, life and positivity.

Light comes in all shapes, colors and sizes. So, there is not an acceptable excuse for not lighting up the world. This world is filled with enough sorrow, despair, and hopelessness. We need to let our lights shine brightly. You are a unique light with your own gifts, so embrace your luminosity, and share it with the world today.

~Daily Inspiration by Elda Robinson, Teacher

17.

Choose to Flourish

"Every man has a right to decide his own destiny."
– BOB MARLEY

December seems wrought with decisions. What to buy? Where to go? Who to invite? How to find the time and how to finance it all? While the holidays are designed to be enjoyed, December seems to be one of the most stressful months of the year. However, you do have the opportunity to decide right now how you want your month to go. Your decision starts with defining the difference between decision and choice. While decision is the act or need for making up one's mind, choice gives you the right, the power and the opportunity to choose the path you want to take right now. While decision is more process based, choice is more of a mindset. **You get to choose who you want to be amongst all the stress and hustle of December, and in life overall.**

Who you choose to be determines how your December and each month after will be for you. **Today, decide what you want your destiny to be, and choose an attitude that allows you to flourish.**

~Daily Inspiration by Bonnie Bonadeo, The Connection Coach

18.

Thought for the Day

"Our hearts grow tender with childhood memories and love of kindred, and we are better throughout the year for having, in spirit, become a child again at Christmas-time."
– LAURA INGALLS WILDER

19.

World Peace Can Happen

Would you be inspired to affect global peace in a positive way? I thought you might, as peace in our world crosses all borders and touches all humanity.

My friends were on an important trek to the Middle East, where peace has been elusive for centuries. Their goal was to raise the vibration to a higher level to affect peace in the region in a powerful and positive manner.

While visiting ancient holy places, my friends searched to locate tiny crevices to place small pieces of rose quartz, a stone known as the stone of love and relationships.

As they located those special places and placed just the right sized rose quartz stone in its perfect location, each set the intention for a positive peace to radiate throughout the land and beyond all borders.

Now close your eyes for a moment and imagine if each one of us were to have that identical intention to radiate global peace from the holiest places on the planet throughout our world. Can you feel the positive vibrations magnificently being sent to our populations everywhere like a vibrant aurora borealis? I have goosebumps feeling the possibilities of us collectively changing our world in such a powerful way to benefit not only humankind, but also every plant and animal that lives here with us.

If we can each imagine that, we can create global peace. Yes we can. I beg you to close your eyes and fill your heart and intention to charge each of those rose quartz stones, and to radiate your intention of global peace out to our world. Just imagine the possibilities we can collectively bring to reality. Peace to you and everyone.

~Daily Inspiration by Syndee Hendricks, Certified Business Consultant and Intuitive Coach

20.

Meditation Can Be Life-Changing!

One of my dear friends, who is also a client, asked me to work with one of her friends who was having a hard time with her life and business. I want to share her story with you to highlight the importance of meditation in your life. Though everyone needs to find the meditations that speak to them, the one I'll share in another part of this book is one that has been life-changing for many.

Cassandra was so devastated with the relationship with her estranged husband, that she had to discontinue working in her business and move herself and her twelve year old daughter into her parent's home.

After spending time reviewing her situation and her business, an action plan was developed. One of the things in her action plan was for Cassandra to do the Empowering Meditation mentioned above twice a day. She agreed to work on her action plan, and do the meditation.

A year had passed when I was meeting my dear friend at a coffee house. As I saw her and a second woman coming toward my table, I was shocked to see that it was Cassandra! When they approached me, I said, "Cassandra, you look amazing! What have you been doing?" She exclaimed with a huge smile that she had completed everything we discussed on her action plan, and that her life was now back on track! I felt that my work with her was done, and the Empowering Meditation was a big turning point for Cassandra!

Find the meditation that speaks to you, and you, too can keep your life on track.

~Daily Inspiration by Syndee Hendricks, Certified Business Consultant and Intuitive Coach

21.

Knowing Ourselves

"Until you make the unconscious conscious, it will direct your life and you will call it fate."
– C.G JUNG

You will uncover a whole new world if you watch yourself do the things you do and then ask yourself: "Why do I do it this way?" With this awareness, you may be able to make new choices that could change the course of your day for the better.

Especially in this season of light when life can get very hectic, you want to pay special attention to your own unconscious thoughts and feelings. It might feel counterintuitive to take extra time to be by yourself so that you can explore why you react the way you react. However, in the end, if you can accomplish this, your new insights and your positive energy will influence your family and the December events in a good way.

~Daily Inspiration by Mooniek Seebregts and Martina Caviezel, The Parent Empowerment Coaches

22.

Thought for the Day

"Do you want to love your life? Look in the mirror."
– BYRON KATIE

23.

Greater Gifts

We all have the ability to create a powerful future. We can't change the past and dwelling in it doesn't change it…. never let your past be your **p-r-e-s-e-n-t**. It can never replace my future. WE can't change, take back, nor replay any moment. You can participate in healthier decisions, enjoy a positive outlook on life, and look forward to an awesome future. **Enjoy the "present" and make choices that build the future you want.**

~Daily Inspiration by Kri' Shawn Terrell, Motivational Speaker

24.

Spreading Love Through Light

Church service on Christmas Eve is a special tradition for me. Familiar Christmas carols bring tears of nostalgia and listening to my loved ones singing makes me want time to stand still.

My favorite moment of the night is the finale when the lights are dimmed, the congregation hushes, and the only light in the sanctuary is from one candle. This flame is passed down the rows as each person lights a neighbor's candle. This continues until everyone's candles are lit, children included under the watchful eyes of parents. The congregation looks like a heavenly choir as each face is illuminated by a candle. Silent Night is sung softly and with reverence. The organ, now much louder, plays the opening notes to Joy to the World and everyone raises their candles to shoulder height. Jubilant singing continues, and I stand in awe and wonder for the remainder of the song. Finally, the lights come on, and we are encouraged to blow out our candles. I would prefer to remain in this heavenly choir and not dispel the peaceful scene.

The candle lighting service is a reminder to me that each of us brings our own light to the darkness around us. By sharing our love and positive energies with others, we do not diminish our own light but are emboldened by the synergy of our flames in concert with theirs. I am reminded to be the light that can help illuminate the way for those who are standing in their own darkness. **This Christmas Eve, may we share the gift of love and let our brilliance shine into a world that is desperate for the light.**

"Thousands of candles can be lighted from a single candle, and the life of the candle will not be shortened."
- BUDDHA

~Daily Inspiration by Dr. Ruth Anderson, Spiritual Counselor

25.

Do You Believe?

At this time of year, we are asked to believe in something that seems impossible ... an elderly man dressed up in a red suit traveling around the world bestowing presents to all the good girls and boys — in a 24-hour period with only flying reindeer to make sure it happens without any problems.

Who of us have not had requests in our life that seem almost as impossible. Your project sponsor calls to let you know that management is expecting deliverables 2-weeks earlier than previously planned. A family member suddenly requests help with your parents and you are thousands of miles away. You have it all – a great career, money in the bank, wonderful loved ones, the home, the kids, and the dog – yet you can't seem to believe that you should have all this.

When did you stop believing? Believing in yourselves and your abilities? As children, you were told that you could have it all ... just imagine it and it will happen. How do you get back to that?

Go back to your childhood ... feel the joy of belief in all things – Santa Claus, the Easter Bunny, the Fairy Godmother and the fairy tale ending. Keep a journal, write down all the dreams you have and all that you have accomplished. **Believe in your gifts, your abilities and let go of the negative thoughts** you have been conditioned to think because of hurts and pains and disappointments you have had.

I still believe in the elderly man dressed up in a red suit traveling around the world bestowing presents to all the good girls and boys. I carry this spirit of believing in me all the time. That is what you can do. **Believe!**

~Daily Inspiration by Denise Hansard, Empowerment Expert

26.

Thought for the Day

*"I will honor Christmas in my heart,
and try to keep it all the year."*
- CHARLES DICKENS

27.

As You Give, You Receive

When you release any limitation to receiving your Good, you dissolve discomfort and fear, and you expand your willingness to receive. You manifest that which you are open to receive and your commitment expands that which you can hold.

As you give and receive freely you are allowing your true heart to express through you. Giving creates a vacuum, which the Universe automatically fills with Greater Good. As you allow the Universe to give freely through you, you automatically place yourself in the position of receiving, allowing the receiver the opportunity to give. All things accepted are all things given, for giving and receiving are the same.

Life is a circle with no one left out. The unconditional love you give creates the experience of the unconditional love you receive, and that which you receive reflects your relationship with Source. Therefore, when giving to others you simultaneously receive fulfillment from the act of giving.

Today open your heart fully to giving and receiving ... you will naturally want to serve others — knowing that Who You Are, is One with all others.

~Daily Inspiration by Kathleen E. Sims, D.D., C.H.T

28.

Thought for the Day

"Life is not measured by the number of breaths we take, but by the moments that take our breath away."
– MAYA ANGELOU

29.

My Gift is Love

Everyone loves a holiday bargain, right? Do you know anyone who gets up at 4:00 AM and stands in line for hours just to get a good price on a TV? Or clips coupons to save on all their food items?

Funny thing... The best gift of all is hidden everywhere in plain sight. And it's free! It is.... You guessed it. Love!

Love is like the quantum gift. The more love you give, the more love is created. So why don't more people give love freely? It requires us to be vulnerable.

> *"Vulnerability is the birthplace of love, belonging, joy, courage, empathy, and creativity. It is the source of hope, empathy, accountability, and authenticity. If we want greater clarity in our purpose or deeper and more meaningful spiritual lives, vulnerability is the path."*
> – BRENÉ BROWN

The next time someone cuts you off in traffic, I invite you to try this: Notice any anger. Breathe. Imagine this person is experiencing some intense stress. See if you can feel some compassion for their situation. Visualize sending love energy from you heart to theirs.

It might feel awkward at first. If that is the case, pretend you are acting in a play... just experiment with the idea. Don't judge your actions. Just try it.

Afterwards, notice how you feel. I suspect you will feel a little relief. Maybe even some joy?

The miracle of giving the gift of love is that just the giving of it can heal us. We have to experience love to offer it as a gift. I encourage you to embrace giving the gift of love every minute of every day. It will change your life!

~Daily Inspiration by Olivia Parr-Rud, Corporate Love Ambassador

30.

Empowering Meditation

This mediation works best if done at first wake and before sleep. If at any time your mind wanders, gently bring it back to where you were and continue. Some people do get distracted. Should you fall asleep, when you wake, just return to where you left off. You may alter any part of this meditation that does not resonate with you.

1. Relax
2. Breathe
3. Pray
4. Give Gratitude
5. Bring in your higher power, angels, guides, etc.
6. Envision a cord attached to the base of your spine going to the center of the earth.
7. Envision one thing to release. See it and or the energy around it going to the center of the earth
   Through that cord to dissipate with no harm to anyone.
8. Begin releasing the emotions around that one thing. Release fear, negative emotions, all that no longer serves you.
9. Ask your higher power, angels, guides, etc. to assist you.
10. Allow all the energy you've been holding around that one thing to be released into the cord. Feel the feelings and let them go. Put them on the wings of a favorite animal if you need help...
11. Envision all the emotional cords attached to you to be sent down the cord you created—each time you have a negative experience, it can create an invisible emotional cord connecting you to the person or feeling.
12. Once released, call in earth energy.
13. Call in your own light.
14. Feel the joy as both energies mix throughout your body.
15. Thank those you called in to help you.
16. Give gratitude again.

Tips for "Higher Vibrational Living":
- Live in high integrity
- Do the work for the issue, the relationship, the job, etc. for success.
- Forgiveness brings release to you; otherwise, you are the one it hurts!
- Create your own "Personal Code of Ethics".

~Daily Inspiration by Syndee Hendricks, Certified Business Consultant and Intuitive Coach

31.

How Will You SHINE in the New Year?

> *"It's not that we aim too high and miss, it's that we aim too low and hit."*
> - LES BROWN

Now is the time to look at your future - where are you going, what are you called to be, where are you called to stretch? I encourage you to...

Aim high and far, aim further than you can even see where it will land! Set goals for yourself that scare you a little bit, that aren't the safe route. Remember, you don't have to know the "how" (you can figure that out later). Set those goals that are further than you have ever been before. Look for opportunities, that thing that's so far out there you can hardly believe you're claiming it. There is room in the sky for all of us to SHINE! One Shining star can light the path for more. Let's fill the sky and world with our powerful, positive and purposeful light!

Check in on your plan to go forward in the new year. As you take in all that you've learned this year, explore: **Where do you want to be seen more, so you can serve more?**

Have fun! By the way, fun and scary goals and strategies are not mutually exclusive! There's a joy in discovery, in showing up, in shining, in stretching to a new, exciting place.

All because ... you were made for such a time as this, therefore SHINE!

~Daily Inspiration by Rebecca Hall Gruyter, Influencer & Empowerment Leader

A NOTE FROM REBECCA

Dear Powerful Reader,

Thank you for reading our anthology. I hope it has touched your heart and spirit; encouraging and inspiring you!

I wanted to share a little bit more about our organizations, Your Purpose Driven Practice™ and RHG Media Productions™. We are passionate about helping others live on purpose and with purpose in their life and business. I hope this book has supported and inspired you to choose to live on purpose, and with great purpose!

If you are wanting to reach more people and be part of inspiring and supporting others with your message, your gifts, and the work that you bring to the world; then I want to share some opportunities for you to consider.

Each year we compile and produce anthology book projects, support authors in publishing their own powerful books as best sellers, produce and publish an international magazine, launch TV shows, facilitate women's empowerment conferences, launch radio and podcast shows, help experts and speakers step into a place of powerful influence to make a global difference. We provide programs and strategies to help you reach more people, and facilitate the Speaker Talent Search (which helps speakers, experts, and influencers connect with more speaking opportunities.) We would love to support you in reaching more people. Please take a moment to learn a little bit more about us at the sites listed below, and then reach out to us for a conversation. **We would love to have you join us as we seek to make a positive global difference.**

You can learn more about each of these things are our main website:
www.YourPurposeDrivenPractice.com
Enjoy our powerful **TV and podcast shows**: www.RHGTVNetwork.com
Learn more about the **Speaker Talent Search™**:
www.SpeakerTalentSearch.com

Learn more about our **writing opportunities**:
http://yourpurposedrivenpractice.com/writing-opportunities/
If you would like to connect with me personally to explore some of our opportunities in upcoming book projects, podcast/radio shows, and/or TV, then here is the link to schedule a time to speak with me directly: www.MeetWithRebecca.com or you can email me at: Rebecca@YourPuposeDrivenPractice.com
May you always choose to Step Forward and SHINE!

Warmly,
Rebecca Hall Gruyter

BY SUBJECT

Balance/Support
February: 3, 25, 27
March: 31
April: 19, 30
May: 1, 2, 8, 17, 26, 29, 31
June: 6, 7, 9, 16, 26, 27
July: 1, 19, 21
August: 7, 17, 24
September: 23
October: 14, 16, 17, 19, 25
November: 3, 6, 8, 14, 20, 24, 29
December: 2, 7, 15, 20, 24, 29

Choice
January: 19, 25, 26, 27, 28, 29, 31
February: 1, 6, 15, 19, 21, 26, 28
March: 2, 3, 6, 11, 12, 15, 16, 18, 19, 22, 23
April: 2, 3, 5, 8, 10, 24, 27
May: 7, 14, 16, 30
June: 9, 10, 15, 21, 30
July: 2, 3, 4, 13, 14, 15, 18, 24, 25, 31
August: 14
September: 7, 16, 18, 20, 29, 30
October: 5, 8, 10, 12, 13, 15, 17, 18, 21, 24, 25, 26, 27, 29, 30, 31
November: 1, 2, 3, 5, 12, 15, 16, 17, 19, 22, 26
December: 1, 11, 12, 14, 17, 20, 24, 29, 30, 31, 25

Clarity
January: 22, 30
February: 22
April: 19
May: 14, 16
July: 22, 29
August: 23
September: 8, 28
October: 12, 22, 27
November: 1, 4, 5, 11, 15, 18
December: 16, 17, 21, 23

Commitment
January: 7, 8, 9
March: 17, 23, 27
April: 8, 22
May: 18, 23, 29
June: 4, 14, 24, 29
July: 8, 11, 16, 23
September: 11
October: 3, 8, 12, 18, 26
November: 4, 5, 8, 14, 22, 28
December: 5, 31

Encouragement/Inspiration/Empowerment
January: 9, 22, 14
February: 16, 17
March: 14, 17, 19, 21, 22, 23, 28
May: 5, 26, 29

Encouragement/Inspiration/Empowerment (continued)
June: 8
July: 5, 8, 12, 15, 29
August: 13, 18
September: 4, 21, 23, 24, 27
October: 1, 11, 14, 15, 16, 23, 26
November: 2, 4, 5, 12, 15, 29
December: 3, 7, 8, 15, 24, 25, 30, 31

Faith
January: 13
April: 7
May: 14, 18, 23
June: 10
September: 1, 10, 23
October: 17
November: 11, 15, 16, 23
December: 6, 9, 14

Family/Relationships
February: 4, 18, 20
March: 29
April: 17, 23, 26
May: 9, 12, 31
June: 6, 9, 11, 19, 23
July: 10, 31
August: 4, 11, 21
September: 5, 6, 8, 29
October: 19, 22, 29
November: 2, 9, 18, 19, 24, 26, 29
December: 2, 6, 10, 18, 27, 29

Fear/Courage
January: 5
February: 5
March: 9
April: 4, 5, 14
May: 25
June: 22
July: 5, 9
September: 17, 19

Fear/Courage (continued)
October: 4, 6, 8, 15, 24, 25, 26
November: 5, 11, 14, 24, 27

Gratitude
January: 28
February: 26
March: 13
May: 2, 20, 21
June: 9
August: 24
September: 6, 23
October: 2, 7
November: 3, 8, 10, 13, 16, 21, 27
December: 23, 27

Growth
January: 23
March: 1, 4, 5, 14
April: 2, 9, 12, 13
May: 17, 22, 26, 28
June: 16, 17, 26, 27
July: 1, 11, 28, 29, 31
August: 17, 19
September: 9, 11, 13, 16
October: 3, 4, 10, 13, 28
November: 18, 22, 23, 24, 27, 29
December: 1, 3, 8, 10, 20, 23, 30, 31

Love
February: 2, 8, 9, 10, 14, 24
March: 7, 29, 30
June: 20
July: 17
August: 30
September: 5, 6, 21
November: 9, 25
December: 22, 24, 27, 29

Mindset/Perspective
January: 4, 10, 12, 23, 29
February: 6, 7, 9, 19, 28

Mindset/Perspective (continued)
March: 5, 11, 15, 16, 18, 19, 20, 25, 30
April: 12, 19, 28
May: 8, 13
June: 3, 15
July: 16, 17, 24, 27, 31
August: 2, 28
September: 1, 7
October: 1, 20, 22, 23, 24, 26, 29, 31
November: 1, 3, 4, 11, 13, 15, 17, 22, 24, 29
December: 1, 7, 8, 13, 14, 18, 20, 21, 23, 25, 26, 28, 29, 31

Peace/Joy
January: 16
April: 8, 29
May: 6, 14, 17, 28
June: 28
July: 26, 30, 31
August: 8, 9, 10, 14, 29
September: 2, 10, 22
October: 2, 7, 17, 20, 27, 28, 29
November: 3, 4, 6, 10, 14, 24
December: 6, 11, 13, 18, 19, 24, 25

Persistence
January: 21
March: 5, 10, 19
April: 3, 11, 16, 18
May: 10
June: 24
July: 8
September: 4, 22
October: 7
November: 5, 7, 11, 12, 28, 30
December: 5, 14, 15

Potential
January: 4, 6, 18
February: 17
March: 23, 25

Potential (continued)
April: 29
May: 4, 5, 8, 13, 20, 21
June: 2, 3, 4, 18
July: 18, 20, 26
August: 20
September: 25, 26
October: 1, 6, 8, 9, 12, 13, 21
November: 3, 5, 11, 20, 22, 24, 29, 30
December: 9, 15, 21, 24, 30, 31

Purpose
January: 1, 11, 15
February: 11, 17, 22
March: 1
April: 15, 26
May: 3, 4, 8, 15, 18, 19
June: 2, 23, 25
July: 1, 2, 4
August: 1, 3, 5, 16, 26, 28
September: 8, 9, 24, 25, 28
October: 5, 8, 9, 13, 18, 20, 21, 23, 28, 31
November: 1, 5, 30
December: 16, 21, 30, 31

Saying "YES"
January: 1, 11, 12, 14, 17, 18, 19, 20, 24
February: 1, 3
April: 6, 8, 27, 29
May: 8, 27
June: 3, 29, 30
July: 9, 12
September: 26, 29
October: 10, 12, 16, 21, 31
November: 1, 5, 15, 29, 30
December: 14, 31

Success
January: 3, 12, 14, 17, 20, 30
February: 13, 16, 23
March: 1, 2, 8, 9, 12, 14, 17, 18, 19, 23, 24, 26

Success
April: 1, 6, 7, 10, 11, 20
May: 5, 7, 26, 29
June: 5, 16, 17, 29
July: 1, 17, 18, 20, 22, 23, 29, 31
August: 8, 12, 14, 15
September: 9, 11, 12, 19, 27, 29
October: 2, 3, 6, 11, 12, 23
November: 1, 12, 22, 27, 28
December: 8, 13, 15, 20, 31

Wonderfully Made
January: 2, 3, 11
February: 12, 28
April: 21, 25, 27, 28
May: 3, 4, 11, 13, 24
June: 1, 3, 28
July: 31
August: 6, 24, 28, 31
September: 1, 3, 14, 15, 21, 23, 28, 29
October: 1, 9, 12, 14, 18, 21, 22, 24, 25, 31
November: 3, 4, 14, 20, 26, 30
December: 6, 9, 14, 20, 21, 22, 29, 31

LEARN MORE ABOUT OUR AUTHORS

Dr. Ruth Anderson is a lifelong student, teacher, and multi-award-winning author. Retired after a satisfying and worthwhile career in special education and public school administration, Ruth was given the life-changing opportunity to redefine how she saw herself and grow into her soul's purpose. After a myriad of classes and hours meditating, she embraced her second calling, that of an author, intuitive, and transformational facilitator. Ruth walks in connection with Spirit and spends time daily listening to her angelic guides including Divine Mother, and Archangels Michael, Gabrielle, and Raphael. She freely shares the lessons that she has learned during her meditative sessions via her writing and with her clients. Ruth is an ordained minister with The Church of Inner Light and uses her books, website, and Facebook to share her ministry of inspiring others to connect with their higher selves and embrace their soul's calling. Her goal is to live an authentic life that is worthy of her soul's calling and help transform lives through her work. Ruth lives in Colorado, adores her family and friends, and is passionate about her pets Tucker, Jack, Maddie, Izzy, and Lola. Above all else, Ruth strives to make the world a more compassionate place.

openclinic1@outlook.com
303 726-7095
www.theministryonline.com

Social Media Links
Facebook: https://www.facebook.com/theministryonline1
Twitter: https://www.twitter-com/TheMinistryRA

Bonnie May Best is a Wellness Consultant, Author and Inspirational Coach. She has over 40 years' experience in education, mediation, and corporate systems analysis and planning. She has 20 years' experience as a Wellness Consultant. Blending her teaching and coaching skills, Bonnie enjoys helping people experience more in life -- more joy, passion, love and success. She believes that every person has a dream, and loves to support people as they explore and manifest their dreams for REAL SUCCESS. Bonnie has published five books: *Inspirational Poems Vol 1 and 2*, *Haiku Poems for All Seasons*, *Weave the Threads of Your Life*, and *Daily Inspirational Poems*.

bonnie@bbest.com
Phone Number: 510-761-0439
http://bbest.com

Social Media Links
Facebook:
https://www.facebook.com/BBest.Wellness
https://www.facebook.com/BBest.Coach
https://www.facebook.com/AuthorBonnieBest
LinkedIn: http://www.linkedin.com/in/bonniebest
Twitter: @bbest4u - link: https://twitter.com/#!/bbest4u
YouTube: http://www.youtube.com/c/BonnieBest

Other Social Media Channels
Amazon Author Page: amazon.com/author/bonnie-best

Bonnie Bonadeo – Speaker-Coach-Author-Audio Influencer. Bonnie is known as The Connection Coach plus Founder of The Beauty Agent Network Speaker –Education Resource Company, BonnieBonadeo.com- Connection Coach, Speaker, Author and Syndicated Host of BEaUty Inside and Out Radio. Bonnie focuses on the people part of leadership, personal branding and public speaking. By eliminating "overused and overrated techniques" and layers of "how to's" she coaches others to uncover and discover their greatness and what is takes to elicit greatness in others. A Beauty and wellness industry professional with over 25 years' experience, she has mastered many levels and achievements. As a 2013 Enterprising Women and 2016 Cover of Salon Today Coaches Guide, she is a Certified Emotional Intelligent Speaker, Executive Business Coach, 2x International bestselling Author of Success in Beauty. Bonnie speaks authentically on her struggles and successes as a person, leader and entrepreneur to foster growth and awareness in others. She is the essence of her brand and all about Connecting You to You.

http://www.bonniebonadeo.com

Social Media Links
Facebook: https://www.facebook.com/BonnieBonadeoCoach/
Twitter: http://www.twitter.com/bonniebonadeo1
Instagram: http://www.instagram.com/bonniebonadeo
Linkedin: http://www.linkedin.com/bonniebonadeo

Carmen Bryant is a serial entrepreneur who has had several small businesses over the last 25+ years. Carmen has been an entrepreneur since 1991 when she started her first business creating art and selling it at the local Wine and Art festivals. She has started 4 other businesses since then. She currently owns and operates two businesses: Altos Mobile Massage, a Silicon Valley based company bringing massage therapy and yoga to small and mid-sized companies and Bryant Business Ventures Inc. which umbrellas both BBV Coaching and BBV Real Estate Investment.

As a Success Coach, Carmen focuses on empowering and motivating other women entrepreneurs who are starting a new business or taking their businesses and their personal lives to their next level of greatness. Carmen has completed Tony Robbin's Mastery University and Business Mastery and will begin the TR Leadership Mastery Courses in 2018. She has learned from some of the most successful coaches; Tony Robbins, Dr. Wayne Dyer, Brendon Burchard, Dean Graziosi, and Mary Morrissey are favorites. She uses methods, tools and teachings from all of these thought leaders in her coaching sessions.

Carmen started her career as a cell biologist in the biotechnology industry and after earning her MBA, moved out of the lab to product and project management for biotech and medical device firms. She has a B.S. in Marine Biology from San Jose State University and an MBA from Santa Clara University. Carmen is an active member of the Mindvalley Community founded by Vishen Lakhiani. Favorite personal activities include creating kiln-fused Glass Art. learning through online course-work, reading, long walks on the beach, travel and meditation.

Carmen M. Bryant M.B.A.
650-279-7013
AltosMobileMassage.com

Social Media Links
Facebook:
https://www.facebook.com/Carmen7377
https://www.facebook.com/AltosMobileMassage/
LinkedIn:
https://www.linkedin.com/in/carmenbryant/
https://www.linkedin.com/company/altos-mobile-massage/
Twitter: @Carmen7377 @AltosMobileMass

Sunday Burquest is Grit Girl.

Sunday is a wife, mother of four, inspirational speaker, breast cancer survivor and reality tv personality. Diagnosed with breast cancer in April of 2012, she endured multiple surgeries, chemotherapy, radiation and a bout with depression. A culmination of difficult life circumstances, led Sunday to the realization she was much stronger than she imagined; *she discovered her grit.*

Taking her new-found strength to the next level, she followed a life-long dream to audition for and was then cast to compete on the television series Survivor: Millennials vs Gen-X (2016). After Survivor, she knew she had a message others needed to hear. Sunday made the decision to step away from 25 years of ministry to pursue speaking full-time and by drawing on her personal experiences, she is reaching audiences of all ages with a message of strength, hope and grit.

Sunday is the author of, "Grit Girl Power to Survive, Inspired by Grace", walking the reader through her journey to finding grit while, providing a path for them to do the same. She is passionate about audience's understanding her grit is a direct result of her relationship with Jesus. He equips every person with the strength and confidence to follow their dreams and ultimately, His plan for their lives - *in Him we discover our GRIT.*

Sburquest@gmail.com
612-270-8687
http://iamgritgirl.com/

Social Media Links
Facebook:
https://www.facebook.com/sundayburquest/
https://www.facebook.com/profile.php?id=100012752731769
https://www.facebook.com/groups/gritgirltribe/
LinkedIn: https://www.linkedin.com/in/sundaysurvivor/
Twitter: https://twitter.com/sundaysurvivor
Instagram:
https://www.instagram.com/wearegritgirl/
https://www.instagram.com/sundaysurvivor/

Adrian Jefferson Chofor, a global mobility lifestyle expert helping people that want to live abroad or currently living abroad with challenges work and live strategically and successfully. She used to live abroad and loved the global mobile lifestyle of an expatriate. She is also a personal transformation strategist and speaker, helping people to live their best lives. She is the owner and founder of Aspire2Inspire Transformational Practice, LLC helping clients transform their aspirations into reality with outcomes that inspires others to reach their dreams as well. She empowers people to step forward and live a phenomenal life.

Adrian is a travel and cultural enthusiast having travelled extensively all over the globe and lived abroad herself and married to an expatriate. Her passion for travel and observing cultures from all over the world has driven her as a life strategist to bridge cultural gaps to foster communication, understanding, and deeper relationships within corporate teams and on an individual basis. Her mission is help expatriates, entrepreneurs, and people from all walks of life tools and skillsets gain more clarity, confidence, and focus to master their life. Adrian is an award-winning speaker and soon to be published author of Aspire to your Greatness!

connect@adrianjeffersonchofor.com
415-523-6680
www.adrianjeffersonchofor.com

Social Media Links
Facebook:
https://www.facebook.com/adrian.jeffersonchofor
https://www.facebook.com/expat2go
Linkedin: https://www.linkedin.com/in/adrianjeffersonchofor
Twitter: https://twitter.com/expat2go
Instagram: https://instagram.com/expat2go

Ron Coquia has been an explorer of personal growth and transformation since 1988. Ron left a "successful" career as a technology leader in the heart of Silicon Valley to embark on a journey to uncover true success, true joy, and true fulfillment. On his transformational journey, he discovered that lasting fulfillment is not something we find outside of us, but rather deep within our core. Hidden behind our desires, fears, and self-judgement lies the most powerful and beautiful part of who we are – our Radiance. When we allow our radiance to shine through us and out into the world, we experience the truth of our joy, our love and our passion for life.

As Ron uncovered his radiance and gifts, he discovered his core passion was to serve the world as a transformational coach and producer. Ron founded Transformational Productions to support his clients to uncover their radiance in front of camera and create transformational videos. In 2019, Ron will be launching a powerful new program called "Journey to Radiance" to support those that are on a journey of dissolving their fears, self-judgment and inner barriers to uncover their true inner power, joy and radiance.

Ron believes that it is not what you achieve, but how you hold the light within you that can bring more joy, love and freedom in your life. It is your beautiful and authentic Radiance that empowers your unique gifts that our world needs.

ron@transformationalproductions.com
925-322-0049
www.TransformationalProductions.com
www.JourneyToRadiance.com **launching in 2019**

Social Media Links
Facebook:
https://www.facebook.com/ron.coquia
https://www.facebook.com/TransformationalProductions
Linkedin: https://www.linkedin.com/in/RonCoquia
Twitter: https://www.twitter.com/RonCoquia
YouTube Channel: Transformational Productions

Previously the Chief Operating Officer for an Australian international franchise organisation, **Shirley Dalton** was responsible for coaching and training over 200 franchisees to run profitable and successful businesses before moving on to start her first business where she continues to coach and consult to small business owners on a one to one basis. Focussing on the 3P's to business success (People, Processes and Possibilities), Shirley works with business owners to systematize and streamline their businesses, lead and manage their teams and manage their mindset to create a business and a life they love. Passionate about personal growth and development, Shirley created and produced a TV and radio show where she has interviewed hundreds of successful entrepreneurs and business owners who share their success tips to help entrepreneurs and business owners grow and scale their businesses. Building on her superior organisation skills, degrees in Education and Psychology, business knowledge and understanding of people and processes, today Shirley uses her proprietary methodology that allows her to use her best gifts in coaching, consulting, interviewing and understanding of processes to grow and expand your business in today's crowded marketplace.

Shirley@shirleydalton.com
+61402281146
www.ShirleyDalton.com

Social Media Links
Facebook:
https://www.facebook.com/shirley.dalton.79
https://www.facebook.com/shirleydaltoncom/
Linkedin: https://www.linkedin.com/in/shirleydalton
Twitter: https://twitter.com/shirley_dalton

Julz DeFant grew up in Washington State living in poverty with addicts for parents. She was surrounded by abuse of every kind, being labeled as a "nothing", and an overpowering victim-mentality. She decided, at the early age of four, that she would NOT live this way. She spent her childhood fighting against the circumstances she was born into, all the while knowing, there was a greater purpose in her life and that she had a choice in who she would be. By age 11, she was abandoned and homeless, but still determined not to give up. She worked hard to get herself through school and became the first person in her family to graduate high school. After earning her degree in Dental Hygiene in 2009, she dedicated herself to helping others grow in their potential, be inspired in life, and in preventing burn-out. Julz has been working in healthcare for the past 20 plus years, gaining the experience and training to not only facilitate quality care for patients, but also in building teams that are motivated and last. She now lives in Olympia, WA with her husband and 7-year-old daughter. She continues to work part-time clinically while she peruses her calling as an author and public speaker, sharing truth, creating smiles, and empowering others to shine.

happyjuliegirl@comcast.net
1 (360) 556-6499

Social Media Links
Facebook: fb.me/julz_rdh
Twitter: https://twitter.com/JulzRDH
Instagram: https://www.instagram.com/julz_rdh

Marlene Elizabeth is a Certified Money Coach, Mama-preneur and Founder of MONEYWINGS™. Marlene believes every woman deserves to unfold her financial dream. She is on a mission to help women rewrite the stars of their money story, one brave feather through her podcast *Let's Get Tender: Money Conversations that Matter*, speaking events and private coaching. Deeply inspired by her daughter to transform her relationship to money as a single-Mom, Marlene helps women see money differently and equips them with life-changing strategies to breakthrough limiting beliefs around money and success. Her clients uncover their unique, untapped natural gifts and strengths while developing a powerful sense of confidence, clarity and purpose to thrive.

She earned her Master's degree in Religious Education from Boston College, B.A. in International Relations from U.C. Davis and is a Certified Brain Personality Specialist. Marlene is the bestselling author of MONEYWINGS™ : *Unfold Your Financial Potential One Brave Feather At A Time*, and bestselling co-author of *Bloom Where You Are Planted and Shine!* and *Step Forward and Shine!* Her forthcoming co-authored book *Step Into Your Brilliance* is due for release Fall 2019.

marlene@marleneelizabeth.com
909.247.1127
www.marleneelizabeth.com

Social Media Links
Facebook: www.facebook.com/growmoneywings

Kathy Fairbanks leads the Klemmer corporate team providing experiential training introductions to clients worldwide in order to support them in achieving their desired goals. She's honored to serve as the weekly host of "The Compassionate Samurai Business Hour" on Voice America Talk Radio where Kathy and guests share stories and tools for overcoming obstacles and creating shortcuts for sustainable results in business.

Prior to Team Klemmer, her dynamic 20-year career in the financial services industry focused on new business development for CitiGroup and GE Capital, where her boldest accomplishment was winning, losing and then winning again a $96 million-dollar equipment finance deal. Prior to entering the financial services arena, Kathy attended Indiana University's Kelley School of Business and received a B.S. in Transportation & Public Utilities Management. She is honored to serve on the Advisory Board at Pathways for Veterans, in support of veterans and their families to create full and abundant lives post-military service. Kathy and her husband of 30 years live in Marin County, California and are the blessed parents of two young adults who are both Klemmer Leadership graduates.

Email: kathy@klemmer.com
Phone: 415-250-4444
Website: www.klemmer.com

Social Media Links
Facebook: https://www.facebook.com/kathy.m.fairbanks
LinkedIn: https://www.linkedin.com/in/kathyfairbanks
Twitter: https://www.twitter.com/KathyLFairbanks

Cassandra Garabedian is a style consultant, CEO and the owner of Making Statements `N Style. She is uniquely skilled in women's apparel and accessories.

A former runaway model, she has sashayed from the San Francisco Bay catwalk to the catwalks of the fashion houses of Milan, Italy. She has studied fashion design in San Francisco and worked side by side with her mother, Georgia Franklin a former head seamstress at Levi Strauss, Co., SF. An entrepreneur in her own right, she was also Cassandra's mentor and inspiration. To complete the circle of one day owning a successful business, Cassandra went back to school at the University of San Francisco, where she received a BS degree in Business Management double majoring in Marketing.

Cassandra has been in business for over fifteen years assisting women and men on Dressing for Success. Together they would create a poised, polished, "put-together", effortless signature look that resonated with confidence and would be instrumental in making the right impression at the right time, when it matters the most.

Cassandra is currently a member with the Commonwealth in San Francisco, National Association of Women Business Owners (NAWBO) Oakland/San Francisco Chapter, National Association of Professional Women (NAPW) Oakland/Walnut Creek Chapter, Women Speakers Association(WSA), Global Shine Community: Empowering Women-Transforming Lives, Voice America Network, and the Step Forward and Shine Community.

Outside her professional life she participates in a variety of organizations, such as the public television network KQED, donating her time and cash to support their humanitarian drives, Love A Child, the Center for Battered Women, Bay Point and her church, Unity Church of Richmond with their food drives to help feed their cities homeless.

www.makingstatementsnstyle.com
cgarabedian@gmail.com
(510) 755-5903
(510) 841-6800

Social Media Links
Facebook:
https://www.facebook.com/Making-Statements-N-Style-2053964941541986/
Twitter: Making Statements `N Style
Linkedin: https://www.linkedin.com/in/cassandra-f-garabedian-16ab62148

Bettyanne Green is a Content Marketing Strategist and Copywriter who helps heart-centered business owners give voice to the purpose behind their products, through marketing messaging that matters - to the marketplace, to their bottom line, and toward a world that works for everyone.

With more than 35 years' experience in marketing communications, writing and graphic design, Bettyanne offers wraparound services for a distinctive and effective content marketing program. She adapts time-tested communication and behavioral principles (that outlast the next 'shiny new object') for today's dynamic online and offline marketing world, while honoring and lifting up the truth her clients yearn to tell.

Bettyanne's business model: an ongoing relationship with clients so they can safely deep-dive together to uncover the message, the story, the voice that are uniquely their own. Together they craft the messaging that will connect with their dream client, and formulate a practical content marketing strategy and calendar. Then she provides ongoing support with copywriting/editing, repurposing content, and consultation. She's the go-to for anything written that will deliver a message that matters, where it matters.

If it has words, Bettyanne can help you! With a degree in Public Communications, she has worked in almost every aspect of marketing communications, ranging from The New York Times, the League of Women Voters, international development magazines, The Cleveland Orchestra, political campaigns and civic change efforts, to emerging authors writing in English as a second language. Bettyanne Green can be reached at Bettyanne@Heart2HeartMarketing.com to schedule a free 30-minute phone consult.

Bettyanne@Heart2HeartMarketing.com
216-255-2223
www.Heart2HeartMarketing.com

Social Media Links
Facebook page(s):
https://www.facebook.com/bettyanne.green
https://www.facebook.com/Bettyanne.Green.Copywriter/
LinkedIn: https://www.linkedin.com/in/bettyannegreen
Twitter: https://twitter.com/mixedbag1

John Hall has a servant's heart.

He was born in Kentucky and spent much of his childhood helping on his grandparents' farm in southern Ohio. There he learned a lot about the interaction of humans and nature, and to serve at the mercy of the uncontrollable events of nature. The crops were dependant on nature, and sometimes nature didn't always cooperate (or more truthfully, the other way around).

His serving continued when he enlisted in the Navy to serve his country. He was promoted through the enlisted ranks and earned a commission as a Naval Officer and retired from this era of serving others as a Lieutenant Commander.

He earned a Bachelor of Science Degree in electrical engineering from the University of Washington, a Master of Business Administration (MBA) from John F. Kennedy University, and a Master of Science degree in Computer Science from The Navy Postgraduate School.

Today, John is a successful business owner, entrepreneur, and author who draws upon his vast life experience of serving others to mentor people who are looking for independence. John fiercely believes in personal independence and he helps people improve their lives to become less dependent on others for their well being.

sailor180@hotmail.com
(707) 372-8282

Denise Hansard (pronounced "Hanserd")
Life Architect & Motivational Speaker
Author of *Suffering In Comfort*
Radio Host of *The Denise Hansard Show*

3 Things to know about Denise Hansard.
1. Didn't just hang her shingle out as a coach … Masters in Counseling (working therapeutically & in the personal development growth arena), Certified Pricing Professional (those 20+ years in the corporate world teaching the art, science and value of pricing … your worth in it), Life Coaching Certification (getting back to her gift as a Life Architect, helping women design their one life from the inside out)
2. Been there, done that … successfully started 2 businesses and climbed the corporate ladder. Have coached hundreds of women to generate 6 figure incomes, find the love of their life and take back their power. Have spoken on stages to groups of 5 to over 300 … transforming the minds and hearts of CEOs, Executive Sales, Sales Teams, and anyone who would listen.
3. G.R.I.T.S … Girl Raised in the South and owning every bit of that label. Knowing exactly who she is, what she brings to the table coming from the heart … pushing clients to do and be more … to take action in spite of every mean girl thought and story they have.

denise@denisehansard.com
847-485-8446
http://denisehansard.com

Social Media Links
Facebook: https://www.facebook.com/Coaching2Dream
LinkedIn: https://www.linkedin.com/in/denisehansard
Twitter: https://twitter.com/DeniseHansard_
Youtube: http://tinyurl.com/Denise-Hansard-YouTube
Soundcloud: https://soundcloud.com/user-499912013
Radio: http://boldbravemedia.com/shows/the-denise-hansard-show/

Jaimie Harnagel is a Certified Reiki Master and Shamanic Practitioner. She has studied Animal Communication, as well as crystal healing.

Blending her background in mind, body and spirit, she has experience in many areas of healing with both inner and outer environments. Whether working with Chakras or Feng Shui, energy healing or essential oils, she takes every opportunity to encourage others to shine.

She has years of experience in retail, sales and customer service as well as owning her own businesses. She enjoys being in nature, beadwork and reading.

Jaimie has been featured in the book "*Step Forward and Shine*" and was featured in RGH Magazine. She will also be participating in the upcoming anthology "*Animal Legacies*" in 2019.

Her mission is to lift and inspire others so that they can share their own beautiful light with the world.

Jaimie lives in Northern California with her husband and two animal friends who rule the roost.

bjharnagel@msn.com

Social Media Links
https://www.facebook.com/jaimie.harnagel

 **Lisa Teresi Harris** is an author, professional keynote speaker, fitness coach, and an award-winning entrepreneur. A Registered Dietitian since 1978, she started her second career as a Certified Personal Trainer, specializing in Baby Boomers and older adults, at age 59. Currently, she's the owner of Enduring Fitness 4U, where she provides senior exercise classes and in-home fitness training and nutrition coaching.

Lisa was inspired to start helping others realize their best lives after battling her own incurable autoimmune disease and then witnessing her mother's strength start to deteriorate.

Lisa's goal - her undying "why" – is to empower folks to live out their lives with as much strength and independence as possible. Through her coaching and speaking, she's inspired hundreds of people to get stronger and live longer.

Lisa resides in the southern California wine community of Temecula with her husband Terry, close to their two daughters and three grandchildren.

Lisa@EnduringFitness4U.com
(951) 533-2612
EnduringFitness4U.com

Social Media Links
Facebook: www.facebook.com/lisateresiharris
LinkedIn: www.linkedin.com/in/lisa-harris-58920a62/
Twitter: https://www.twitter.com/lteresiharris

 **Nancy Tarr Hart** has a wide and varied history of personal and professional experience, encompassing 40+ years of business experience combined with theatre experience as a performer, director, costumer, educator, and administrator. An intuitive and mystic, the understanding of her gifts fully ignited in 1999 when she enrolled in a part time undergrad program for adult students from which, in 2005, she earned a BA in Philosophy and Religious Studies, *summa cum laude* from the Notre Dame of Maryland University (NDMU). She continued on her Spirit/Sophia guided academic journey and, in 2013, was awarded a PhD in Religious Studies with a concentration in feminist theory, the Divine Feminine, and Marian studies from the University of Trinity Saint David, Lampeter, Wales. Recently she has come full circle academically (and according to Spirit/Sophia's plan), and is back at NDMU—this time as an Assistant Professor teaching courses in philosophy and religious studies. Nancy is also an ardent fiber artist who enjoys traveling, writing, gardening, reading, and sharing her home with her beautiful black kitties, Kali and Bastet.

ntarrhart@gmail.com

Social Media Links
Facebook: https://www.facebook.com/nancy.t.hart.9

Syndee Hendricks, award winning, certified business consultant, multiple author, corporate trainer, and philanthropist, Syndee Hendricks provides invaluable insight, inspiration, and action plans that catapult her clients from struggling to thriving in her international coaching/consulting practice. She finds hidden money.

While managing her business, she parlayed her knowledge and expertise to help her husband with Alzheimer's disease, and shares their success of keeping him coherent for over a decade in her new book.

She is CEO of Imagine More Success, LLC, and is co-hosting IMSpodcast, which is syndicated internationally. Her 2019 projects include publishing three books and introducing Essential Entrepreneur Skills Training Courses.

Business: Imagine More Success & Insightful Coaching
syndeehendricks@gmail.com
www.SyndeeHendricks.com
www.ImagineMoreSuccess.com
916.835.4123

Social Media Links
Facebook:
https://www.facebook.com/syndeehendricks
https://www.facebook.com/Insightfulcoaching
Twitter: https://www.twitter.com/Syndeehendricks
Linked In: https://www.linkedin.com/in/syndeehendricks
Instagram: https://www.instagram.com/syndeehendricks
Pinterest: https://www.pinterest.com/syndeehendricks

Teresa Hawley-Howard is an international best-selling author and publisher. Her mission in life is to help others find their voices and share their stories! She also wants to help them walk through their pain, limitations, and their own doubt to live the life they deserve. She knows their words, stories, scars, and their pain can inspire, heal and give hope to another person. She is an empowerment/writing coach, publisher, speaker, #1 international best-selling author, radio host, and CASA volunteer. She is also Co-Founder of Tribute Magazine, spotlighting entrepreneurs.

Founder of Women On A Mission, inspiring and uplifting women to live the life they desire. Radio Host of WOM Radio show, and host of Modern Day Woman and Words Have Power Podcasts! Teresa's goal is to help 10k people share their stories! Reach out and let Teresa help you share your story!

She is also the founder of WOM Enterprises. WOM Enterprises offers complete publishing packages for authors! The company offers several ways to become an author! You can write in one of many anthologies or you can write your own book! Either way you will become a published author! Share your story, promote your business and create your legacy! WOM Enterprises will help you make your dream become a reality. So, stop procrastinating and become an author today with WOM Enterprises!

www.teresahawleyhoward.com
teresa@takeactionwithteresa.com
903-910-9635

Best-selling author **Mary E. Knippel**, Writer Unleashed at YourWritingMentor.com, publisher at Authentic Grace Publishing and inspirational speaker, is fiercely committed to guiding you to unleash your story worth writing. With a firm philosophy that *No one can tell your story but YOU*, Mary invites you to take pen in hand to deliver your expertise to the world. Using her 30 years as a journalist, and the power of storytelling, she is on a mission to support you to be visible, vibrant and prosperous. Someone is waiting to hear your story… the story only you can tell.

As a journal writer since the age of 11, Mary knows the enormous power and healing capabilities of the written word. A two-time breast cancer survivor, she used writing and other creative tools in her recovery and chronicles the results in her upcoming book, *The Secret Artist*, where she shares what she has learned to help you move from survive to thrive. Learn more about Mary's virtual classes and workshops, receive free writing tips and techniques as well as what to do about writer's block, or invite her to speak to your group, by visiting her website at www.yourwritingmentor.com.

mary@yourwritingmentor.com
650-440-5616
https://yourwritingmentor.com

Social Media Links
Facebook:
https://facebook.com/maryeknippel.author
https://facebook.com/maryeknippel
LinkedIn: https://www.linkedin.com/in/maryeknippel
Twitter: https://twitter.com/MEKnippelAuthor
Youtube: https://www.youtube.com/user/maryeknippel
Instagram: https://www.instagram.com/maryeknippelauthor

As an advocate for mental health and stress resolution **Catherine M. Laub** has a campaign, Brighten Your Day with Turquoise, where turquoise is a calming color, uplifts us and helps us think clearly. She shares her own journey with mental illness on her self-produced podcast, The Celestial Spoon, and by talking to groups inspiring them to reach out for support if they require it. Catherine is an Award-Winning Author for her book: "Journey of Angelic Healing, Stories to Feed Your Soul" and continues her writing in anthologies.

As a Psychic/Medium and Turquoise Angel Guide Catherine also psychically delivers information to people from the spiritual realm, their guides and angels that benefits them greatly with their lives. She does readings at local events, as well as performing sessions with clients worldwide, via phone and Skype, email and in person.

Catherine is available to speak at your event about mental health and how turquoise can uplift you.

Her ideal client may be struggling with stress, deep depression or anxiety and would like an inspirational and spiritual view on overcoming their stress. She uses angelic psychic guidance to work closely with others as their mentor.

catherine@catherinemlaub.com
631-619-2040
www.catherinemlaub.com

Social Media Links
Facebook:
https://www.facebook.com/catherine.laub.54
https://www.facebook.com/CatherinesCelestialSpoon
LinkedIn: https://www.linkedin.com/in/catherinemlaub
Twitter: cathysquests
YouTube: https://www.youtube.com/channel/UCeWwroCru4uRiZds-FAEVgw
Amazon: http://www.amazon.com/-/e/B014M7GZA0

A decorated Navy Veteran with over 25 years of Diversity & Inclusion experience, **Tresté Loving** has trained over 76,000 globally. Specializing in Law Enforcement Relations & Corporate Culture, Tresté's interactive and informative approach to difficult topics such as racism, captivates audiences filled with Senior Executives and Recruits alike!

During her military service, Tresté received the admirable Meritorious Service Medal, as well as a prominent Diversity & Inclusion award. Her expertise was utilized in drafting the Department of the Navy's first Diversity Policy, and her leadership called upon to manage victim-family relations for the Pentagon on 9/11. Tresté's educational background includes a Bachelor's Degree in International Business, as well as an Equal Opportunity/Diversity Officer designation.

With a passion to help individuals understand why they think the way they do, Tresté's main objective is to alleviate racial discourse, while developing highly effective teams. Her expertise transcends local law enforcement, having trained CEOs for some of the nation's top corporations, the Federal Police, NCIS and the Department of the Navy.

www.tiredofhate.com
http://tiredofhate.com/blog/
tresteloving@tiredofhate.com
757.748.2590

Social Media Links
Facebook: https://www.facebook.com/breakthroughhate
Twitter: https://twitter.com/t resteloving
LinkedIn: https://www.linkedin.com/in/tresteloving

Dr. Liz Lyster, Women's Midlife Health Expert, is passionate about helping women feel like their best selves, so they can bring health and happiness to the world.

Since 1990, Dr. Liz has helped women and men regain energy, reignite their sex drive, clear up hormonal imbalance, and lose hundreds of pounds. She is the author of "Dr. Liz's Easy Guide to Menopause: 5 Simple Steps to Balancing Your Hormones and Feeling Like Yourself Again".

After graduating from Cornell University with honors, Dr. Liz completed medical school at the University of California, Irvine, followed by her OB/GYN residency in Los Angeles. To expand her commitment to teaching, Dr. Liz achieved a Masters of Public Health degree from UCLA in Community Health Education. In addition to her private medical practice, Dr. Liz also currently also teaches at Notre Dame de Namur University in Belmont, California.

Dr. Liz practices what she preaches. To model growing older with grace, agility and power, Dr. Liz celebrated turning 50 by climbing Mt. Kilimanjaro. She is a continuous learner, having logged thousands of hours as a leader, participant, or volunteer in personal development programs since the age of 19. She is a wife, a mother of two sons, and an avid hiker and Argentine tango dancer. She is fluent in Spanish.

Dr. Liz is dedicated to people expanding their idea of optimal health beyond medicine to include nutrition, physical activity, and spirit. You can contact Dr. Liz through her web site at www.DrLizMD.com.

You are invited to join her online community at www.DrLizMD.com and receive free monthly updates on latest health information and inspiration!

drliz@drlizmd.com
(844) 375-4963
www.DrLizMD.com

Social Media Links
Facebook:
https://www.facebook.com/DrLizLyster/
https://www.facebook.com/doctorliz
LinkedIn: https://www.linkedin.com/in/drlizmd/
Twitter: https://www.twitter.com/drlizlyster
YouTube: https://www.youtube.com/channel/UC4rNfJmg7aCWeoqdEBP5iRA
Instagram: https://www.instagram.com/drlizlyster
Pinterest: https://www.pinterest.it/drlizlyster

 **Nicolas C. Pacheco** is a church planter in the San Francisco, CA. Bay Area. He is a graduate of the Gateway Seminary, formerly known as Golden Gate Baptist Theological Seminary. He is a PREPARE & ENRICH facilitator, and founder of "Destruyendo Barreras", a marriage restoration ministry. He is also an independent certified coach, teacher, and speaker for the John Maxwell Team. Pastor Pacheco is also a certified Life Coach, Life Impact LLC. As of 2017 Pastor Pacheco was recruited to teach at California Crosspoint Academy; he teaches both middle and high school students Spanish and Bible Studies. Also, in 2017 he began coaching at Cardinal Education. He currently serves as director of the Hispanic extension of the seminary, CLD, and as Pastor of Iglesia Bautista Dulce Refugio in Oakland, CA.

pastornpacheco@nicolascpacheco.com
pastornpacheco@hotmail.com
510-228-7255
www.nicolascpacheco.com

Social Media Links
Facebook: https://www.facebook.com/profile.php?id=100013458371939
Linkedin: https://www.linkedin.com/in/nicolascpacheco

**Olivia Parr-Rud**, Corporate Love Ambassador, is a global thought leader, data scientist, and award-winning and best-selling author. Her unique approach to business success draws on her passion for data science, holistic leadership, and personal growth through a blending of quantitative and qualitative methods and practices. Her latest research unveils the relationship between loving behavior (i.e. compassion, connection, and caring) and long-term corporate profits.

Olivia's successful career in data science led to the writing of her international best-seller, Data Mining Cookbook, Modeling for Acquisition, Risk and Customer Relationship Management (Wiley 2001). Recognizing the need for higher emotional intelligence to thrive in our increasingly complex global economy, she was inspired to conduct research in the areas the communication, collaboration and leadership – highlighted in her second book, Business Intelligence Success Factors, Aligning for Success in a Global Economy (Wiley/SAS, 2009). Her third book, Business Analysis Using SAS® Enterprise Miner® and SAS® Enterprise Guide®, A Beginner's Guide, won Best of Show at the Carolina Technical Book competition. In her 4th book, Love@Work, A Corporate Journey to Self-Love and a Life of Inspired Purpose, Olivia shares her personal story and offers a 4-step method for healing yourself, unveiling and embracing your unique gifts, and stepping into your inspired purpose – available in early 2019.

Olivia lectures and consults with clients in the areas of data science and holistic leadership. She is currently developing courses for bringing love into business. Olivia holds a BA in Mathematics, an MS in Statistics and is a Certified Passion Test Facilitator. Clients include Cisco, Clorox, Walmart, Wells Fargo, Genentech, State Farm, Nationwide, Liberty Mutual, Royal Bank of Scotland, Citizen's Bank, HP, IBM, SAS, and Xerox.

olivia@lovemakeityourbusiness.com
215 948-3500
www.LoveMakeItYourBusiness.com

Social Media Links
Facebook: https://www.facebook.com/LoveMakeItYourBusiness/
LinkedIn: https://www.linkedin.com/in/oliviagroup/
Twitter: https://twitter.com/ParrRud
YouTube: www.OliviaOnYouTube.com

**Linda Patten** is founder of *Dare2Lead with Linda*, international speaker and best-selling author, talk radio show host on the VoiceAmerica Women's Channel, leadership expert, coach, and trainer. Her life's work is challenging women to dare to lead: whether it is for navigating the often-daunting entrepreneurial world, building strong teams for a thriving business, stepping out of the shadows into the light as a leader of one's life, or learning the leadership skills that will grow the seeds of change into a world-level movement.

With 40 years of leadership experience spanning the military (including protocol officer to a 4-star general), corporate, and entrepreneurial arenas, Linda is uniquely qualified to guide women on their journey of self-discovery, skills development, and a charted course toward becoming an extraordinary leader. Her book and 12-step program, *The Art of Herding Cats: Leading Teams of Leaders*, are rooted in her heartfelt vision to empower women to step out, step up, and step into the kind of leadership that creates positive change in the world.

Linda is a gifted communicator who is regularly featured live and online on business panels, interviewed as a leadership expert, and as a popular speaker and seminar leader on topics related to women in business and leadership. She holds an MBA in Organizational Behavior and Leadership, a Certificate in Meeting Management, as well as leadership positions in numerous professional management associations and women's business networking groups.

linda@dare2leadwithlinda.com
925-954-3239
www.dare2leadwithlinda.com

Social Media Links
Facebook:
https://www.facebook.com/dare2leadwithlinda
https://www.facebook.com/linda.patten.311
LinkedIn: https://www.linkedin.com/in/lindapatten
Twitter: https://www.twitter.com/patten_linda
You Tube Channel: http://www.youtube.com/c/LindaPatten
Google+: https://plus.google.com/+LindaPatten
Pinterest: https://www.pinterest.com/lindapatten311/

Carmell Pelly is a Mindset Coach, Business Strategist, Social Media Influencer, Bestselling Author, Creator of The Inspired Sisterhood, Professional Photographer, and Recovery Advocate.

Passionate about spreading the power of Self-Love, Carmell speaks and teaches Women globally to fully accept themselves by trusting in their higher callings and not giving in to fear. Her encouragement helps you see the blocks to your own empowerment and move through them to Abundance.

Creative enterprise comes naturally to Carmell who has had the enthusiasm and tenacity to build a lifestyle that is purposeful and happy. Coming from the experiences of recovery, Carmell is an advocate for self-transformation and success.

www.carmellpelly.com

Social Media Links
Facebook:
https://www.facebook.com/CarmellPelly3
https://www.facebook.com/CarmellPelly
Instagram: https://www.instagram.com/carmellpelly

 **Mark Edward Pyle** is the Scribe Prophet, Mastered Self Initiate and Soul (Karma) Reader, with 40+ years of study and Master Level experience with Numerology, Astrology, Card Sciences (Standard & Tarot). Mark also has extensive knowledge of Sacred Frequency Tuning Forks. Mark began having Prophetic Visions at an early age. At the age of 13, Mark began his 40+-year Esoteric Journey. In 1995, Mark went through a major personal transformation (Ascension) and because of this, Mark was Ordained as a Minister in July 1996. He founded an Outreach Ministry that serviced Skid Row Los Angeles for 13 years. During that time, Mark also served, briefly, in the capacity of Pastor and Mission Department President for 2 churches in South Los Angeles, CA. Mark's Prophetic Gift helped countless people during his time of dedicated service. ON May 1, 2009, Mark was diagnosed with Colon Cancer. He immediately stepped away from his ministry and was unable to continue working. This Life Pivot progressed during the 3 year radically intensive recovery period. During the Fall 2012, Mark became aware of his I AM Presence, his Mastered Self. He embraced his Mastered Self and began a Journey that has Expanded as he has Ascended. As a result, he discovered his Mastered Self Life Guidance System and incorporated it into his daily life and developed it for delivery to the People.

Mark consistently provides you with Your Real-Life Solutions for Your Real-Life Problems, equipping you to make better informed decisions that serve your Highest Good.

awakenings@iamascensions.com
510-329-1076
www.iamascensions.com

Social Media Links
Facebook:
https://www.facebook.com/profile.php?id=100009851492668
LinkedIn: https://www.linkedin.com/in/mark-edward-pyle-8a495911

Tish Reese, MA, LMFT, is a health and wellness mentor. She is the mother of two, a licensed psychotherapist, experienced mediator, divorce and child custody expert, and transformational coach. Tish loves to empower successful, health-conscious women to improve their physical health and emotional well-being using natural solutions.

Tish is a cancer survivor who is thriving in her life. She understands the importance of optimal health, which includes building and maintaining a strong immune system. She believes good health is the foundation of a quality life.

Tish's approach to physical and emotional well-being is holistic. This means that all aspects of the individual are taken into consideration — body, mind and spirit — to restore wholeness and harmony. Tish will inspire and guide you to achieve optimal whole body and mind wellness so that you can be your most radiant and thriving self.

Tish will help you Transform Your Health, Find Your Happy and Love Your Life!

tish@tishreese.com
(925) 849-0515
https://www.tishreese.com

Social Media Links
Facebook: https://www.facebook.com/tish.reesemft
LinkedIn: https://wlw.linkedin.com/in/tish-reese-ma-lmft-033b888b

Elda Robinson was born and raised in Northern California. She graduated from Western Baptist Bible College (now Corban University) and moved to Wisconsin to work at a home and care facility for mentally challenged children and adults. She and her husband worked there for seven years before moving back to California and beginning careers in Christian school education. That career choice has continued for over 30 years. She has taught in every grade level; kindergarten through high school. She has also served as an elementary principal. In 2009 she received the American Heart Association's Principal of the Year for her work with Jump Rope for Heart. She has also been a seminar speaker at several education conventions. She received her Masters in Curriculum Development to help improve her unit studies in the classroom which led to being a co-author of a science curriculum that is currently being used in private schools across the United States as well as other parts of the world. At the encouragement of her husband and her sisters, she has also written children's books. One, *Nathanial's Family*, has been published. The others are waiting "until she has time"! Until then she and her husband of 48 years continue to teach, travel, and enjoy learning.

erscimom589@gmail.com

Mooniek Seebregts and **Martina Caviezel** are both recognized as The Parent Empowerment coaches with GreatParentsEmpower.com. As coaches, they specialize in empowering moms and dads to be the parents they have always aspired to be, helping them to succeed in the demanding "job" of raising confident, capable, and loving kids.

Over the years, these two talented coaches have noticed that many parents unconsciously rely on the use of outmoded systems and counter-productive behaviors that were carried forward from their own upbringing. "Often, when starting a family, new parents realize that they don't understand exactly what parenting entails. Soon, the list of must-do tasks ends up dominating life, work, and relationships, and slowly, parents lose track of who and how they really would like to be as parents."

In the 7-week GreatParentsEmpower online course, Mooniek and Martina help parents learn the skills needed to be a great parent. This is accomplished by dismantling old ideas and unreal fantasies. The following results are achieved: participants make better choices; they cope better with challenging situations (family drama or kid drama); they acquire more confidence and patience; they create a great connection with their kid(s); they know how to deal with expectations, unhelpful thoughts, feelings of guilt, stress, and the all-too- often-held sense of being overwhelmed--and more. Mooniek: "Acquiring the appropriate education and tools prepares parents to better teach their kids how to become loving, capable, and confident individuals ..."

info@greatparentsempower.com
415-848-9013
Greatparentsempower.com

Get the course:
https://greatparentsempower.com/course/7-class-audio-course-plus/

Social Media Links
Twitter: https://www.instagram.com/greatparentsempower/

Mary Shores spends her career as an author, speaker, and entrepreneur, generating positive and pragmatic solutions for people who are freaking out. Mary blends personal experience with her extensive knowledge of neuroscience and human behavior to guide businesses and individuals to defeat the freak out and create their ideal life.

Social Media Links
Twitter: https://www.twitter.com/Mary_Shores
Instagram: https://www.instagram.com/Mary_Shores
Facebook: https://www.facebook.com/shoresmary

Kathleen E. Sims, D.D.,C.H.T., is Co-Founder of The Center for Conscious Living, in Pleasant Hill, CA, and the creator of the website, www.kathleenthelovecoach.com. Serving client globally, she brings her 'Body of Work' forth in many forms - Soul-based counseling, spiritual healing, hypnotherapy, EMDR, mentoring, life and love coaching and transformational workshops. Clients see her in person at her Center, or access her powerful Love Teachings worldwide through Skype. Her work is mystical, yet practical, based on Universal Spiritual Principles and Transformational Coaching Technologies, resulting in permanent change – where clients see all things are possible.

Manifesting her Soulmate in high school at the age of 16, they evolved their relationship into a conscious and mature deep love - lasting 4 decades. After Jim's sudden transition she attracted a second amazing Soulmate at 61. Kathleen has been gifted with the unique ability to draw from deep personal experiences translating them into 'The Legacy of Love Teachings', so others can attract deep abiding Love.

Co-authoring 5 personal growth books that have hit #1 on the Best Seller List, lead to an interview on Voice America Radio and TV – sharing her inspiring Love Story, along with being the Featured Love Coach on Selfgrowth.com and on Arielle Ford's Soulmate Secrets' site. In addition, she has her own YouTube Channel with many educational videos bringing more Love into the world.

Her Vision is that every person whose heart innately yearns for a loving, fulfilling relationship has one, transforming our world into Love & Light.

Social Media Links
Facebook:
Professional Page: www.facebook.com/kathleenthelovecoach/
Personal Page: https://www.facebook.com/kathleen.e.sims
Twitter: https://twitter.com/2melifesadance
Linkedin
https://www.linkedin.com/in/kathleen-e-sims-a879259
YouTube Channel:
https://www.youtube.com/user/KathleentheLoveCoach
Video Link:
http://player.voiceamerica.tv/video/C517E07542/youre-never-too-young-or-old-for-everlasting-love
Radio Interview Link: with Rebecca Hall Gruyter – Empowering Women - Transforming Lives
http://cdn.voiceamerica.com/women/011357/gruyter021616.mp3

Inguss Strikaitis moved to USA from small beautiful Baltic Country Latvia in Eastern Europe. He loves people, animals and adventures. Inguss is true entrepreneur, from owning his own beauty salons to know growing his international health and wellness business helping people stay young and beautiful inside out. He has passion for people and this world. Inguss has open heart for everyone, you need some encouragement on any day, he is the guy to talk. He also has a traveling bug, he is on the road or air very often, by learning other cultures, and bringing back experiences to share with others.

Inguss@inguss.com
+1 (213) 327-8345
www.inguss.com

Social Media Links
Facebook: https://www.facebook.com/ingusss
LinkedIn: https://www.linkedin.com/in/ingussstrikaitis
Twitter: https://twitter.com/IStrikaitis
YouTube: https://youtube.com/GetRichAndSkinny
Instagram: https://www.instagram.com/thecrazywrapguy

Kri' Shawn Terrell is a native of NC. She is a public speaker, a member of The John Maxwell Team with an extensive background in business management and entertainment. She studies the arts, and loves to write. She won her first award, The Burlington Women's Writing Award at age 13. Some of her interests include fashion, cooking, scripture, and technology. She's a big fan of math formulas, and logic puzzles. In her downtime she enjoys predicting patterns in the stock market.

krishawnterrell@icloud.com
336-350-4531

Social Media Links
Facebook: http://www.facebook.com/Nichole.terrell.98
Twitter: https://www.twitter.com/flawless_bitty7
Instagram: https://www.instagram.com/Niki_S_Fellowz

India White was born in Sarasota, Florida on to a family of 10 children and low SES. Enduring physical and mental abuse from her mother who struggled with alcoholism, at the age of 16, India was kicked out of the house on Christmas Eve. Shortly following this hardship, she moved to the Sarasota YMCA Youth shelter her last two years of high school as an honors student. At graduation, India moved to Gainesville from a homeless shelter into a college dorm overnight as a Gates Millennium Scholar and majored in math at the University of Florida. She has paid it forward as a motivational speaker, educator and administrator and has authored several books and was also featured on news shows, and in magazines. Currently as a McKnight Fellow, White is pursuing her Doctorate in Educational Leadership from UF's Department of Educational Administration and Policy. White was profiled in Senator Marco Rubio's book "American Dreams" as an "Inspirational Story for America". India's business, Rising Glory Productions has been a dream come true as she continues to help pay it forward as a motivational speaker, coach and world changer with other leaders.

India.White.123@gmail.com
www.india-white.com

Social Media Links
Facebook: https://www.facebook.com/indiawhitetsic
LinkedIn: https://www.linkedin.com/in/theindiawhite
Twitter: https://www.twitter.com/Indispeaknteach
Youtube (In progress) : Willie Mae White
Instagram: https://www.instagram.com/Indi238

CLOSING THOUGHTS

I hope you have been touched by these powerful inspirations have encouraged, equipped and empowered you to live on purpose and with purpose each day of the year! We hope you have been encouraged on your journey and are inspired to apply the practical and profound tips, advice, and great wisdom into your life. We can't wait to see you, hear from you, and celebrate you as you share the gift of you with the world! May you always choose to **live on purpose and with great purpose; one day and one inspiration at a time.**

~Rebecca Hall Gruyter, Compiler

Books compiled or written by Rebecca Hall Gruyter to be released in 2018 and 2019:

The Expert and Influencers Series: Leadership Edition

This powerful anthology will feature over 25 experts and influencers committed to empowering you in the area of Leadership. They will share tips, advice, powerful insight to help you step forward as a leader in your life and business. *(To be released June* 2019)

Step Into Your Brilliance!

This anthology featuring over 25 authors (the first book in the "Step Into" anthology series) will empower readers to discover and embrace their brilliance. This book will then equip and empower the reader to share their own brilliance with the world. The world needs you and your brilliance! (To be released in September of 2019).

The Animal Legacies!

This anthology featuring over 20 authors will share heart-warming, inspiring, empowering true stories of how animals have powerfully touched their lives. They will share a profound lesson they learned, a powerful truth, a powerful legacy, encouraging messages, a celebration and honor of our animal friends. Every reader will be encouraged, their heart touched; as each writer shares and passes to you their own animal legacy. We know this book will touch your heart and life. (To be released December 2019).

Anthologies Available Now That Are Compiled by Rebecca Hall Gruyter:

Special "SHINE Series" (Compiled and led by Rebecca Hall Gruyter)

"Come out of Hiding and SHINE!" (Book 1 in the SHINE Series)

"Bloom Where You are Planted and SHINE!" (Book 2 in the SHINE Series)

"Step Forward and SHINE!" (This book, the 3rd and final book in the SHINE Series)

"The Grandmother Legacies" (Anthology Compiled by Rebecca Hall Gruyter)

Books Available Now Featuring a Chapter by Rebecca Hall Gruyter:

"Becoming Outrageously Successful" Anthology compiled by Dr. Anita Jackson

"Catch Your Star" Anthology published by THRIVE Publishing

"Discover Your Destiny" Anthology compiled by Denise Joy Thompson

"I Am Beautiful" Anthology compiled by Teresa Hawley-Howard

"The Power of Our Voices, Sharing Our Story" Anthology, compiled by Teresa Hawley-Howard

"Succeeding Against All Odds" Anthology compiled by Sandra Yancey

"Success Secrets for Today's Feminine Entrepreneurs" Anthology compiled by Dr. Anita Jackson

"Unstoppable Woman of Purpose" Anthology and workbook, compiled by Nella Chikwe

"Women on a Mission" Anthology compiled by Teresa Hawley-Howard

"Women of Courage, Women of Destiny" Anthology compiled by Dr. Anita Jackson

"Women Warriors Who Make It Rock" Anthology compiled by Nichole Peters

"You Are Whole, Perfect, and Complete - Just As You Are" compiled by Carol Plummer and Susan Driscoll